ECONOMIC INTEGRATION IN AFRICA

In this work, Richard E. Mshomba offers an in-depth analysis of economic integration in Africa with a focus on the East African Community (EAC), arguably the most ambitious of all the regional economic blocs currently in existence in Africa. *Economic Integration in Africa* provides more than just an overview of regional economic blocs in Africa; it also offers a rich historical discussion on the birth and death of the first EAC starting with the onset of colonialism in the 1890s, and a systematic analysis of the birth, growth, and aspirations of the current EAC. Those objectives include forming a monetary union and eventually an East African political federation. This book also examines the African Union's aspirations for continent-wide integration as envisioned by the Abuja Treaty. Mshomba carefully argues that maturity of democracy and good governance in each country are prerequisites for the formation of a viable and sustainable East African federation and genuine continent-wide integration.

Richard E. Mshomba is Professor of Economics at La Salle University in Philadelphia. Born and raised in Tanzania, he received a PhD in economics from the University of Illinois at Urbana-Champaign. He is the author of *Africa in the Global Economy* (2000), a Choice Outstanding Academic Book, and *Africa and the World Trade Organization* (2009).

Economic Integration in Africa

The East African Community in Comparative Perspective

RICHARD E. MSHOMBA
La Salle University, Philadelphia

CAMBRIDGE
UNIVERSITY PRESS

CAMBRIDGE
UNIVERSITY PRESS

University Printing House, Cambridge CB2 8BS, United Kingdom

One Liberty Plaza, 20th Floor, New York, NY 10006, USA

477 Williamstown Road, Port Melbourne, VIC 3207, Australia

314–321, 3rd Floor, Plot 3, Splendor Forum, Jasola District Centre, New Delhi – 110025, India

79 Anson Road, #06–04/06, Singapore 079906

Cambridge University Press is part of the University of Cambridge.

It furthers the University's mission by disseminating knowledge in the pursuit of education, learning, and research at the highest international levels of excellence.

www.cambridge.org
Information on this title: www.cambridge.org/9781107186262
DOI: 10.1017/9781316888896

First published 2017
Reprinted 2018

Printed in the United States of America by G.H. Soho Inc.

A catalogue record for this publication is available from the British Library.

Library of Congress Cataloging-in-Publication Data
Names: Mshomba, Richard Elias, 1954– author.
Title: Economic Integration in Africa : the East African Community in comparative perspective / Richard E. Mshomba.
Description: New York, NY. : Cambridge University Press, 2017. | Includes bibliographical references.
Identifiers: LCCN 2017026033 | ISBN 9781107186262 | ISBN 1107186269
Subjects: LCSH: East African Community – History. | Africa, Eastern – Economic integration – History. | Africa, East – Economic integration – History. | Africa – Economic integration. | Federal government – Africa, Eastern.
Classification: LCC HC860 .M77 2017 | DDC 330.9676–dc23
LC record available at https://lccn.loc.gov/2017026033

ISBN 978-1-107-18626-2 Hardback

To my mentors:

Bishop Dennis V. Durning, C.S.Sp.

Dr. Richard Geruson

Professor Harvey Glickman

Contents

Figures

Tables

Acknowledgments

Bless the Lord, O my soul; and all my being, praise his holy name.
(Psalm 103:1)

As an undergraduate at La Salle University, my professors gave me many opportunities to study the economy of Africa, in general, and Tanzania, in particular. One of my philosophy professors, Michael Kerlin, even revised his syllabus when he learned I was taking his class to include works by the first president of Tanzania, Julius Nyerere, a respected political leader and philosopher.

My master's thesis and PhD dissertation at the University of Delaware and the University of Illinois at Urbana-Champaign, respectively, were on the Tanzanian economy. Since I returned to La Salle University 26 years ago as a faculty member, the university has generously supported my research, which has focused on Africa.

Thus, while this book provides only a glimpse of African countries' fascinating economic and political dynamics, it is, in fact, the culmination of a lifetime of learning. It also provides an opportunity for me to express my gratitude to special people in my life and schools and universities that have believed in me, supported me, and encouraged me over the years.

I do not have adequate words to thank my parents. They worked very hard as subsistent farmers just to be able to provide the basic necessities. They had almost no formal education themselves, but they had the love, fortitude, and vision to send me and my siblings to school. *Asanteni sana, Mama na Baba!*

It is truly a blessing that I can count on the support and prayers of my friends and my immediate and extended families: the Mshombas, the Durnings, and the O'Hallorans.

I will be forever grateful to Brothers Patrick Ellis and Emery Mollenhauer and La Salle University for taking a chance on me and offering me a full tuition scholarship for my undergraduate studies. As if that were not enough, La Salle also gave me a job! I must add that La Salle also gave me a research leave to work on this book. I am very grateful. I also commend and thank La Salle's librarians for their expertise and dedication.

I sincerely wish to thank my colleagues in the Economics Department for their friendship and support and being flexible with schedules to allow me to take a research leave. My special thanks to Dave Robison who has consistently passed along to me materials on Africa. In addition, the Dean (Emeritus) of the School of Arts and Sciences, Thomas Keagy, was all one could wish for in a dean. I am grateful for his constant support and enthusiastic encouragement.

In conducting research for this book, I spent time in Nairobi, Kenya and Arusha, Tanzania at the headquarters of the East African Community (EAC). I consulted with business associations, traders, politicians, and many government and EAC officials. I am thankful for their time, information, and insight. I thank Jason Braganza for helping me with his own observations and also for introducing me to a number of government officials in Nairobi. My special gratitude goes to Philip Wambugu of the EAC for his insights and also for assisting me, tirelessly, in making appointments with other officials.

My students' interest in my work is a constant source of inspiration. I am grateful for their questions and observations. In particular, I want to thank Robert McDonough and Emily Schmitt for their assistance in preparing tables and graphs for this book.

I owe special thanks to Voxi Amavilah who was very generous with his time in reviewing the whole manuscript and providing very insightful comments. I have also benefited a great deal from my discussions and correspondence with my dear friend, Daniel Ole Njoolay. In addition, I want to offer my sincere thanks to anonymous reviewers for their extremely useful comments and for their support for publication.

I literally could not have completed this manuscript in a timely manner without the loving and constant support of my wife, Elaine. She is my number one cheerleader and trusted in-house editor. With her legal training and extensive experience as a language teacher, Elaine pays close attention to detail and organization. I cannot thank her enough. I am also grateful to our sons – Alphonce, Dennis, and Charles – and our daughter-in-law, Kelley, for their support. Alphonce and Dennis both majored in Economics, and their interest in the field in general, and my work in particular, has always been a source of joy for me. Charles, who is in high school, has also enjoyed learning about economics and Tanzania.

The three people to whom I have dedicated this book are very special to me. Each one, in his own way, has played a significant and direct role in helping and guiding me through my education and professional life. They have been a true blessing in my life.

The individuals who helped me with this book or who are close to me may not necessarily agree with my analysis and conclusions. I also take full responsibility for any errors or omissions.

–Richard E. Mshomba

Abbreviations

ACP	African, Caribbean, and Pacific Countries
AERC	African Economic Research Consortium
AGOA	African Growth and Opportunity Act
ANAW	African Network for Animal Welfare
ASEAN	Association of Southeast Asian Nations
AU	African Union
BoT	Bank of Tanzania
CAT	Coffee Authority of Tanzania
CCM	Chama Cha Mapinduzi
CEMAC	Economic and Monetary Community of Central Africa
CEN-SAD	Community of Sahel-Saharan States
CES-TFTA	COMESA-EAC-SADC Tripartite Free Trade Area
CETs	Common External Tariffs
CFTA	Continental Free Trade Area
CIF	Cost, Insurance, and Freight
CMA	Common Monetary Area
CNDD-FDD	National Council for the Defense of Democracy-Forces for the Defense of Democracy
COMESA	Common Market for Eastern and Southern Africa
CPI	Corruption Perceptions Index
CUF	Civic United Front
DSU	Dispute Settlement Understanding
EAC	East African Community
EACB	East African Central Bank
EACJ	East African Court of Justice
EACSO	East African Common Services Organization
EADB	East African Development Bank

EAHC	East African High Commission
EAMU	East African Monetary Union
EBA	Everything But Arms
ECA	Economic Commission for Africa
ECCAS	Economic Community of Central African States
ECGLC	Economic Community of Great Lakes Countries
ECOMOG	Economic Community of West African States Monitoring Group
ECOWAS	Economic Community of West African States
EPA	Economic Partnership Agreement
EPZs	Export Processing Zones
EU	European Union
FDLR	Democratic Forces for the Liberation of Rwanda
FTAAP	Free Trade Area of the Asia-Pacific
GATT	General Agreement on Tariffs and Trade
GATS	General Agreement on Trade in Services
GDP	Gross Domestic Product
GNI	Gross National Income
GSP	Generalized System of Preferences
HDI	Human Development Index
HIPC	Heavily Indebted Poor Countries
ICC	International Criminal Court
ICGLR	International Conference on the Great Lakes Region
ICTSD	International Centre for Trade and Sustainable Development
IGAD	Intergovernmental Authority on Development
IGADD	Inter-Governmental Authority on Drought and Development
IMF	International Monetary Fund
IOC	Indian Ocean Commission
JKIA	Jomo Kenyatta International Airport
KANU	Kenya African National Union
LDCs	Least Developed Countries
MDC	Maputo Development Corridor
MDRI	Multilateral Debt Relief Initiative
MNC	Multinational Corporation
MFN	Most Favored Nation
MPs	Members of Parliament
MRU	Mano River Union
NAFTA	North America Free Trade Area

NATO	North Atlantic Treaty Organization
NGO	Non-Governmental Organization
NPV	Net Present Value
OAU	Organization of African Unity
PAP	Pan-African Parliament
PPP	Purchasing Power Parity
PRSPs	Poverty Reduction Strategy Papers
PTA	Preferential Trade Area
REBs	Regional Economic Blocs
SACU	Southern Africa Customs Union
SADC	Southern African Development Community
SADCC	Southern African Development Coordination Conference
SPLM	Sudanese People's Liberation Movement
TANU	Tanganyika African National Union
TCCIA	Tanzania Chamber of Commerce, Industry and Agriculture
TAZAMA	Tanzania-Zambia Mafuta Pipeline
TPP	Trans-Pacific Partnership
TRIPS	Trade-Related Aspects of Intellectual Property Rights
UEMOA	West African Customs and Economic Union
UMA	Arab Maghreb Union
UN	United Nations
UNCTAD	United Nations Conference on Trade and Development
UNDP	United Nations Development Program
WAMZ	West African Monetary Zone
WTO	World Trade Organization
ZEC	Zanzibar Electoral Commission

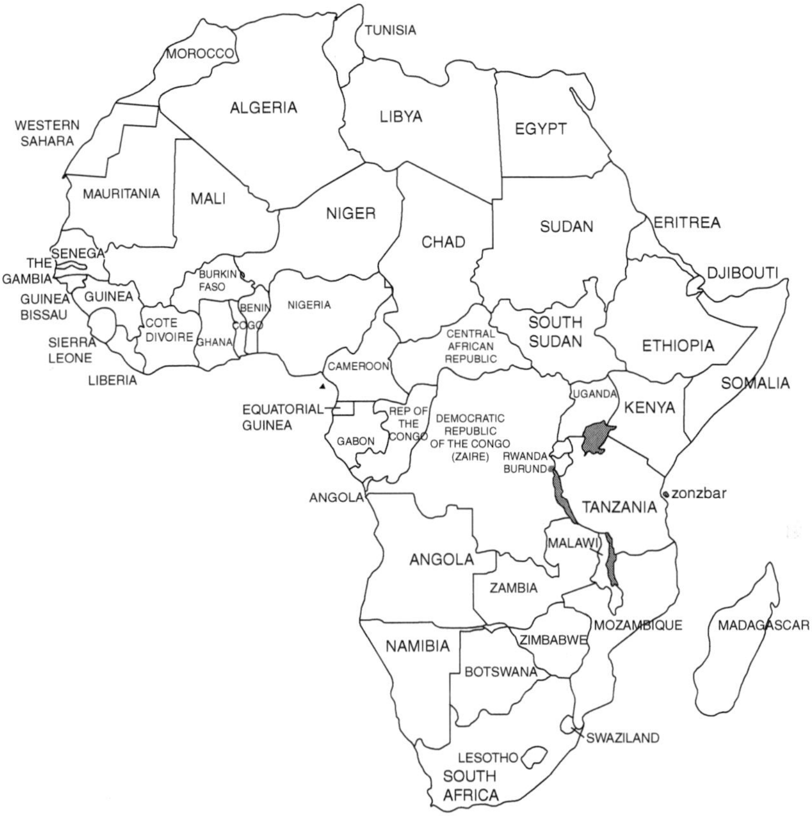

Figure I Map of Africa
Source: Bruce Jones Design Inc. Reprinted by permission.

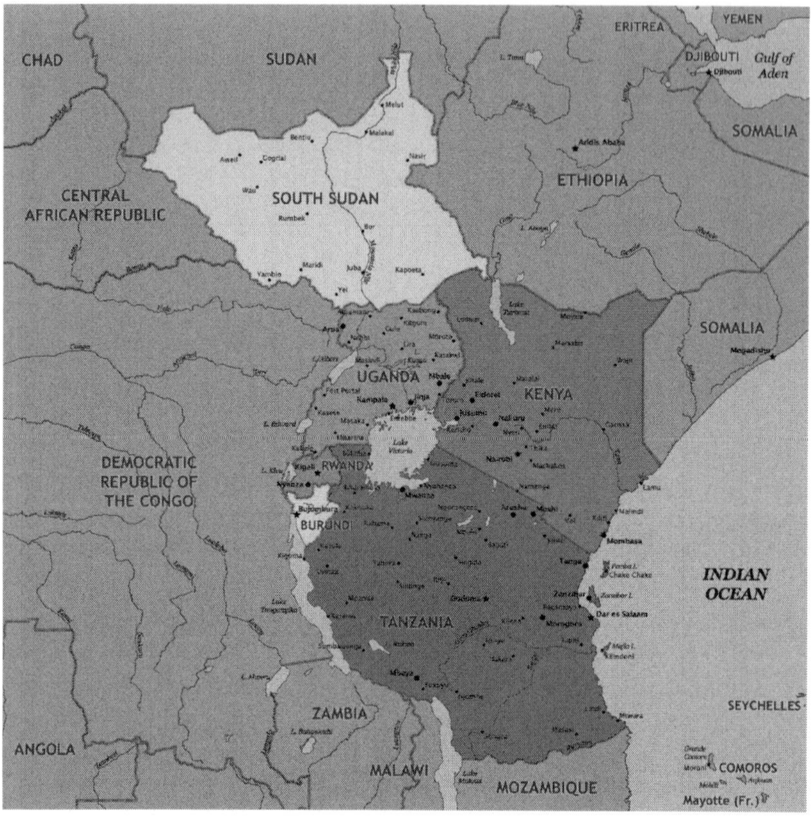

Figure II Map of East Africa
Source: Sitesatlas.com. Reprinted by permission.

1

Introduction

In the struggle against Colonialism the fundamental unity of the people of Africa is evident and is deeply felt. It is, however, a unity forged in adversity in a battle against an outside Government. If the triumph in this battle is to be followed by an equal triumph against the forces of neo-colonialism and also against poverty, ignorance and disease, then this unity must be strengthened and maintained. *Julius Nyerere*

Of all the potential strategies for development for Africa, it is hard to find one that receives more widespread rhetorical support than that of creating and strengthening regional economic blocs. The case for economic integration in Africa is so easy to make that pronouncements about it are often made with prophetic optimism and even political euphoria. It is taken for granted these days that regional economic integration is important for African development.

Given that this strategy seems to be unquestioned and accepted categorically, some leaders may try to speed up the process to gratify their personal political ambitions. They may forget that the benefits of economic integration, though many, are not guaranteed. Important social and development goals, such as achieving an equitable income distribution, must always be taken into consideration. Thus, it is important for governments to conduct an in-depth evaluation of the impact of joining a regional bloc or of moving a regional bloc to a higher level of integration.

Regarding efforts to integrate Mozambique and South African economies under what came to be known as the Maputo Development Corridor (MDC), Taylor (2003, 313) concludes that

the form of regionalization being currently promoted in Southern Africa is premised on an unquestioned belief that integration of their territories into the global economy is absolutely crucial and inevitable. The structural limitations of this are never probed as, it is apparent, "there is no alternative."

Taylor argues that the regionalization agenda has been set mainly by "elites," referring to specific African leaders. He explains that those leaders were influenced by the neoliberal economics ideology – freer private sector and greater openness to international trade and investment. Indeed economic openness in general gained momentum in the late 1980s and early 1990s following the neoliberal economic policies encouraged by the International Monetary Fund (IMF) and the World Bank. However, while not everyone is enthusiastic about regional integration, regionalism has come to receive broader internal support in African countries. Neoliberal economic policies have become entrenched in some countries to the point that now, for example, it is the IMF that is cautioning the East African Community (EAC) not to rush into a monetary union (Omondi, 2014).

The EAC, the primary focus of this book, aspires not only to form a monetary union, but also a political union. This aspiration to form a political federation goes beyond that of any other regional bloc currently in existence anywhere in the world.

The potential impact of economic integration can be divided into two types: static and dynamic. The *static impact* refers to the change in equilibrium of the market price and quantity of goods before and after the movement towards free trade. Theoretically, the potential static impact of economic integration can be analyzed in terms of trade creation or trade diversion.

Trade creation occurs when economic integration leads a product source to shift from high-cost domestic producers to low-cost producers in a member country. It is a movement towards free trade. As an example, consider Kenya before and after the EAC was formed.[1] The EAC is comprised of Burundi, Kenya, Rwanda, South Sudan[2], Tanzania, and Uganda. Suppose that before the EAC was established, Kenya applied a tariff on onions it imported from Tanzania. Following the establishment of the EAC, if Kenya eliminates or reduces the tariff rate on onions from Tanzania, Kenya will reduce price distortion at home and will import more onions from Tanzania. This would be a case of trade creation. Trade creation would produce a net welfare gain for Kenya.

Trade diversion occurs when integration causes a product source to shift from a low-cost non-member country to a high-cost member country. Suppose, before the EAC was formed, Kenya had a tariff on imports of rice, and Kenya could potentially import rice from Pakistan or Uganda. Suppose further that Kenya in fact imported rice from Pakistan because Pakistan produced it at a lower cost and, thus, sold it at a lower price than Uganda. Following the establishment of the EAC, Kenya removes the tariff on imports of rice from Uganda, but not on rice imported from Pakistan. Trade diversion happens if Kenya begins to import rice from Uganda instead of Pakistan. Note that this diversion happens not because Uganda is a lower cost producer, but because a tariff distorts the actual price of rice from Pakistan. Trade diversion can cause a net welfare gain or a net welfare loss for Kenya. Removing the tariff removes price distortion for imports from Uganda. However, there is the possibility of a net welfare loss because the terms of trade for Kenya deteriorate as it switches its source of rice from a low-cost producer to a high-cost producer, that is, from Pakistan to Uganda.[3] Nonetheless, even with trade diversion, it is highly unlikely for regional economic integration to cause an overall net welfare loss, considering its dynamic impact.

The *dynamic impact* of economic integration includes increased competition, economies of scale, increased investment, political stability, and political and economic leverage. Economic integration exposes domestic producers to competition from their counterparts in the region. At the same time, it allows domestic producers to acquire knowledge and technical skills from others, all of which leads to a more efficient use of resources and production in line with comparative advantage.

Economic integration allows producers to take advantage of economies of scale. Economies of scale refers to the reduction of a firm's long-run average cost of production as the firm expands and produces more (internal economies) or as more firms enter the industry (external economies). Economic integration enlarges the markets for products and inputs, thus allowing firms to expand production. Increased production allows for more specialization, greater spread of fixed costs, the use of better equipment, and the acquisition of inputs at a discount price. Expanded markets attract new firms. This, in turn, brings external economies of scale by increasing the speed at which new techniques are generated and diffused throughout the industry and attracting suppliers of inputs to locate into the region. Individually, the economies of most African countries are too small to attract large foreign direct investments and, therefore, economic integration helps to enlarge the sources of inputs and the markets for final products.

Economic integration is not performed in a political vacuum. Asante (1997, 26) has argued that "[economic] integration is political as well as economic in both objectives and procedures." Economic integration and political stability support one another. Successful integration, even if economic in nature, will tend to forge political stability in the region. Likewise, political stability enhances economic integration. The underlying objective behind the creation of the European Union was political stability and peace in the region.

The Association of Southeast Asian Nations (ASEAN) was formed in 1967 by Indonesia, Malaysia, the Philippines, Singapore, and Thailand, primarily to bring political stability to the sub-region. The initial primary objective of the members of this regional group was to reduce conflicts among themselves and forge unity against the threats of their Communist neighbors, Vietnam, the former USSR, and China. In fact, the threat of outside forces, although requiring a reallocation of resources to address, solidified the unity of ASEAN members. The political stability achieved within the ASEAN countries fostered a greater commitment to economic cooperation and development (Simon, 1982; Leifer, 1989).

The Economic Community of West African States Monitoring Group (ECOMOG) was able to reduce the level of political instability in the West African region in the 1990s (Yabi, 2010). Most notable was ECOMOG's leadership in containing the civil war in Liberia and in restoring a democratically elected president of Sierra Leone, Ahmad Kabbal, to power in 1998. Kabbal had been overthrown in 1997 in a coup d'état.

In 2014, ECOWAS helped to reduce political tensions in Burkina Faso following the resignation of President Blaise Compaore. Compaore had been Burkina Faso's president for 27 years, and he had been trying to force a change in its constitution to allow him to run for another term.

The Intergovernmental Authority on Development (IGAD) attempted unsuccessfully to mediate conflicts in South Sudan in 2014. Nonetheless, Tanzanian leaders joined in those efforts, leading to a peace agreement in early 2015 between the rival factions of the ruling Sudanese People's Liberation Movement (SPLM). That agreement fell apart, but pressure from the United Nations Security Council and continued efforts by regional leaders led to another peace agreement in August of 2015. Unfortunately, that was only an agreement on paper. Fighting resumed in 2016.

Even when an economic bloc is not organized and strong enough to suppress conflicts in its region, it can provide an organizational structure through which external support can flow in. That said, some economic blocs, such as the Economic Community of Central African States (ECCAS), are too weak even to be effective conduits of external support (Elowson and Wiklund, 2011).

Regional economic integration also enhances negotiations with international organizations and other countries by sharing costs and expertise. This has particularly been the case in the negotiation and signing of the Economic Partnership Agreements (EPAs) with the European Union (EU).

To put EPAs in historical context, in 1963, the European Economic Community and African countries signed the Yaoundé Convention, which allowed most dutiable imports from African countries to enter the European market duty-free. The Lomé Convention signed in 1975 replaced the Yaoundé Convention and formalized all preferential treatments of imports by the European countries from the African, Caribbean and Pacific (ACP) countries. However, in the late 1990s, developing countries that are not part of the ACP group argued, successfully, that the EU was discriminating against them, by providing non-reciprocal preferential treatment to a select group of developing countries. Subsequently, in 2000, the Lomé Convention was replaced by the Cotonou Agreement between the EU and ACP countries with the understanding that the arrangement would evolve into EPAs, that is, reciprocal agreements between the EU and the ACP countries (African Trade Policy Centre, 2007).

The call for African unity is a constant in African politics. The Organization of African Unity (OAU) in 1980 in its Lagos Plan of Action for the development of Africa set the year 2000 as the time by which an African Common Market would be established (Organization of African Unity, 1980). Ten years into the Lagos Plan of Action, it was obvious that Africa would not even come close to the realization of this level of integration by the turn of the century. In 1991, the OAU established a new road map for African unity with its Abuja Treaty (Organization of African Unity, 1991). The Abuja Treaty, also known as the African Economic Community Treaty, was signed by fifty-one members of the OAU and took effect in 1994.[4] It sets six stages of implementation through which existing and new regional economic communities would gradually move to deeper levels of integration. Table 1.1 provides a summary of those stages.[5] It was envisioned that the regional economic communities would be the building blocks of the African Economic Community, creating a continental economic and monetary union by 2028. Given the level of integration at which most regional blocs in Africa are currently, it is safe to say that history will prove the Abuja Treaty to have been overly optimistic.

Regional economic integration faces many challenges, including countries having membership in multiple regional economic groups, a lack of political commitment, unrealistic schedules, political instability in some regions, authoritarian leadership in some countries, dependence on foreign aid, and differences in the levels of economic development between member countries. Notwithstanding these challenges, the Abuja Treaty provides important reference points with which to assess the progress, or lack thereof, towards deeper levels of economic integration in Africa.

Table 1.1 *Stages to Establish the African Economic Community*

Stage	Task	Time period
First	Strengthen existing regional economic communities and establish new ones where they do not exist.	5 years (1994–1999)
Second	Conduct studies to determine timetables for removal of tariffs and non-tariff barriers on intra-regional trade.	8 years (1999–2007)
Third	Deepen integration in each regional economic community to the level of a customs union.	10 years (2007–2017)
Fourth	Establish a continental customs union.	2 years (2017–2019)
Fifth	Establish a continental common market.	4 years (2019–2023)
Sixth	Establish a continental economic and monetary union with a single African currency.	5 years (2023–2028)

Source: Organization of African Unity (1991).

This book examines the EAC as a way through which to understand the benefits, challenges, and complexities of creating an African Economic Community. Even if regional economic integration were to be accepted as a necessary condition for African development, questions about membership, size, speed, the level of integration, and its potential impact must always be carefully considered. As important as it is for geographical neighbors to be neighborly to each other, relationships must be forged thoughtfully, constitutionally and democratically.

The EAC provides a unique and rare example from which to learn because, in a sense, it is a regional bloc that rose from its own ashes. The former EAC, established in 1967, was comprised of Kenya, Tanzania, and Uganda. In the early 1970s, the EAC was hailed as an exemplary customs union to be emulated by other African countries. Notwithstanding its promise, the EAC collapsed in 1977 following a bitter war of words and the closure of the border between Kenya and Tanzania, followed in 1978 by an actual war between Tanzania and Uganda.

The relationship between the three countries normalized in the 1990s, and in 1996 they established what they called the East African Co-operation. In 2004, Kenya, Tanzania, and Uganda signed an agreement for the establishment of the East African Community Customs Union. In 2007, Burundi and Rwanda acceded to the EAC, increasing its membership from three to five countries. South Sudan, which officially became an independent state on July 9, 2011, applied to join the EAC in the same year (Uma, 2011).

However, the civil war that broke out in South Sudan in late 2013 increased the doubts, which were there from the start, about its institutional capacity to function adequately in a dynamic regional economic bloc like the EAC. Nonetheless, South Sudan was admitted into the EAC in 2016.

Considering that regional economic blocs are expected to be the building blocks of the African Economic Community, the EAC is also a useful case to study because it joined two other blocs, the Common Market for Eastern and Southern Africa (COMESA) and the Southern African Development Community (SADC), to form a tripartite free trade area (ICTSD, 2014). The combined membership in these three regional groups is 27 countries.

Yet another reason the EAC is a good case to study is that it is arguably the most ambitious of all the regional economic blocs currently in existence in Africa. While it is still learning from its own past experience and the experiences of other economic blocs such as the European Union, the EAC may come to serve as a model to be emulated, fine-tuned, or avoided by other African regional blocs. After a transitional period of five years, the EAC officially became a customs union in 2010 – 33 years after the collapse of the former EAC. In the same year, a protocol signed in 2009 to establish a common market came into force. In late 2013, the five leaders of the EAC signed a protocol to establish a monetary union by 2023. The ultimate goal of the EAC is to form a political federation. Considering the collapse of the former EAC and the progress the new one is making, discussion about the EAC is both cautionary and inspiring.

Even the most basic level of regional economic integration, let alone an economic bloc like the EAC that is envisioning a federation in a few years, encompasses many areas of cooperation, monitoring and regulation. This book does not attempt to be all-inclusive or meticulously comprehensive regarding economic integration in Africa. Instead it endeavors to understand economic integration in Africa generally, while focusing on the dynamics and trajectory of economic and political integration in the EAC, incorporating a historical framework, and considering the key agreements.

Chapter 2 describes various levels of economic integration and highlights regional economic blocs in Africa. This chapter also provides pertinent information about five members of the EAC, thereby serving as an introduction to subsequent chapters. Since South Sudan is a relatively new country and has just joined the EAC, it is not included in the comparative analysis of the members of the EAC. However, some basic information and analysis about South Sudan is included.

Chapter 3 provides the colonial history of the former EAC. It analyzes the breadth and depth of integration between Kenya, Tanganyika (now mainland Tanzania), and Uganda when the countries were under British rule and how that economic cooperation set the stage for the former EAC.

Chapter 4 discusses the establishment of the former EAC and explores factors that contributed to its collapse. The troubled economic relations that developed following the collapse of the former EAC are also examined, especially those between Kenya and Tanzania. In addition, the study considers how Kenyans and Tanzanians coped with the closure of the border.

Chapter 5 considers the political and economic dynamics in East Africa (and in the African continent generally) and initiatives that lead to normalized relations between the original members of the EAC. This chapter examines how the EAC has operated as a customs union. Special attention is given to observable disparity between the depth of integration officially agreed upon and the actual practice, such as the declared and actual reductions in trade barriers for intra-group trade.

Chapter 6 analyzes the Protocol on the Establishment of the EAC Common Market which came into force in 2010. It presents the barriers to labor mobility in the EAC and questions whether there is real commitment to this level of integration.

Chapter 7 considers the costs and benefits of a monetary union and analyzes the macroeconomic convergence criteria established as necessary conditions before a monetary union can be established. In 2013, the five leaders of the EAC signed a protocol to establish a monetary union by 2023.

Chapter 8 examines whether or not democracy in East African countries has matured enough to allow for the formation of a viable and sustainable East African federation. The EAC's ultimate goal is to establish a political federation. This chapter analyzes the political landscape of the member countries. This includes land conflicts, the politics of oil and natural gas reserves, internal and border conflicts and presidential term limits.

Chapter 9 explores the trade dynamics between the EAC and other regional blocs whose membership overlaps with the EAC's membership. The EAC is considering accepting new members and deepening its trade relations with COMESA and SADC under what is called the COMESA-EAC-SADC Tripartite. The chapter also examines Africa's overall aspirations for Pan-Africanism as envisioned by the Abuja Treaty and analyzes the role of the African Union (AU).

Chapter 10 is the conclusion. It considers future prospects for economic integration in East Africa in particular and Africa in general.

Notes

1. While a few regional economic blocs are mentioned in this introductory chapter, a full list of all African regional economic blocs is provided in Chapter 2.
2. South Sudan was admitted into the EAC in 2016.
3. The terms of trade refer to a country's price of exports relative to the price of its imports. Deterioration in the terms of trade is a fall in the price of exports relative to the price of imports (or an increase in the price of imports relative to the price of exports).
4. In 1991, when the Abuja Treaty was signed, Eritrea and South Sudan did not exist as independent states, and South Africa was not a member of the OAU.
5. The various levels of integration are described in Chapter 2.

2

Regional Economic Integration in Africa

To place the discussion of this chapter in context, a brief discussion about the General Agreement on Tariffs and Trade (GATT) and the World Trade Organization (WTO) is warranted. GATT was established in 1947 with the mission to liberalize global trade. The WTO replaced GATT in 1995. Through the WTO, governments of member countries engage in multilateral negotiations to reduce trade barriers.

A basic principle of the WTO and its predecessor, GATT, is non-differentiated treatment, commonly called the *most favored nation* (MFN) principle. The MFN principle means a member country must treat all other members equally in respect to trade policy. If a member country lowers the tariff rate on a commodity entering from one member country, for example, it must likewise lower the tariff rate on that commodity from all other member countries. An exception to the MFN rule is made by GATT Article XXIV for free trade areas and other levels of economic integration. Thus, forming regional economic blocs is allowed by this exception.

STAGES OF ECONOMIC INTEGRATION

It takes time for countries to develop deeper levels of integration. There are several levels of economic integration, ranging from preferential trading arrangements to a political union.

Preferential Trading Arrangement

Under this lowest level of integration, member countries agree to lower some trade barriers between themselves. Each country sets its own trade policies vis-à-vis non-members, though a most-favored-nation clause usually precludes preferential treatment by any member country to a non-member. In other words, a member country cannot offer more favorable access to its market to a non-member.[1] An example is the Preferential Trade Area (PTA) for eastern and southern African states, established in 1981, before it became the Common Market for Eastern and Southern Africa (COMESA) in 1994.

Free Trade Area

At this level of integration, members remove all trade barriers on intra-group trade. Similar to preferential trading arrangements, member states set their own national barriers on trade with non-members.

While most regional blocs in Africa declare themselves to be free trade areas, they actually still maintain a number of trade barriers between member countries. In January 2012, African leaders meeting at the African Union summit that focused on ways to boost intra-African trade "endorsed a plan to set up a Continental Free Trade Area (CFTA) by 2017" (ICTSD, 2012). There seems to be something captivating about a five- or ten-year period in planning for the future, but suggesting a *genuine* CFTA for Africa by 2017 was wishful thinking, to say the least.

Since member countries under preferential trading arrangements or free trade areas are allowed to set their own external barriers, there is the potential for exporters to transship their goods to avoid high tariffs. Transshipment involves two steps. First, the product is exported from a non-member country to a member country with relatively low external protection. Second, the product is re-exported to another member country that has higher external protection. This type of "cheating" in trade must not be confused with benign and transparent transshipment of goods from one country to another through an intermediary country, for example, from South Africa to Rwanda, through Tanzania, or from Nigeria to Togo, through Benin.

Preferential trading or free trade agreements usually try to prevent trade "cheating" through transshipment by including a "rules of origin" provision. The goods must be imported directly from another member state in which they were produced. For example, COMESA stipulates that for goods to qualify as originating from a member country, they must meet one of two criteria – the material-content criterion or the value-added criterion (COMESA, 2002). Under the material-content criterion, if the exporting country used inputs imported from non-members, the cost, insurance, and freight (CIF) value of those inputs must not exceed

60 percent of the total cost of materials used in production. That is, a minimum of 40 percent local material content must be achieved under that criterion. The value-added criterion requires that the value added from processing or assembling inputs be at least 35 percent of the post-factory cost of the finished product. For products deemed of particular importance for the economic development of member states, the value-added requirement is set at 25 percent. Note that whether the value-added minimum requirement is 25 percent, 35 percent, or even slightly higher, it is still possible to meet the criterion even when the domestic material content is practically zero. It depends on the relative costs of processing and assembling. Other regional economic blocs in Africa, such as the EAC, Economic Community of West African States (ECOWAS), and Southern African Development Community (SADC), have similar rules of origin requirements with some variations in the percentages.

It can be expected that some traders will try to circumvent the rules of origin requirements to increase their profits. In its strategic plan for 2010–2014, the Kenya Sugar Board (2010) points to the problem of transshipment of sugar into Kenya through other COMESA countries, such as Egypt, from non-COMESA countries. Mayoyo and Marete (2011) report that

> [t]he Kenya Sugar Board has unearthed a multi-billion shilling sugar importation racket at the Mombasa port in which the government could have lost more than Sh. 1.6 billion [$18.3 million] in revenue . . . The sugar, which is suspected to be from Thailand and Brazil, is shipped to ports in Egypt from where it is transshipped to Mombasa as originating from there . . . Egyptian Sugar Integrated Industries, a state corporation that deals with sugar exports from Egypt has confirmed that falsified documents were used to show the imports were from here.

This sugar that was allegedly transshipped through Egypt entered into Kenya duty-free. However, Kenya had an ad valorem tariff of 100 percent on sugar from non-COMESA and non-EAC countries.

A challenge related to "country of origin" certification is to get member countries to agree on which products require certification and which ones do not. For those that require "country of origin" certification, countries may not agree on the procedures used to certify products or may not trust the organizations that issue those certifications and, thus, may refuse to accept rules of origin certificates. Likewise, countries typically have difficulties agreeing on the equivalence of each other's sanitary and phytosanitary procedures. Ngo-Eyok (2013) points to some of the bottlenecks of intra-regional trade of grain in ECOWAS caused by confusion regarding what is to be certified and who makes that decision.

Customs Union

In a customs union, member countries not only remove trade barriers among themselves but also maintain common trade barriers for goods imported from non-members. Currently three regional blocs in Africa are customs unions. These are the Economic and Monetary Community of Central Africa, also known as *Communauté Economique et Monétaire de l'Afrique Centrale* (CEMAC), the Southern African Customs Union (SACU), and the West African Economic and Monetary Union, also known as *Union Economique et Monétaire Ouest Africaine* (UEMOA) (UNCTAD, 2009).

COMESA had originally planned to establish a customs union by 2004 but failed to do so. It renewed its efforts in 2009. However, the EAC countries have not yet signed the COMESA customs union protocol. All EAC members, except South Sudan and Tanzania, are also members of COMESA. A country cannot belong to more than one customs union, unless those customs unions have the same external trade barriers. However, that would, in effect, make them a single customs union. This is the vision of the three eastern and southern African regional blocs, COMESA, the EAC, and SADC, under what is called the COMESA-EAC-SADC Tripartite.

Common Market

This level of integration extends the customs union by allowing free movement of factors of production – labor and capital – within the bloc. The first EAC was a common market. It existed from 1967 to 1977. In 2009, the EAC members signed a protocol to establish a new common market. Its implementation started gingerly in July 2010, though in reality the EAC continues to function more like a customs union, or even an advanced free trade area, as discussed in Chapter 5. Despite its name, COMESA is not a common market. As for the continent of Africa as a whole, the Abuja Treaty, which entered into force in 1994, set 2023 as the target year for an African common market.

Monetary Union

A monetary union adopts a single currency and, thus, a unified monetary policy. During the colonial era, African countries were unified by colonial currencies and institutions (O'Connell, 1997). For example, three British colonies in East Africa – Kenya, Tanganyika (now mainland Tanzania), and Uganda – had a common currency from 1921 to 1965 (Delupis, 1969). Initially, the EAC planned to establish a monetary union in 2012. Clearly that did not happen. The plan now is to establish a monetary union by 2023.

The Common Monetary Area (CMA), comprised of Lesotho, Namibia, South Africa, and Swaziland, is a quasi-monetary union. The CMA agreement allows the South African rand to circulate freely in all four countries. At the same time, it provides the three small economies freedom to issue national currencies which float freely in their respective countries.[2] Those currencies are pegged on par (on a one-to-one basis) with the rand. South Africa compensates Lesotho and Namibia for the loss of seigniorage revenue (Central Bank of Lesotho, 2006; Metzger, 2008).[3]

CEMAC and UEMOA each have a common currency. The two currencies, which were initially pegged to the French franc, are now pegged to the euro and are at parity with each other, but restricted to their respective monetary blocs (Metzger, 2008). These two blocs and the Comoros Islands form what is known as the CFA zone.[4] The West African Monetary Zone (WAMZ) has already set and missed four target dates for a single currency – 2003, 2005, 2009, and 2015. The newest target date is 2020. It seems new target dates are set just to keep the idea alive, but there has not been a real commitment to a single currency. The member countries have failed to meet macroeconomic convergence criteria, and there seems to be no leadership to move things forward. Given its relatively vast economic size, Nigeria was expected to be an obvious leader of this group of six countries. Nigeria's economy is about nine times the combined size of the other five members of WAMZ – Gambia, Ghana, Guinea, Liberia, and Sierra Leone. However, Nigeria has had its hands full dealing with attacks by Boko Haram and Niger Delta Avengers.

Economic Union

A full-fledged economic union has all the features of a monetary union plus explicit unification of fiscal policy. No single regional bloc in Africa is an economic union yet. It is the stated goal of the Abuja Treaty to have all regional economic blocs in Africa reach the level of an economic union and merge for an all-continent economic union by 2028. However, targets for early levels of integration have come and gone, only to be replaced with new ones. In 1980, the Organization of African Unity (OAU), in its Lagos Plan of Action for the economic development of Africa, set the year 2000 as the time by which an African common market would be established. Interestingly, this target was set when most African countries had inward-looking policies.

Their economies at the time were marked by monopolies and monopsonies created and shielded by their governments. Many of the so-called democracies were in fact one-party systems and dictatorships. It was in that economic context and political environment that these projections of economic integration were made.

The African Union (AU) replaced the OAU in 2002 and aimed to accelerate the integration process that had been outlined by the Abuja Treaty. Interestingly, yet not completely surprising in African politics, the major lobbyist for the unification of Africa was the Libyan dictator, Muammar Gaddafi. In fact, the precursor to the establishment of the AU was a special OAU summit of African heads of state initiated and hosted by Gaddafi in Sirte, Libya, in 1999, at which point it was declared (in the Sirte Declaration) that steps towards integration must be accelerated.[5] However, given the level at which most regional economic blocs are currently and that some states are failed states, it is totally unrealistic to imagine that Africa will be an economic union by 2028.

It is important to note that, in practice, beyond the customs union stage, economic integration towards an economic union does not follow a specific path. Regional economic blocs in Africa with a single currency have not achieved the common market stage yet. In addition, even where there is a common currency in the bloc, fiscal policy has not yet been unified to create an economic union. This is not unlike the situation in the euro zone, where countries have relinquished their power to implement monetary policy individually, but fiscal policy is still in their control.

Federation

Beyond economic union, the full "marriage" of nations is a political federation. That is the ultimate goal of the EAC – to establish the Federation of East Africa. Given the current membership of the EAC, an East African federation of all members would be a system of government that has a single national authority and six state authorities – Burundi, Kenya, Rwanda, South Sudan, Tanzania, and Uganda. If and when that happens, it will be a historical event of monumental proportion. In the early 2000s, there were calls from EAC leaders to fast-track the establishment of a federation. They thought they could establish an East African federation by 2015. An in-depth discussion about the path to a federation is provided in Chapter 8.

On April 26, 1964, Tanganyika and Zanzibar moved directly to the establishment of a single nation, Tanzania, skipping all the preliminary stages of integration. It was an arranged marriage between two leaders,

President Julius Nyerere of Tanganyika and President Abeid Amani Karume of Zanzibar.[6] It happened just a few months after Zanzibar won independence from the British (December 10, 1963) and overthrew the Sultan (January 12, 1964). The union of Tanganyika and Zanzibar (to form Tanzania) is unique, and, perhaps for good reasons, no other countries have taken such a bold move. Although the union has, by and large, remained intact, its legitimacy has come to be questioned and some would even like to see it dissolved (Mwakikagile, 2008).

REGIONAL ECONOMIC BLOCS IN AFRICA

Currently there are 17 African regional economic blocs, as shown in Figure 2.1 and Tables 2.1 and 2.2, with varying levels of integration (UNCTAD 2009, 2012, 2013). However, as of 2017, only eight of them were officially considered by the AU to be the building blocks of the African Economic Community. Those eight are listed in Table 2.1 below in bold. The level of integration indicated in parentheses does not necessarily mean that the group has actually attained it. For example, the Community of Sahel-Saharan States (CEN-SAD) is not anywhere near having a genuine free trade area yet, but that is its aspiration as of 2017.

Table 2.1 *Regional Economic Blocs in Africa*[a]

CEMAC	Economic and Monetary Community of Central Africa (monetary union)
CEN-SAD	Community of Sahel-Saharan States (free trade area)
CMA	Common Monetary Agreement (monetary union)
COMESA	Common Market for Eastern and Southern Africa (free trade area)
EAC	East African Community (common market)
ECCAS	Economic Community of Central African States (free trade area)
ECGLC	Economic Community of Great Lakes Countries (free trade area)
ECOWAS	Economic Community of West African States (free trade area)
ICGLR	International Conference on the Great Lakes Region (free trade area)
IGAD	Intergovernmental Authority on Development (free trade area)
IOC	Indian Ocean Commission (free trade area)
MRU	Mano River Union (free trade area)
SACU	Southern Africa Customs Union (customs union)
SADC	Southern African Development Community (free trade area)
UEMOA	West African Customs and Economic Union (monetary union)
UMA	Arab Maghreb Union (free trade area)
WAMZ	West African Monetary Zone (free trade area)

[a] The regional blocs in **bold** are those that are officially considered by the AU to be the "building blocks" of the African Economic Community.

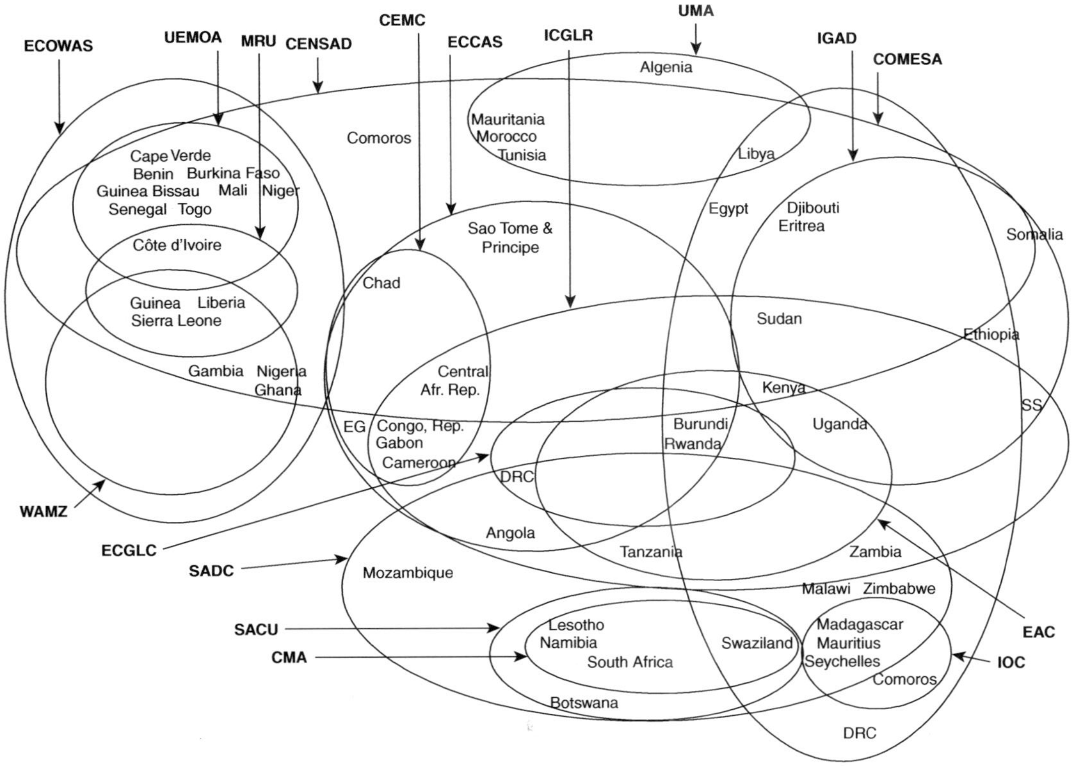

Figure 2.1 Regional Economic Blocs in Africa
Note: EG – Equatorial Guinea. SS – South Sudan; South Sudan is also a member of the EAC. Comoros and DRC (Democratic Republic of Congo) are listed at two different places in this figure.

Table 2.2 *Membership of African Countries in Regional Economic Blocs (REBs)*

	CEMAC	CENSAD	CMA	COMESA	EAC	ECCAS	ECGLC	ECOWAS	ICGLR	IGAD	IOC	MRU	SACU	SADC	UEMOA	UMA	WAMZ	REBs
Algeria																X		1
Angola						X			X					X				3
Benin		X						X							X			3
Botswana													X	X				2
Burkina Faso		X						X							X			3
Burundi				X	X	X	X		X									5
Cameroon	X					X												2
Cape Verde		X						X										2
Central African Republic	X	X				X			X									4
Chad	X	X				X												3
Comoros		X		X							X							3
Congo, Democratic Republic				X		X	X		X					X				5
Congo, Republic	X					X			X									3
Côte d'Ivoire		X						X				X			X			4
Djibouti		X		X						X								3
Egypt		X		X														2

Equatorial Guinea	X					X												2
Eritrea		X		X						X								3
Ethiopia				X						X								2
Gabon	X					X												2
Gambia		X						X									X	3
Ghana		X						X									X	3
Guinea		X						X				X					X	4
Guinea-Bissau		X						X							X			3
Kenya		X		X	X				X	X								5
Lesotho			X										X	X				3
Liberia		X						X				X					X	4
Libya		X		X												X		3
Madagascar				X							X			X				3
Malawi				X										X				2
Mali		X						X							X			3
Mauritania		X														X		2
Mauritius				X							X			X				3
Morocco		X														X		2
Mozambique														X				1
Namibia			X										X	X				3
Niger		X						X							X			3
Nigeria		X						X									X	3
Rwanda				X	X	X	X		X									5
Sao Tomé and Principe		X				X												2
Senegal		X						X							X			3

(continued)

Table 2.2 *(continued)*

	CEMAC	CENSAD	CMA	COMESA	EAC	ECCAS	ECGLC	ECOWAS	ICGLR	IGAD	IOC	MRU	SACU	SADC	UEMOA	UMA	WAMZ	REBs
Seychelles				X							X			X				3
Sierra Leone		X						X				X					X	4
Somalia		X								X								2
South Africa			X										X	X				3
South Sudan					X				X	X								3
Sudan		X		X					X	X								4
Swaziland			X	X									X	X				4
Tanzania					X				X					X				3
Togo		X						X							X			3
Tunisia		X														X		2
Uganda				X	X				X	X								4
Zambia				X					X					X				3
Zimbabwe				X										X				2
Number of members	6	29	4	19	6	11	3	15	12	8	4	4	5	15	8	5	6	160

If each country in Africa maintained membership only in one regional bloc, Africa would need 160 countries to maintain the current 17 groupings at the same levels of membership.[7] Given the total number of African countries – 54 – one could also say that, using a rounded average, every country belongs to three regional economic blocs. Except for Algeria and Mozambique, which only belong to UMA and SADC, respectively, all other African countries belong to more than one African regional economic bloc. Eight countries belong to four regional blocs, and Burundi, the Democratic Republic of Congo, Kenya, and Rwanda belong to five.

The membership of economic blocs has remained highly fluid. Accessions and withdrawals are rather common occurrences. For example, Lesotho (1997), Mozambique (1997), Tanzania (2000), and Namibia (2004) withdrew from COMESA in the years shown in parentheses. Angola suspended its membership in COMESA in 2007. Rwanda withdrew from ECCAS in 2007 and returned to it in 2014. Seychelles acceded to COMESA in 2001. Seychelles withdrew from SADC in 2004 and rejoined it in 2007. Libya acceded to COMESA in 2005. Eritrea suspended its membership in IGAD in 2007. When Eritrea wanted to rejoin IGAD in 2011, it found that it was not welcome, at least not so readily. Liberia acceded to WAMZ in 2010. Comoros and Guinea joined the CEN-SAD in 2007. Cape Verde joined the CEN-SAD in 2009. Purely in terms of membership, the CEN-SAD has grown faster than any other regional economic bloc in Africa. Founded in 1998 by six countries (at the urging of Libya's dictator, Muammar Gaddafi), it grew to 29 members by the end of 2009. Madagascar was suspended from SADC in 2009 after a coup d'état which removed President Marc Ravalomanana from office. Madagascar was also suspended from the African Union for the same reason. The AU and SADC lifted their suspensions on Madagascar in 2014 following the installment of President Hery Rajaonarimampianina who was democratically elected. South Sudan joined the EAC in 2016.

In addition to regional economic blocs, there is a multitude of bilateral trade agreements between African countries and developed countries. There are also special trade arrangements, such as the US African Growth and Opportunity Act (AGOA), the EU Everything But Arms (EBA), and the Generalized System of Preferences (GSP), which add their own complexities.

AGOA is a 2000 US trade law that gives preferential treatment to goods originating from Sub-Saharan Africa. In 2001, the EU expanded its already relatively open policy towards the least developed countries with what they call the EBA initiative. The EBA removes quotas and tariffs on all products, except for weapons and ammunitions, coming from the LDCs, including 34 African countries. The GSP is a program under which developed countries provide preferential reduction or removal of trade barriers for products from designated developing countries.

On top of everything else, the evolution of the Cotonou Agreement into Economic Partnership Agreements (EPAs) has added even more "noodles" into what was already referred to as a "spaghetti bowl" of regionalism. As if that were not enough, in 2016 the United Kingdom decided to leave the EU. That means that once the United Kingdom officially exits the EU, in addition to EPAs between the EU and ACP countries, EPAs would need to be established between the United Kingdom and ACP countries.

Negotiations between the EU and ACP countries on EPAs started in 2002, and by 2016 the EU had concluded EPA deals with the Southern African Development Community (SADC), ECOWAS, and the EAC (ICTSD, 2014a).[8] After signing an EPA, an ACP country has a 15-year transition period to liberalize at least 80 percent of its imports from the EU.

Negotiating EPAs as economic blocs is rather complicated because member countries in every bloc are quite diverse. That is part of the reason why it is taking so many years for African countries to sign EPAs with the EU. In the EAC, for example, Kenya is a middle-income country while the other five countries are categorized as least developed countries.[9] The least developed countries do not need an EPA to receive preferential treatment from the EU because they already benefit from the EBA. The same can be said about the least developed countries in ECOWAS and SADC. By having to negotiate as a group, member countries must first overcome the differences that tend to divide them and create an "us" attitude when negotiating with other countries.

But the "us" attitude can be elusive. While all EAC countries joined together to negotiate an EPA deal that was concluded in 2014, just a few days before the signing ceremony in 2016, Tanzania (followed by Burundi and Uganda) pulled out of the deal (Olingo, 2016; Viljoen, 2016). Later Uganda changed its mind and agreed to sign the deal. The future of the EPA deal between the EAC and the EU became uncertain because the EAC had negotiated as a regional bloc. While the decision in 2016 by the United Kingdom to leave the EU may have been a factor in the decision by Tanzania, the most likely explanation is that it had nothing to lose by not signing the EPA deal, at least not right away. As a least developed country, Tanzania has access to the EU market through the EBA, without being required to provide reciprocity, unlike an EPA agreement. What is not clear is why it agreed to the EPA deal in the first place. Needless to say, the decision by Tanzania was not well received by Kenya, which does not qualify for the EBA. The rules of origin used by the EU to determine which goods qualify for the EBA essentially eliminate the possibility of Kenya transshipping its goods through its EAC partners.[10]

It is worth noting that African countries' membership in multiple regional economic blocs is itself another challenge in negotiating EPAs. ACP countries were to negotiate with the EU as regional groups and not as individual ACP countries in order to streamline the process. The 76 ACP countries were divided into seven negotiating regions, roughly in line with regional economic blocs. In some cases, members of a given regional bloc were split into different groups in negotiating the EPAs. For example, the SADC-EU EPA applies to only seven of the fifteen SADC countries. The other eight SADC members are negotiating an EPA with the EU through other regional blocs. In addition, in the Common Market for Eastern and Southern Africa (COMESA), for example, Egypt is not an ACP country.

The five largest economic blocs in Africa are the CEN-SAD, COMESA, ECCAS, ECOWAS, and SADC. All African countries, except Algeria, belong to at least one of these regional blocs. Some regional blocs are subsets of others, as shown in Figure 2.1 and Table 2.2. All members of ECOWAS and UMA, except Algeria in the latter, are members of the CEN-SAD. All members of UEMOA and WAMZ are members of ECOWAS. All members of IGAD, except Somalia and South Sudan, are members of COMESA. All members of SACU are members of SADC. There is also an overlapping of membership in the COMESA-EAC-SADC Tripartite. For example, all members of the EAC, except Tanzania, are members of COMESA. Seven members of SADC are also members of COMESA.

Needless to say, the overall picture with respect to regional economic integration in Africa is that of considerable duplication and complexity. Administratively, that can be very costly. This is the reason some SADC members withdrew from COMESA. However, it is important to note that the subsets within larger blocs allow countries to deepen their level of integration at different speeds until they can all join together at a higher level of integration, as envisioned by the Abuja Treaty. For example, in ECOWAS, UEMOA already has a common currency. WAMZ is working on having a common currency for its sub-region. If and when WAMZ reaches that goal, attaining a common currency for the whole ECOWAS region would become more of a possibility. Moreover, when groups have some countries in common, the probability of those groups joining together to form one large group may be enhanced.

Regarding the number of regional economic blocs in Africa, it is important to note that (a) many of them were the result of colonialism or reactions to colonialism, and (b) some of them were initially established with a specific objective. Chapter 3 demonstrates how British colonial rule was clearly the foundation for and architect of the former EAC. CEMAC and UEMOA are directly linked to French colonial rule, which was keen in establishing economic unions of its colonies from the very start of colonialism. SACU, the oldest customs union in the world, was established by the 1910 agreement between South Africa and the High Commission Territories of Bechuanaland (Botswana), Basutoland (Lesotho), and Swaziland.[11] Namibia joined SACU formally in 1990 when it gained independence, but it was a *de facto* member of SACU all along as a South African colony (McCarthy, 2003). The CMA was an offshoot of SACU when, in 1921, South Africa established its central bank (South African Reserve Bank) and its currency became the only medium of exchange and legal tender in the SACU region (Wang, Jian-Ye, et al., 2007).

SADC is a child of the Southern African Development Coordination Conference (SADCC). SADCC was born out of the 1980 Lusaka Declaration of nine countries – Angola, Botswana, Lesotho, Malawi, Mozambique, Swaziland, Tanzania, Zambia, and Zimbabwe. The Lusaka Declaration itself resulted from the coalition of the Frontline States (Angola, Botswana, Mozambique, Tanzania, and Zambia) formed in 1970. The efforts of the Frontline States were instrumental in bringing political freedom to Zimbabwe (then Southern Rhodesia) and Namibia and ending apartheid in South Africa. Namibia joined SADCC in 1990 immediately following its independence. SADCC functioned effectively as a political forum, particularly against South Africa's apartheid regime.

Whether it was a restructured economic bloc of what was left behind by the colonialists or a newly created one, such as the CEN-SAD, COMESA, ECCAS, and ECOWAS, one goal has always been to use economic integration as a way to reduce economic dependence, especially on former colonial powers. Moreover, regional economic integration was anticipated to produce political and economic leverage in multilateral negotiations.

In addition to the predecessor of SADC, another example of a regional economic bloc that was initially established with a specific goal is IGAD. IGAD is the successor of the Inter-Governmental Authority on Drought and Development (IGADD), which was formed in 1986 to coordinate the efforts of member countries, primarily to deal with drought and other related disasters in the region (Review of African Political Economy, 1994). As the areas of cooperation expanded, especially in trying to resolve political conflicts in the region, "drought" was dropped out of IGADD in 1996, and the bloc was renamed the Inter-Governmental Authority on

Development (IGAD). In 2012, IGAD members announced their intention to transform IGAD into a full-fledged free trade area (Mbogo, 2012).

All regional economic blocs are dynamic and, unlike in the past when external influence was dominant, African countries have increasingly taken charge of their economies. In pursuing economic integration, African countries have also moved from being reactive to proactive. One can argue that from the 1960s up to the early 1990s, the approach of African countries to economic integration was mostly a reaction to colonialism. The tone in trade policy rhetoric was almost isolationist – divert trade from developed countries to African countries, irrespective of the differences in opportunity costs. Likewise, reacting to an uneven distribution of benefits of trade among African countries (partly an outcome of colonialism), regional economic blocs were setting up complicated compensation schemes and making bureaucratic decisions regarding the location of certain industries (that is, in which countries to locate). In many ways, the approach was against what economic integration is supposed to promote – freer trade.

It is important to note that, generally speaking, being reactive can be the response needed at a given time. It was the reaction to colonialism that led 13 American colonies to unite and fight the British to win their freedom. That reactive approach in Africa, while not abandoned altogether, started to fade away in the 1990s. Many African countries started to institute economic and political reforms that gave the private sector more freedom to grow and brought some degree of accountability to governance. Around the same time, the IMF and World Bank responded to the mounting criticism over their high-handed structural adjustment programs. In an apparent effort to repair their images, in 1999, the IMF and World Bank developed a new mechanism for issuing loans – Poverty Reduction Strategy Papers (PRSPs). Under this framework, countries were invited to take the initiative to prepare nationally owned PRSPs (IMF, 2000). Developing countries were given more policy space to determine their own economic destinies.

While the availability of outside technical and financial assistance will continue to be among the factors that determine programs in a regional bloc, African countries have gained a good level of ownership of the direction of their regional blocs. As a result, policy recommendations relating to economic integration have become more proactive rather than reactive. Emphasis is now on reducing non-trade barriers and improving the infrastructure and trade facilitation in the region as ways to increase intra-regional trade. This may lead to reduced trade with former colonial masters, but that is not the overarching objective.

As can be expected, each economic region has its own dynamism determined by many factors, including the differences in the economic size of the member countries, economic growth, internal political stability, the role of the private sector, and, importantly, the personalities of the leaders. The huge difference in economic size between member countries often creates natural leaders in the group, such as South Africa in SACU and Nigeria in ECOWAS. These countries are conspicuously hegemonic powers in these groups. They can lead their groups to higher levels of integration or be the major stumbling block. At the same time, a lack of hegemonic power is evident in a group such as ECCAS, where there seem to be no leadership in furthering economic integration (Elowson and Wiklund, 2011).

In the last few years, nowhere has the dynamism of regional economic integration in Africa been more apparent than in the EAC. It is mainly for this reason that the EAC is being used as a case study in this book. As will be clear in the succeeding chapters, some leaders in the EAC have been more proactive than others, creating what came to be known as the "coalition of the willing." This is comprised of the presidents of Kenya, Rwanda, and Uganda and, by extension, refers to the coalition of those three countries.

CURRENT MEMBERS OF THE EAST AFRICAN COMMUNITY, EXCLUDING SOUTH SUDAN

Most of the analytical comparison excludes South Sudan due to its newness in the EAC. Moreover, as a relatively new country, very little data is available. The founding members of the EAC are Kenya, Tanzania, and Uganda. Burundi and Rwanda joined the EAC in 2007. South Sudan joined the EAC in 2016. All members of the EAC, except Kenya, are officially categorized as least developed countries (LDCs), and Burundi, Rwanda, and Uganda are also landlocked. In fact, after Kenya rebased its gross domestic product (GDP) in 2014, revealing that its GDP in 2013 was actually $55 billion (25 percent higher than before the statistical revision), it was elevated from a developing country to a low middle-income country.[12] Rebasing increased Kenya's GDP per capita in 2013 from $994 to $1,246.

The GDP of the EAC in 2014 was $147 billion or about 9 percent of Sub-Saharan Africa's GDP. Burundi has by far the smallest economy and is the poorest country in the EAC, as shown in Table 2.3. Its share of GDP in the EAC in 2014 was only 2.1 percent. Although Rwanda and Burundi are comparable in geographical size and population, Rwanda's GDP was 250 percent larger than that of Burundi's. Burundi's GDP per capita is about 30 percent of the weighted average GDP per capita of the other four members and only one-fifth that of Kenya's.

All members of the EAC had respectable real GDP growth rates in the last 15 years, even when developed countries were in a recession. The average annual growth rate of the real GDP for the EAC from 2000–2014 was 6.3 percent.

The EAC countries also vary significantly in geographical size and population, as shown in Table 2.3. For example, you can fit Burundi, Kenya, Rwanda, and Uganda into Tanzania, and have enough area left to easily accommodate another Burundi and Rwanda. Some of these differences may be inconsequential. However, in general, these differences can be opportunities for mutually beneficial economic endeavors or sources of fear regarding deeper integration. Kenyans, for example, whose arable land per capita is half that of Tanzanians, may see the vast underutilized arable land in Tanzania as a golden opportunity to invest there in agriculture and livestock. However, Tanzanians may see an agreement that makes it easier for Kenyans and other "outsiders" to buy land in Tanzania as frightening. It should be pointed out that this kind of fear is neither unique to Tanzania nor to Africa.

Table 2.3 includes the Corruption Perception Index (CPI), produced annually by Transparency International (an NGO), because corruption is an insidious form of non-tariff barrier, as discussed in Chapter 5. The CPI is a good broad measure of corruption, which is an endemic and persistent problem in Africa, and the EAC bloc is not spared from it.

> The index defines corruption as the abuse of public office for private gain, and measures the degree to which corruption is perceived to exist among a country's public officials and politicians. It is a composite index, drawing on 16 surveys from 10 independent institutions, which gathered the opinions of businesspeople and country analysts. (Transparency International, 2006)

The CPI ranges from 0 to 100, from highly corrupt to highly clean, respectively. The smaller the CPI, the higher the level of corruption. Transparency International considers a CPI of 50 as the borderline number that separates countries that do and do not have serious problems with corruption. Countries are also ranked, starting with the least corrupt to the most corrupt. Out of 168 countries in the 2015 survey by Transparent International, 54 countries had a CPI of 50 or above, including only six African countries: Mauritius and Namibia (CPI of 53, ranked 45th), Rwanda (CPI of 54, ranked 44th), Cape Verde and Seychelles (CPI of 55, ranked 40th), and Botswana (CPI of 63, ranked 28th). Rwanda's CPI was above 50 from 2012–2015, except in 2014 when it dropped to 49.

Table 2.3 *Selected Features of EAC Countries*

	GDP 2014		Real GDP per Capita 2014 Current ($)	Real GDP Annual Average Growth Rate 2000–2014	Population 2014		Land Area		Corruption Perception Index			
	Current ($) (billions)	Share of EAC (Percentage)			(millions)	Share of EAC (Percentage)	Square km. (thousands)	Share of EAC (Percentage)	2012	2013	2014	2015
Sub-Saharan Africa	1,729		1,776	4.9	973.4		23,616					
EAC	147.0		939	6.3	156.6		1,707					
Burundi	3.1	2.11	287	3.7	10.8	6.90	26	1.5	19	21	20	21
Kenya	60.9	41.42	1,356	4.8	44.9	28.67	569	33.3	26	25	26	25
Rwanda	7.9	5.37	699	7.7	11.3	7.22	25	1.5	53	53	49	54
Tanzania	48.1	32.72	929	6.7	51.8	33.10	886	52.0	35	33	31	30
Uganda	27.0	18.37	714	7.3	37.8	24.14	201	11.8	29	26	26	25

Sources: Transparency International (2015) and World Bank (2015).

As the CPI suggests, Rwanda is a clear exception within the EAC. Rwanda has climbed steadily from a CPI of 25 (ranked 131st) in 2006 to 54 in 2015. That trend suggests there is a culture of transparency and accountability developing in Rwanda. Of course, it may be too early to say whether or not that trend will be sustained, especially given that its CPI dropped in 2014 (ranked 55th). The remaining members of the EAC have noticeably low CPIs. In 2015, they ranged from 21 (Burundi) to 30 (Tanzania), as shown in Table 2.3.

The EAC countries are plagued by "big time" corruption at all levels of government and also by what the World Bank has called "quiet corruption." Quiet corruption indicates "various types of malpractice of frontline providers (teachers, doctors, inspectors, and other government representatives) that do not [necessarily] involve monetary exchange" (World Bank, 2010, p. xi). Kenya, Tanzania, and Uganda are mentioned repeatedly in the World Bank study in highlighting absenteeism of teachers and health care providers. (See a review of the World Bank study by Tandon, 2010.) It is worth mentioning that in October 2015, Tanzania elected a new president who has declared war on corruption. If he is successful, the level of corruption in Tanzania will decrease and its CPI will start to climb.

The structure of merchandise exports of the EAC members is shown in Table 2.4. It is important to note that the structure of merchandise exports is very sensitive to exogenous variables such as the terms of trade and the weather, especially considering that all of these countries still rely heavily on agricultural exports. Incidentally, the structure of merchandise exports may change significantly in a few years in Uganda, and prospectively in Kenya and Tanzania, if the oil and natural gas discoveries in these countries lead to

Table 2.4 *The Structure of EAC Exports, 2014*

		Main Categories of Exports (Percentage)				
Country	Total Value in US $ (millions)	All Foods	Agricultural Raw Materials	Fuels	Ores and Metals	Manufactures
Burundi	130	72.1	0.4	0.0	3.3	24.2
Kenya	6,133	46.2	12.2	1.0	2.2	36.9
Rwanda	736	36.9	4.1	0.2	46.5	12.3
Tanzania	4,645	45.2	7.1	3.5	15.5	28.5
Uganda	2,270	66.1	5.9	1.1	0.9	25.7

Source: World Bank (2015).

Table 2.5 *Intra-regional Exports, 2008–2014*

	Exports as Percent of Total Intra-EAC Exports				
	Burundi	Kenya	Rwanda	Tanzania	Uganda
2008	0.3	54.6	6.5	11.9	26.7
2009	0.3	54.7	2.3	15.2	27.6
2010	0.5	54.3	2.3	16.7	26.1
2011	0.9	56.8	3.0	15.3	24.0
2012	0.5	49.3	10.6	16.1	23.6
2013	0.9	41.3	3.5	31.9	22.3
2014	0.9	47.7	4.7	20.1	26.7

Source: East African Community (2015).

production of exportable oil and natural gas. However, an increase in the percentage of exports contributed by fuels, for example, does not necessarily imply a decrease in the exports of other products. It can simply mean that fuel exports are growing faster than the exports of other products. In fact, depending on how fuel revenues are invested in the economy, fuel exports can promote the growth of other sectors. Unfortunately, such an optimistic outlook for Africa has often proven to be naïve.

In many African countries, oil has proven to be both a blessing and a curse (Kron, 2011). The discussion on oil discoveries in East Africa is extended in Chapter 8 because oil production has the potential to transform a country's economy and politics, for better or worse. In addition, oil production and the distribution of its proceeds will undoubtedly be a factor in determining the direction of economic and political integration in East Africa.

As can be expected, given its relative economic size, Kenya provides the largest share of intra-regional exports, as shown in Table 2.5.[13] Intra-regional trade is discussed in more detail in subsequent chapters, but it is worth noting at this point that a considerable amount of trade within East Africa is not recorded (Lesser and Moisé-Leeman, 2009).

SOUTH SUDAN

The number of member countries in the EAC increased to six when the newest country in the world, South Sudan, joined the bloc in 2016. South Sudan officially separated from Sudan and became an independent country on July 9, 2011. South Sudan has a population of 12 million people, bringing the population of the EAC to 165 million people. With an area of 644,000 square kilometers, South Sudan becomes the second largest country in the EAC. It is landlocked, and it is a least developed country.

According to the World Bank, South Sudan's GDP and GDP per capita in 2014 were, respectively, $13.3 billion and $1,100. However, the civil war that broke out in late 2013 and the free fall of oil prices from an average of $100 a barrel between 2012 and 2014 to less than $40 a barrel in early 2016 caused its GDP to fall precipitously. South Sudan is rich in arable land, and the vast majority of the population depends on subsistence farming. However, the overall economy of South Sudan is highly dependent on oil. Oil production accounts for almost 100 percent of export revenue, 95 percent of government revenue, and 50 percent of GDP (African Development Bank Group, 2015).

South Sudan is among the most corrupt countries in the world, even worse than Burundi. Out of 168 countries in the 2015 survey by Transparent International, South Sudan (tied with Angola) was ranked 163rd with a CPI of 15. Only four other countries in the survey had a CPI lower than that of South Sudan – Sudan, Afghanistan, North Korea, and Somalia.

South Sudan's major trading partners are Ethiopia, Kenya, Sudan, and Uganda (African Development Bank Group, 2013). The formal trade is highly lopsided, with South Sudan exporting much less than what it imports from the four major trading partners. However, it should be noted that economic activities in South Sudan are dominated by subsistence farmers and informal entrepreneurs. Even cross-border trade with neighboring counties is dominated by informal traders.

But even this subsistence farming and informal trade are threatened by the seemingly endless civil war in South Sudan. Peace agreements have been reached only to be ignored after a short period. After two-and-a-half years of a brutal civil war, in 2015, South Sudan's leaders agreed to form a transitional coalition government. The coalition government was mandated to administer free elections within 30 months of its existence. While the peace deal and the transitional government were tenuous, at best, they helped to convince the EAC leaders to admit South Sudan into their regional bloc in March of 2016. Nonetheless, fighting resumed in South Sudan in July of 2016 with no clear, permanent solution in sight. That led to the United Nations Secretary General Ban Ki-moon warning that South Sudan was "poised on the brink of an abyss" (The New York Times, 2016).

Notes

1. It is not clear how enforceable the most-favored nation clause is in this context when countries often belong to a number of economic blocs that have different levels of integration.
2. The South African economy is at least 20 times the size of the three small economies combined.
3. The Central Bank of South Africa, like other central banks, issues currency by buying government securities. Central banks earn interest revenue on those securities. Seigniorage is the difference between that interest revenue and the cost of producing and distributing currency. When a country adopts another country's currency, it loses seigniorage. South Africa's compensation for the loss of seigniorage is based on the annual yield of South African government bonds and the amount of rands circulating in Lesotho and Namibia (Tavlas, 2007). In 1986, Swaziland withdrew from a commitment to peg its currency (lilangeni) to the rand. However, for practical reasons it has continued to peg its currency on par with the rand and also to allow rands to circulate freely in Swaziland. Nonetheless, since Swaziland has rescinded the obligation to link its currency with the South African rand, it cannot claim compensation from South Africa for any loss in seigniorage.
4. CFA stands for *Communauté Financière d'Afrique* – "Financial Community of Africa."
5. The BBC (July 8, 2002) described the [African] union as "the brainchild of Libyan leader Colonel Muammar Gaddafi." Taken literally, the statement disregards the earlier voices of distinguished African leaders such as Kwame Nkrumah of Ghana and Julius Nyerere of Tanzania who promoted the idea of an African union years before Gaddafi was in power. Nonetheless, the timing of the Sirte Declaration and the establishment of the AU had a lot to do with Gaddafi. In fact, paragraph 7 of the Sirte Declaration has explicit admiration for Gaddafi's "inspirational leadership." "In our deliberations, we have been inspired by the important proposals submitted by Colonel Muammar Ghaddafi, Leader of the Great Al Fatah Libyan Revolution, and particularly, by his vision for a strong and united Africa, capable of meeting global challenges and in shouldering its responsibility to harness the human and natural resources of the continent in order to improve the living conditions of its peoples" (African Union, 1999).
6. Mwakikagile (2008) provides an insightful discussion about the political and social environment of the time and the convictions of Nyerere and Karume that shed light on the formation of the union and its timing.
7. South Sudan is not yet an official member of COMESA. However, since it was part of Sudan, which is a member of COMESA, South Sudan has observer status in COMESA.
8. The European Commission provides updates on the status of EPA negotiations on its website: http://ec.europa.eu/trade/policy/countries-and-regions/development/economic-partnerships/.
9. South Sudan joined the EAC after the EPA deal between the EAC and the EU had been concluded. In 2014, Kenya was classified as a middle-income country after a statistical revision of its GDP (rebasing), which increased Kenya's GDP by 25 percent (Gundan, 2014). Uganda also rebased its GDP in 2014, raising it by 13 percent (Mold and Mukwaya, 2014).

10. This is not to suggest that the certification requirements of the rules of origin under EBA can guarantee the prevention of transshipment, but the author is not aware of such transshipment involving any EAC country. Cambodia, Indonesia, Malaysia, Pakistan, the Philippines, Sri Lanka, and Tunisia have been accused of transshipping to the EU bicycles made in China (Official Journal of the European Union, 2015).
11. The three High Commission Territories are referred to as such because they were ruled by the British government through the High Commissioner for South Africa.
12. Rebasing GDP is the process by which an old base year is replaced with a new one. Rebasing is done every few years because the structure of the economy changes over time.
13. It is not clear what explains the outliers for Rwanda's number in 2012 and Tanzania's in 2013.

3

The Colonial Background of the Former East African Community

It is often the case that the present is understood better, and plans for the future are made with a broader perspective, when one considers and learns from the past. It is for this reason that Chapters 3 and 4 are included to provide a detailed historical perspective on the current EAC. While the political environment and economic conditions in East Africa are very different today from those that prevailed during the colonial era and the period of the first EAC, the current EAC is directly tied to the evolution of the economic integration in the region during those periods.

The former East African Community (EAC) was comprised of Kenya, Tanzania, and Uganda and lasted only a decade, 1967–1977. It died while still very young. However, a long history of economic cooperation between these nations preceded this first EAC. In fact, its creation can only be understood and appreciated in the context of that history. Likewise, that history helps to explain, at least in part, why the first EAC collapsed.

It is debatable how far back in history one should go to explain the economic cooperation of the East African countries. However, to analyze the rise and fall of the first EAC, the onset of colonialism may provide a logical starting point. In fact, the history of any regional economic bloc in Africa is deficient if it does not include the colonial history. For example, the Southern Africa Customs Union (SACU) and the Common Market Agreement (CMA) are clearly the offspring of colonialism. The history of the Economic and Monetary Community of Central Africa (CEMAC) can be traced back to 1919, when France established the Federation of French Equatorial Africa comprised of Cameroon, Central African Republic, Chad, the Republic of Congo, and Gabon (Thompson and Adloff, 1960). But even without those developments, the division of Africa by the Europeans in itself is sufficient to make the colonial history relevant to understanding how Africa is striving to unite.

Equipped with survey drawing tools and sharp pencils, and regarding Africa as their inheritance and a continent to be "civilized," major European nations met in Berlin, Germany, in 1884–85 and divided the African continent among themselves (Pakenham, 1991). Tanganyika (today's Tanzanian mainland), Burundi, and Rwanda were claimed by Germany. Kenya became a British colony, that is, a British "possession." Zanzibar and Uganda became British protectorates in 1890 and 1894, respectively. In theory, as a protectorate, a country does not cease to exist as an independent state (Grewe, 2000). However, in practice, protectorates were ruled, more or less, as colonies.

Tanganyika was separated from Kenya and Uganda by straight lines that, in some areas, divided people of the same ethnic groups. After WWI, Germany lost Tanganyika to Britain and Burundi and Rwanda to Belgium. Kenya, Tanganyika, and Uganda were now under one colonial master, the British. However, Tanganyika did not become a British "colony" the same way that Kenya, for example, was. Tanganyika was a "mandated" territory, that is, a territory that the League of Nations placed under the "temporary" administration of one of the victorious nations of WWI.

The League of Nations was established in 1919 following the end of WWI to promote peace and international cooperation. The League of Nations charged the governing country, Britain, in the case of Tanganyika, to improve the standard of living in the territories with which it had been entrusted, and to prepare the territory for self-governance. Self-governance was the end goal and, thus, the guiding principle of the mandate system.

The mandate system was the League of Nations' attempt to regulate colonial administration. But this must not be interpreted as a major change of heart by the European countries about colonialism. The British and other powers did not offer to change the status of their colonies to "mandated" states. Tanganyika was a bonus territory for the British, who were quite happy to get it under less than favorable conditions. It is analogous to someone who had slaves of his own and was rewarded with newly dispossessed slaves. The slave owner is told that he can use these new workers for his economic benefit but should also help them acquire useful skills that would enable them to be economically independent when they are eventually freed. Any slave owner would jump at this offer, given that he was not asked to put his own slaves on the same path to freedom. He would treat his "permanent" slaves differently from the temporary slaves. He would see to it that his permanent slaves acquire skills quickly, without too much fear of losing them. As for the temporary slaves, the master would have to perform some balancing act. He would want to help them develop some skills so they could be profitable to him, but he would do so strategically, regarding the kind and pace of skill development, to prevent those slaves from becoming free and independent too quickly. It should, therefore, not be surprising that the Europeans invested more in Kenya than in Tanganyika (and Uganda), as discussed later in this chapter.

Overall, the colonial economy in East Africa, as in other parts of Africa, was characterized by a number of salient features, the residual impact of which is still present today. The transportation system was disarticulated in a way that increased the dependence of the colonies on its metropolis. Railway lines and major roads were primarily built to facilitate trade with the European countries. Thus, all railway lines and roads lead to ports on the coast.

The monetary system further guaranteed the economic dependence of the territories on Europe. Money supply in the territories was determined by the level of exports from the territories to the European colonial powers. Thus, the supply of East African shillings was determined by the sterling pound reserves generated by exports from East African territories. The colonial powers would hold the foreign reserves generated by those exports and, in turn, supply local currency to their respective territories, equivalent to the foreign reserves. Needless to say, the colonialists invested the foreign currency for their own economic prosperity. Rodney (1989, 188) notes that "Africa's total contribution to Britain's sterling balances in 1945 was £446 million, which went up to £1,446 million by 1955," 68 percent of the total reserves of Britain and the Commonwealth.

If territories wanted to stimulate their own economy by increasing the money supply, they had to increase their exports to Europe. The system was counter-cyclical for the territories' economies. An economic boom that caused an increase in exports led to an increase in the money supply. Likewise, an economic recession that caused exports to fall led to a decrease in the money supply. It was the colonial version of the "export-led" growth model.

In a way, the colonialists took the dictates of comparative advantage and trade to an absurd extreme in their version of capitalism, specialization, and the pattern of trade. Brutal force, usurpation of land, taxes which could only be paid with the currency controlled by the colonialists, and other forms of exploitation, combined to create over-specialization in agricultural production and prevent industrialization. As such, there was neither diversity nor the backward and forward linkages usually associated with a cohesive economic system, where growth in one sector of the economy is transmitted into other sectors. Growth in the production of tobacco and cotton in Tanganyika, for example, did not lead to development of tobacco products and textile industries. The pattern of trade was straightforward – Africa, or more accurately Africans, exported raw materials and imported manufactured goods. The few processing businesses in Africa were owned by Europeans and, in the case of East Africa, by Asians.

Another key feature of the colonial economy was the nurturing of the colonialists' monopolies. These were not natural monopolies or ones that had developed from competition, but rather companies that were protected by the colonial powers. It is important to emphasize that in the early years of colonialism, the British granted the administration of its territories to private, for-profit companies, notably, the British East Africa Company and the British South Africa Company. These companies were solely focused on maximizing profits and dividends for their shareholders. The following remark by Ake (1991, 49) captures the essence of the colonial economy.

> The capitalism of colonial Africa displays a pathological maturity, like a highly accelerated ageing process. It has, so to speak, attained the weakness of old age without having had time to take advantage of the benefits of youthfulness, it suffered disadvantages of monopoly without having enjoyed the benefits of competition.

ECONOMIC COOPERATION DURING THE COLONIAL ERA[1]

Inter-territorial Services Between Kenya and Uganda: 1900–1919

The colonial history of the economic cooperation between Kenya and Uganda from the beginning of the 20th century through independence was directly propelled by the interests of the British, either through the British East Africa Company (up until 1920) or the more direct colonial rule. (Tanganyika fell under the British in 1919.) This history is inextricably linked to the construction of the Uganda Railway (later to be called the Kenya-Uganda Railway), from Mombasa, Kenya, on the Indian Ocean to Kisumu on the shore of Lake Victoria. Kisumu was then part of the Uganda Protectorate. The construction of the railway took six years to complete, from 1896 to 1901.

The railway construction brought an influx of indentured workers from India. It is estimated that as many as 32,000 Indian laborers were employed in the project (Delf, 1963). Many of them decided to stay in East Africa when the project was completed and warmly encouraged their compatriots to come to the "land of opportunity." During the course of the colonial era, the Indian population grew and came to dominate trade in the major cities of East Africa.

The founding of Nairobi in 1899 is attributed directly to the construction of the Kenya-Uganda Railway. During the construction, Nairobi became an important transport depot, a major camp for laborers and engineers, and a place for shifting trains from one track to another. What was described by the opponents of the railway project as the "lunatic line" gave birth to the capital of Kenya, one of the major cities in modern-day Africa. Opponents of the project in the British Parliament were concerned with the potentially high cost of the project, considering a number of challenges confronting it. These included long stretches of water shortage, rough terrain, the resistance to foreign intrusion by Africans, disease, and the lack of "skilled" local labor (Marsh and Kingsnorth, 1972). In the end, the optimists were validated and Britain felt victorious in safeguarding their control of Uganda, a territory which was on Germany's radar as its potential territory.

At the completion of the project, apparently to preempt any potential conflict in the operation of the railway, Kisumu was annexed to Kenya to have the entire railway under one local colonial administration (Byrnes et al., 1992). In fact, even without the annexation of Kisumu into Kenya, from a logistical point of view, the 965-kilometer infrastructure united Kenya and Uganda economically and administratively.

Each territory had a local leader in charge – initially an administrator, then a commissioner, and later, for most of the colonial period, a governor. Governors were accountable to the Colonial Office in London. The colonial office gave directives regarding policies, laws, and programs but still left the governors with substantial administrative power, especially in forging relations with other territories.

The inter-territorial services between Kenya and Uganda began in 1902 with the completion of the Kenya-Uganda Railway (Delupis, 1969). In 1905, an East African Currency Board was established bringing the two territories to a single currency, the East African rupee. Further integration between these territories occurred in 1911 and 1917 with the establishment of a postal union and a customs union, respectively. Throughout this time, Tanganyika was still under German rule.

Britain's Aspiration for an East African Federation: 1919–1945

Tanganyika was handed over to Britain by the League of Nations in 1919 after Germany lost WWI. The League of Nations was supposedly responsible for monitoring British rule to see how it was preparing Tanganyika for independence. However, the contract to hand over Tanganyika to Britain was highly influenced by L. S. Amery, the British representative at the establishment of the League of Nations. His strong lobby for his vision of a federation comprised of Kenya, Tanganyika, and Uganda, resulted in an insertion which asked Britain "to prepare for the immediate, complete amalgamation of the three territories" (Hughes, 1963, p. 51). Thus, on the one hand, Tanganyika was to be nurtured for eventual self-determination and independence, and on the other hand, it was to be cajoled into a federation with Kenya and Uganda on British terms.

Tanganyika joined the East African Currency Board in 1921, and in the same year the East African rupee was replaced by the East African shilling. As noted earlier in this chapter, the supply of money in any given territory was linked to the territory's export revenue, which determined the level of foreign reserves. When Kenya and Uganda formed a customs union in 1917, their customs authorities were unified into a single one. Tanganyika joined that customs union in 1923, signaling further integration. However, Tanganyika's customs union remained a separate entity until 1949. Tanganyika joined the postal union in 1933.

Focused on his goal, when L. S. Amery became Colonial Secretary in 1924, he commissioned a study on the potential for a federation of Britain's five territories in Eastern Africa: Kenya (a colony), Nyasaland, Northern Rhodesia, and Uganda (protectorates), and Tanganyika (a mandated territory). Nyasaland and Northern Rhodesia are present-day Malawi and Zambia, respectively. The study was headed by Ormsby-Gore, a British Member of Parliament. The Ormsby-Gore Commission produced a 200-page report which concluded that a federation should not be pursued. Considering that calls for forming an East African Federation and warnings against rushing into such a political union are recurring themes, a lengthy quote of the Ormsby-Gore conclusion is provided here.

> We should like to state at the outset that we are impressed with the need for greater co-operation and understanding, not only between the five Administrations but between unofficial residents in the territories as well. Few things struck us more than the lack of knowledge in each territory of East Africa regarding its neighbours; in fact, we found not merely a lack of knowledge but in many cases complete misunderstanding. But, while there is greater need for mutual understanding, we are of [the] opinion that the day is still far off when such co-operation could be brought about by the imposition of federal government over the whole of the territories.
>
> We found little, if any, support in East Africa for the idea of immediate federation, and in some quarters we found definite hostility. We received a memorial against federation from the King and native government of Buganda, and discussions which had taken place in parts of Kenya immediately prior to our arrival revealed that the suggestion was viewed with more than a little suspicion by all sections of European opinion in Kenya. All shades of opinion in Zanzibar are hostile to federation, and we also received representations against federation from various Indian Associations throughout the three Northern territories. But, apart altogether from these

expressions of opinion, we came definitely to the conclusion that any attempt at federation would be immature. (Secretary of State for the Colonies, 1925, 7–8)

It is interesting that the Colonial Office would try to conduct an opinion poll in some democratic fashion. Of course, millions of East Africans were unaware of the study, let alone what a federation would have meant to them. It is obvious that Britain wanted to benefit from economies of scale associated with governing. In addition, a federation would have given Britain a firm grip on Tanganyika, which Germans repeatedly tried to regain.

Almost as an afterthought, the Ormsby-Gore report added in its conclusion that a "[f]ederation cannot be imposed from without" (p. 9). Instead, the report recommended the modest, yet important, step of having periodic conferences of governors and heads of various departments from these territories. The idea was for the governors to discuss matters of mutual interest such as taxation, communication, agriculture, education, and native administration and to forge paths of cooperation.

The first conference of the five East African Governors and the British Resident (quasi-Governor) of Zanzibar was held in 1926 in Nairobi (Delupis, 1969). From then on, the governors met regularly, although over time Nyasaland and Northern Rhodesia dropped out of these meetings as they were placed under the influence of another commandeered "White Man's Country," Southern Rhodesia (modern-day Zimbabwe). Meanwhile, the Colonial Office in London continued to send commissions to East Africa to explore the possibility of forming a federation. They included the 1927 Hilton Young Commission and the 1929 Sir Samuel Wilson Commission. The fundamental conclusion of these commissions was always the same as the one reached by the Ormsby-Gore Commission: for one reason or another, the territories were not ready for a federation.

Nonetheless, the Conference of Governors produced deeper and wider cooperation. It established the pace and breadth of regional cooperation, as well as the institutions to carry out its plans. Zanzibar joined the East African Currency Board in 1936, replacing rupees with the East African shilling. A joint East African Income Tax Board and a joint Economic Council, as well as a secretariat of the Conference of Governors, were formed in 1940 (East African Community, 2002).

The East African High Commission: 1945–1961

A number of significant events took place in the 1940s at the international level and also in East Africa. The League of Nations, which could not prevent

WWII, faded away. It was later replaced by the United Nations (UN) in 1945, which, in turn, replaced the mandate system with an "international trusteeship system." Tanganyika remained under Britain in this "new" system. WWII rekindled people's conscience about freedom and self-determination. This was reflected clearly in the UN declaration about colonies. Chapter XI of the UN Charter declared that

> Members of the United Nations which have or assume responsibilities for the administration of territories whose peoples have not yet attained a full measure of self-government recognize the principle that the interests of the inhabitants of these territories are paramount, and accept as a sacred trust the obligation to promote to the utmost, within the system of international peace and security established by the present Charter, the well-being of the inhabitants of these territories, and, to this end: to develop self-government, to take due account of the political aspirations of the peoples, and to assist them in the progressive development of their free political institutions, according to the particular circumstances of each territory and its peoples and their varying stages of advancement. (United Nations, 1945, Article 73)

Nonetheless, even with self-governance of the colonies as the ultimate goal, Britain was given considerable latitude to chart the course of history for Tanganyika and its neighbors. The Trusteeship Agreement allowed Britain

> to constitute Tanganyika into a customs, fiscal or administrative union or federation with adjacent territories under his sovereignty or control, and to establish common services between such territories and Tanganyika where such measures are not inconsistent with the basic objectives of the international trusteeship system and with the terms of this Agreement. (United Nations, 1946, p. 2)

Notwithstanding that the Mandate and the Trusteeship agreements permitted the pursuit of integration, it was still not clear how Tanganyika could be brought into a federation with its neighbors without infringing on the key provisions of the agreements. Nonetheless, the Governors' Conference was making strides in integrating the region. The East African Airways Corporation was set up in 1946. In 1948, Tanganyika joined the Kenya-Uganda Railway to form the East African Railways and Harbor (Tulya-Muhika, 1995). Even more profound was the progress made by the Governors' Conference and the prodding from the Colonial Office which brought about the East African High Commission (EAHC) in 1948.

The EAHC had first been proposed by the Sir Samuel Wilson Commission in 1929, but the idea did not gain traction until the mid-1940s. The EAHC replaced the Governors' Conference. It was still comprised of the Governors of Kenya, Tanganyika, and Uganda, but a superior legislative structure and expanded powers were added. The role of the EAHC expanded over time. Its extensive list of areas of cooperation came to include administration, finance, posts and telegraphs, telephone and radio communications, railway and harbors, civil aviation, social services, research and scientific services, economic services, and defense (Delupis, 1969; Hughes, 1963).

Kenya's governor was the Chairman of the EAHC and Nairobi was its headquarters. Kenya's leadership role was to be expected, given that it was the only real colony and that it had a large number of Europeans settlers who wielded substantial influence. While questions arose about moving the headquarters to Dar-es-Salaam or Entebbe (the colonial capitals of Tanganyika and Uganda, respectively), the Colonial Office defended Nairobi as the logical location. Nairobi was already the headquarters of most of the inter-territorial services and was geographically halfway between Dar-es-Salaam and Entebbe. Moreover, it was argued, some High Commission meetings were held in Dar-es-Salaam and Entebbe (Secretary of State for the Colonies, 1956). Of course, that did not prevent Tanganyika and Uganda from complaining about Nairobi's control.

Specifically, Tanganyika and Uganda were dissatisfied with (a) the common fiscal policies applied to the three territories irrespective of their different levels of economic development; (b) Kenya taking the revenues generated from shared common services as its own[2]; (c) lost tariff revenues that could be generated by importing goods from other countries; and (d) the limited opportunity to industrialize, given Kenya's superiority in manufacturing (Ndegwa, 1965). The Europeans invested more in Kenya than in Tanganyika and Uganda, partly because they viewed their stay and dominance in Kenya as long term. From a political point of view, these concerns would always be powerful. However, from an economic point of view, while all these complaints had merit, it would have been wrong to accept them completely at face value.

Regarding fiscal policy, each territory determined its distribution of government expenditures independently, according to its own priorities. This policy space was not compromised in any direct way. Where the complaint had some merit was in the fact that government spending is a function of government revenues, which were determined by common tariff, excise, and income tax rates. But it is not at all clear that if Tanganyika or Uganda had set those rates independently (i.e., if there were no customs union), that their fiscal situation would have been any better. Moreover, while Kenya may have had an upper hand in deciding the tax rates, it is not as if Tanzania and Uganda had no say about them whatsoever.

The concern about lost tariff revenue originated from the reality (which has persisted) that Kenya dominated the intra-regional exports, as shown in Table 3.1. On average, from 1950 to 1961, Kenya contributed 54 percent of

Table 3.1 *Intra-regional Trade in East Africa, 1950–1961*

	Share of Exports of the Total Intra-regional Exports			Intra-regional Exports as a Percent of Each Country's Total Exports			Intra-regional Imports as a Percent of Each Country's Total Imports		
	Kenya	Tanganyika	Uganda	Kenya	Tanganyika	Uganda	Kenya	Tanganyika	Uganda
1950	52	13	35	15	3	8	6	12	8
1951	51	16	33	12	3	5	4	9	8
1952	48	11	41	12	2	7	5	8	8
1953	47	11	42	18	3	12	6	13	11
1954	47	9	44	20	3	11	6	13	11
1955	47	14	39	17	4	10	6	8	10
1956	61	17	22	18	4	6	4	11	13
1957	61	13	26	23	5	8	5	13	16
1958	54	13	33	24	6	13	7	23	20
1959	58	17	25	24	7	11	8	19	20
1960	60	10	29	26	4	13	9	20	20
1961	64	9	27	28	4	14	9	21	22

Sources: Calculated using data in Ndegwa (1963) and Lury (1965).

Table 3.2 *Shares of Intra-regional Exports and Imports of Manufactured Goods in 1959*

	Exports	Imports
Kenya	81	13
Tanganyika	4	50
Uganda	15	37

Source: Ndegwa (1965, 71).

the intra-regional exports; Kenya's contribution was as high as 64 percent in 1961. Although Kenya's dominance would make any trading partner wary, it is important not to emphasize disproportionately the benefits of exports while neglecting the benefits of the lower prices of imports to consumers and firms that use imported inputs, such as cement. Moreover, while the percentage of intra-regional imports to total imports was noticeably lower for Kenya, Tanganyika and Uganda were also highly dependent on imports from outside the East African territories, as suggested by Table 3.1.

Most frustrating to Tanganyika and Uganda was the inherent inequality in industrial development. In the 1950s, Kenya was contributing, on average, 80 percent of the intra-regional exports of manufactured goods. The shares of intra-regional exports and imports of manufactured products for 1959 are shown in Table 3.2.

A number of factors may explain Kenya's dominance in manufacturing, although the cause and effect are not always straightforward. The Europeans had a long view with regard to their dominance and stay in Kenya. Kenya had a much larger population of Europeans compared to Tanganyika and Uganda. They invested in agriculture and industry, including the processing of agricultural products. The infrastructure in Kenya was also more advanced than that of its neighbors, thus making it more attractive to investors. Moreover, Nairobi had already become a very important commercial city and home to many of the inter-territorial services. Firms in Kenya had the advantage of being first in the region and, thus, could take advantage of economies of scale, making it almost impossible for newcomers in Tanganyika and Uganda to survive without some protection.

The trade pattern between Tanganyika, the territory with the least developed manufacturing sector, and Kenya revealed clear roles, similar to those of Tanganyika and its European trading partners. Tanganyika exported raw materials and imported manufactured and processed products. For example, Tanganyika exported tobacco to Kenya and imported cigarettes from Kenya. It exported raw cotton and imported clothing. It exported pyrethrum flowers and imported pyrethrum extract.

Given that Tanganyika and Uganda had only a few highly specialized export products, they were quite vulnerable, compared to Kenya, to the whims of nature, shifts in demand, and even to an unfavorable decision by one investor. For example, the production of cigarettes began in Uganda in 1928, and they became the major export of Uganda to Kenya and Tanganyika. In 1955, cigarette exports contributed 72 percent of Uganda's intra-regional exports. However, in 1956, the manufacturer transferred some of the cigarette production to Kenya, and that alone caused Uganda's exports to Kenya and Tanzania to decrease by 60 percent that year (Hazlewood, 1975).

Whatever the gains of intra-regional trade might have been in each territory, they were not for the benefit of the majority of the population. The colonial economic system was repressive and exploitative by its very design. The benefits of trade to Kenya accrued mostly to the Europeans and Asians and a few African capitalists who controlled the system. But the lack of industrialization in Tanganyika and Uganda is not explained simply by the political and economic leverage of the Europeans in Kenya. The Europeans in Tanganyika and Uganda were not necessarily in favor of industrialization in "their" territories either. They were content with the surpluses they accrued from agriculture and, presumably, opposed to any developments that might put upward pressure on wages.

In 1935, the Japanese proposed to build a blanket factory in Uganda. It was a logical industry and location, given that Uganda had a proven, successful cotton industry. The acting governor of Kenya was in favor of the project. However, the Governor of Uganda, supported by the Governor of Tanganyika, was opposed to the proposal on the grounds that, "so far as Uganda is concerned, it can be definitely stated that it is of great importance to preserve the agricultural population and therefore I do not favor the idea of industrialization" (Nabudere, 1980, 100). It is under these contradictions that the British operated. They wanted development, but they also wanted to preserve the advantages held by the European enterprises. To paraphrase Tulya-Muhika (1995, 1), the Europeans were concerned with ways to deepen the East African integration in favor of the whites and not on the basis of equity. It is in the context of these contradictions that an East African federation was sought and Tanganyika was being prepared for its independence. This is the background against which the former EAC came into existence.

THE DAWN BEFORE THE INDEPENDENCE OF EAC COUNTRIES: 1960–1961

In conjunction with the progress towards economic integration in East Africa, a push towards independence had gained momentum in all of Africa after WWII. As the 1960s approached, it became clear that independence of the East African territories was inevitable, regardless of the resistance by the British, even with regard to Kenya where they had so much to lose. At the dawn of independence, the future of cooperation had to be re-examined and its administration restructured. Moreover, Tanganyika and Uganda were increasingly frustrated with economic cooperation that, in their view, benefited Kenya at their expense. To be fair, some of the complaints by Tanganyika and Uganda were really due to unfavorable global markets since the mid-1950s for their primary products. In addition, Kenya's manufacturing sector itself was not that developed. The manufacturing sector contributed only 10 percent of its GDP. Still, it is all relative.

At the brink of independence, Julius Nyerere, who was expected to become the first president of Tanganyika, threatened to pull his country out of East African cooperative arrangements if inequalities were not satisfactorily addressed. It must not be construed that Nyerere was indifferent to regional cooperation. Nyerere was a nationalist, but also an ardent pioneer of pan-Africanism. In fact, he was willing to postpone Tanganyika's independence to wait for Kenya and Uganda, if that meant East Africa would attain freedom as a federation. He saw that the likelihood of a federation after each country had gained its independence separately was slim, at best. He argued that

> if it is desired to bring about this Federation the right moment to do this is not after each country has separately achieved its own independence but before . . . Surely, if it is difficult now to convince some of our friends that Federation is desirable, when it does not involve surrendering any sovereignty, it is going to be a million times more difficult to convince them later. (Nyerere, 1960, 2 and 4)

But Nyerere also cared deeply about fairness and equality. The inequalities apparent in colonial East African cooperation were not tolerable.

In 1960, the Raisman Commission was established to examine the EAHC and make recommendations. The Raisman Commission reaffirmed the direct and spillover benefits associated with economic cooperation. It was mindful of the challenges threatening East African cooperation, but warned that "no territory would be likely to gain by withdrawing from it. We therefore have no hesitation in recommending that the Common Market be maintained" (Secretary of State for the Colonies, 1961, 62).

The challenges included artificial impediments to trade; the widening divide between the constitutional developments in the territories and the administrative position of the High Commission; inadequate and precarious funding for inter-territorial services; and the perennial complaint by Tanganyika and Uganda about the unequal distribution of the benefits. The Raisman Commission proposed improved economic coordination.

Following the Raisman Report and a meeting in 1961 of UK and East African leaders, it was decided to replace the EAHC with the East African Common Services Organization (EACSO). The EACSO consisted of ministers from the three territories. This came to be known as the system of triumvirates (groups of three). Triumvirates were each responsible for their respective field: communications, finance, commercial and industrial coordination, and social and research services.

The Raisman Report proposed the establishment of a distributable pool of revenue. Each territory would contribute 6 percent of its annual customs and excise revenues and 40 percent of the "income tax charged to companies on profits arising from manufacturing and finance as currently interpreted by the Commissioner of Income Tax" (Secretary of State for the Colonies, 1961, 67). Obviously, the territory that collected the largest amount of a given type of revenue would contribute the most of that revenue, in absolute terms, to the distributable pool. Half of the fund would be allocated to the EACSO for inter-territorial services that could not sustain themselves financially and the other half would be distributed equally to the three territories. The proposed distribution of the common fund was intended to give those services a measure of financial independence and stability.

The equal distribution of half of the distributable fund to the territories was meant to address the fiscal inequalities between the territories. Specifically, it was meant to redistribute revenues from Kenya to Tanganyika and Uganda. Based on the redistribution formula developed by the Raisman Commission, in 1962/63 net transfers from Kenya to Tanganyika and Uganda were £312,000 and £288,000, respectively. In addition, £137,000 was transferred to the EACSO, as shown in Table 3.3.

The formula for redistributing revenues was more or less just an acknowledgment that economic differences existed and not a real game-changer for those inequalities. In economic terms, the formula made only a minor difference. Total revenues in Kenya, Tanganyika, and Uganda, subject to the Raisman Commission's proposal in 1962/63 were, respectively, £22.5 million, £14.4 million, and £12.5 million. The net increases in revenues in Tanganyika and Uganda were only 2 percent in each country and the net loss to Kenya was only 3 percent. Nonetheless, the Raisman formula was

Table 3.3 *Revenue Redistribution Through the Distributable Pool, 1962–63*

		£ thousands			
		Kenya	Tanganyika	Uganda	Total
Contribution From Each Territory	Customs & Excise (6% of total)	1,209	827	723	2,759
	Income Tax (40% of total)	947	236	−189	1,372
	Less Collection Costs	54	27	23	104
	Gross	2,102	1,036	889	4,027
Less Redistribution to Each Territory (50%)		671	671	671	2,013
Net Contribution		1,431	365	218	2,014
Estimated Contribution by Old System to Common Services		694	677	506	1,877
Gain or Loss		−737	+312	+288	
Payments to EACSO under Raisman Formula					2,014
Payments to EACSO under Old System					1,877
Gain or Loss to EACSO					+137

Source: Table VI.3 in Ndegwa (1965, 105).

a diplomatic victory, as all sides accepted it. The Raisman Commission had led to the establishment of the EACSO and a revenue distribution formula which kept regional economic integration going as these three countries entered an exciting new phase in history – independence.

Notes

1. For extended discussions, see Delupis (1969), Hazlewood (1975), Hughes (1963), and Tulya-Muhika (1995) from which some of the information here has been drawn.
2. Tulya-Muhika (1995, 5) points out that the revenue from railway services, which should have been shared by the region, was routinely amalgamated with Kenya's own revenue. In addition, railway fees were set unilaterally by Kenya "as a protective instrument for its own agricultural and industrial development often against economic interests of [the other colonies]."

4

The Rise and Fall of the Former East African Community

EARLY YEARS OF INDEPENDENCE: 1961–1966

Between 1956 and 1958, five African countries (two British colonies and three French colonies) gained independence.[1] In 1960, 17 African countries (one Belgian colony, two British colonies, and 14 French colonies) gained independence. The struggle for independence was not over by any means, but the end of direct colonialism in Africa by the Europeans was in sight. By May of 1963, when the Organization of Africa Unity (OAU) was established, there were 32 independent African countries.

The purpose of the OAU was:

(a) To promote the unity and solidarity of the African States;
(b) To coordinate and intensify their cooperation and efforts to achieve a better life for the peoples of Africa;
(c) To defend their sovereignty, their territorial integrity and independence;
(d) To eradicate all forms of colonialism from Africa; and
(e) To promote international cooperation, having due regard to the Charter of the United Nations and the Universal Declaration of Human Rights (Organization of African Unity, 1963, 3).

The OAU encouraged economic integration as a way to be truly independent. The East African countries were expected to demonstrate leadership in this endeavor, given their history of cooperation. As it happened, the winds of discontent among Kenya, Tanganyika, and Uganda which had already gained momentum before independence were only calmed for a short period by the Raisman Commission. Not even the excitement of establishing the OAU could diffuse the tensions among the three East

African countries. Moreover, as the territories gained their independence, Tanganyika in 1961, Uganda in 1962, and Kenya in 1963, the nationalist sentiment increased, thus magnifying whatever resentments existed between the three countries. Tanganyika and Zanzibar united in 1964 to form Tanzania. National affairs were given priority over matters of the East African Common Services Organization (EACSO). It did not help that the EACSO's power was very limited. While it had authority over common services, individual countries had the power to set tax rates. The effectiveness of the EACSO was determined not so much by its structure, but rather by the member countries' commitment to economic cooperation (or lack thereof).

As it happened, the EACSO was itself a source of contention. The EACSO and all self-sustaining common services were headquartered in Nairobi. Partly due to that geographical reality, Kenyans dominated the administration of the EACSO. On top of that, Nairobi was the headquarters for most of the head offices of companies operating in East Africa. That meant Kenya received the lion's share of income tax revenue. All of these elements that favored Kenya, in conjunction with national politics, made Tanganyika and Uganda even more outspoken about their displeasure with the economic disparity between them and Kenya. The formula to redistribute revenues developed by the Raisman Commission soon came to be seen as inadequate to address the imbalances. It became apparent that to save the common market, a broader scheme to distribute production was needed.

The Kampala Agreement

The Kampala Agreement was reached in 1964 and approved by the Assembly of Heads of States in 1965. Its primary goal was to rectify the trade imbalances in East Africa by steering industrialization from Kenya (the surplus country) to Tanzania and Uganda (the deficit countries). This was to be achieved using five measures:

(a) Immediate action with certain inter-territorially connected firms to increase production in a deficit country and thereby reduce imports from the surplus country.
(b) Agreement as to the immediate allocation of certain major industries.
(c) The application of a system of quotas and suspended quotas, whereby exports from surplus countries would be progressively reduced, and local production would be increased in the deficit countries according to the building up of the productive capacity of the deficit country.

(d) Increased sales from a country in deficit to a country in surplus.
(e) Early agreement within the East African Common Market on a system of inducements and allocations of industry in order to secure the equitable distribution of industrial development between the three countries (Information Service of the United Republic of Tanganyika and Zanzibar, 1964, 3).

If the Kampala Agreement saved the common market, it did so at the price of free trade and free movement of resources. The agreement managed to constrain what it was trying to save. It limited opportunities for intra-regional trade, as well as the role of market factors to determine resource allocation.

Companies that already had production facilities in each country were encouraged to increase production to meet domestic demand, thus eliminating intra-regional trade in those products. These included the East African Tobacco Company, the Bata Shoe Company, the East African Breweries, and the British Standard Portland Cement. There was an exclusive territorial allocation for certain industries. Kenya was given the exclusive right to manufacture electric light bulbs. Tanzania was given the exclusive right to assemble and manufacture Land Rovers and radios and to produce motor vehicle tires and inner tubes. Uganda was given the exclusive right to produce bicycles and nitrogenous fertilizers (Information Service of the United Republic of Tanganyika and Zanzibar, 1964, 6–7). There is no evidence that the allocation of industries was based on comparative advantage. It was regional central planning in action. In effect, the East African countries were myopically creating territorial monopolies, based heavily on trade imbalances.

A country with large intra-regional trade deficits wanting to develop an industry was allowed to set trade barriers on imports from the rest of the region. Overzealous with the green light to institute trade barriers and anxious to expand its beer industry, Tanzania set a quota on imported beer from Kenya that was so restrictive that it had to import beer from outside East Africa to meet demand (Hazlewood, 1975).

One of the potential dynamic consequences of regional economic integration is increased direct investment. Economic integration enlarges the market for products and attracts new firms into the region. However, the question as to which countries investors commit their investment to depends on such factors as the infrastructure, human skills available, domestic policies, the bureaucracy involved in attaining various approvals, and the political conditions in each country. Twisting the arms of investors to locate in a given country based on regional equity may deny the region investors altogether. It is a fallacy to think that a company that wanted to open a subsidiary in Kenya would necessarily agree to open it in Tanzania instead, just because the company would be serving the same East African market. But let's face it, when the general feeling is that your country has been taken advantage of, equity in the distribution of the "pie" baked in a common market arrangement becomes more important than the size of the pie itself. To Tanzania and Uganda, a larger slice of a small pie was better than a small slice of a large pie, even if the latter was larger in absolute terms.

A carefully designed agreement would have limited distortionary policies and still demanded Kenya to contribute more. For example, a regional development bank could have been established to which Kenya would have been asked to contribute a higher proportion of the development fund. But the Kampala Agreement was negotiated under very difficult conditions. The life of the common market hung in the balance. Furthermore, the East African Ministers of Finance, Commerce, and Industry were under pressure from their presidents to come up with quick answers. The ministers saw themselves as "an Emergency Committee to inquire into the measures necessary to bring about a trade balance between the three East African countries" (Information Service of the United Republic of Tanganyika and Zanzibar, 1964, title page). There was no time to consider the nuances of various development policies.

The Kampala Agreement was particularly favorable for Tanzania, not only because of its substance regarding the allocation of industrial activities and safeguard measures on imports, but also because its underlying economic philosophy was that of a centrally planned economy. Tanzania was already leaning towards such an economic system, so its adjustment costs were low. It made its full pronouncement in 1967 in the Arusha Declaration, committing the country to socialism and self-reliance. The Kampala Agreement gave member countries ample policy space to pursue their domestic development policies. In the end, the agreement failed to hold the countries together, as each focused on the shortcomings of the EACSO with respect to its own interests.

Tanzania increased restrictions on imports from Kenya that were far beyond what was envisaged in the Kampala Agreement (Hazlewood, 1975). Tanzania seems to have been emboldened by its own union (Tanganyika and Zanzibar) and disillusioned about the prospects of an East African Federation. In 1965, the East African monetary union which had been in existence since 1921 came to an end. Propelled by Tanzania's desire to control its own monetary policy, the three countries decided to introduce separate currencies. This development was particularly disconcerting for Kenya, which had accepted the Kampala Agreement with the assumption that "the East African Common Market will continue; the common services will continue; [and] in particular, there will continue to be a common single currency" (Information Service of the United Republic of Tanganyika and Zanzibar, 1964, 12). In fact, Kenya had accepted the Kampala Agreement only in principle; it never ratified it.

Tanzania was not reserved about its intention to develop its own monetary policy, but it would be a mischaracterization to suggest that it single-handedly dissolved the common currency. The collapse of the monetary union was not merely the result of a hasty decision by a disgruntled country. It was the result of a long history of inequalities and half-baked solutions. Of course, political independence increased the sensitivity to those inequalities (regardless of their causes) and provided more freedom to pursue one's own domestic development plan.

The introduction of separate currencies was initially thought to be benign and not disruptive, as the three currencies were supposed to be fully convertible and on par with each other. However, the pursuit of different monetary policies, the quest for foreign currency, and the inclination to use foreign exchange controls to limit imports led to divergence between the three currencies. The Kampala Agreement, whose only accomplishment was to condone trade barriers, did not have the force to hold the common market together. If the common market and the provision of common services were to continue, the three countries would have to go back to the drawing board.

The Treaty for the East African Community

In 1965, the heads of state of Kenya, Tanzania, and Uganda established a ministerial commission chaired by an independent consultant, Professor Kjeld Philip of Denmark. The Philip Commission developed the Treaty for East African Cooperation, which was signed by Presidents Jomo Kenyatta (Kenya), Julius Nyerere (Tanzania), and Milton Obote (Uganda) in June 1967. Compared to the "Kampala Commission," the Philip Commission was more composed and took a long-term view. However, just like the commissions that preceded it, it was overly focused on the inequality in industrial development. Nonetheless, it did manage to prolong the life of the common market with the following arrangements: transfer taxes, a development bank, harmonization of policies, monetary arrangements, decentralization of the common services, and institutional restructuring (Hazlewood, 1967).

Table 4.1 *Intra-regional Trade in Manufactured Goods, 1961–1966 (£ million)*

To		Kenya	Tanzania	Uganda
From	Kenya	–	55.2	51.0
	Tanzania	9.0	–	2.2
	Uganda	18.9	10.6	–

Sources: Hazlewood (1967, 7) and Tulya-Muhika (1995, 16–17).

Transfer Taxes

"Transfer taxes" is a euphemism for tariffs (that is, taxes) on intra-regional imports. The adjective, "transfer," was used to emphasize the objective of those taxes – to transfer industrial production from the more advanced to less advanced economies. Transfer taxes could be imposed by a country with an intra-regional trade deficit in manufactured products. Tanzania had a deficit with both Kenya and Uganda. Uganda had a deficit with Kenya but a surplus with Tanzania, as shown in Table 4.1. Thus, Tanzania could impose transfer taxes on imports from Kenya and Uganda; Uganda could impose transfer taxes on imports from Kenya.

The East African Development Bank

In addition to transfer taxes, the Philip Commission proposed a development bank that would also stir up industrial development in the trade deficit countries. Industry was described narrowly to mean only manufacturing and the processing of raw materials. The East African Development Bank (EADB) was to fund only the growth of factories. Although the idea of a development bank was great, its mandate was unfortunate because industrial development involves a chain of complementary initiatives, which includes the production of raw materials, product sorting and grading, storage, transportation, processing (factories), and marketing.

The bank was established, and each country was to contribute the same amount of financial capital to it. However, the bank was to give loans for industrial projects using the following distribution formula: 22.5 percent to Kenya and 38.75 percent each to Tanzania and Uganda. While trying to use a development bank to foster equitable industrial growth was a novel idea, its resources were not sufficient to make a dent. The bank's pool of loanable funds was small to begin with, and even if the bank had been fully loaned up (zero excess reserves), Tanzania and Uganda would have netted only a very small amount in loans. For example, from a pool of £6 million to which each country had contributed £2 million, Tanzania was eligible to receive loans of at most £2.31 million. That implied Tanzania would have had a "net gain" of only £310,000 or the equivalent thereof, an insignificant amount to a sector (industry and manufacturing) that had an annual industrial investment of £10 million in the mid-1960s (Skarstein and Wangwe, 1986).

Harmonization of Policies and Monetary Arrangements

To function as a customs union, the three countries agreed to remove, or more correctly, to *reduce* differences in external barriers enough to prevent transshipment. As Hazlewood (1967, 9) described, "[t]he Treaty can in fact be read not as providing for a rigid standardization of rates of duty, but as providing agreed differences." The treaty provided for harmonization of monetary policies, but it was merely lip service. Differences in economic philosophies were already creating divergence in economic systems between the three countries, particularly between Kenya and Tanzania. Harmonization of policies in other areas, such as agriculture, commerce, research, and transport, was seen as a long-term goal, as there was no inkling of convergence at the time.

Decentralization of the Common Services and Institutional Restructuring

Perhaps the most important element of the treaty was its affirmation of the continual operation of the common services. What was contentious was, again, the apparent dominance of Nairobi (Kenya) as the home of the headquarters of most of the common services. In the spirit of an equitable distribution of administrative headquarters, the EADB was headquartered in Kampala, Uganda. Likewise, the headquarters of the postal and communication services were moved from Nairobi to Kampala. The East African Harbors and Railways Corporation was split into two corporations, one for harbors and the other for railways. The harbors administration was moved to Dar-es-Salaam, Tanzania, and the railways administration remained in Nairobi. The East African Airways Corporation remained in Nairobi. The headquarters of the EAC were established in Arusha, Tanzania, 270 kilometers south of Nairobi.

The system of triumvirates (groups of three ministers) was replaced by a total of three ministers, a Minister of the EAC from each country. These ministers were empowered to make decisions, if unanimous, on issues related to the Community. Matters on which they could not reach a unanimous decision, they referred to the EAC Authority, that is, the Assembly of Heads of State.

THE FORMER EAST AFRICAN COMMUNITY: 1967–1977

The signing of the Treaty for East African Cooperation in June 1967 brought a sigh of relief to the three countries which were at the brink of compromising economic ties that had developed over decades. The treaty signaled new life and kindled optimism about the future.

Table 4.2 gives a glimpse of the intra-regional trade that prevailed during the life of the former EAC and beyond. Clearly, Kenya remained the dominant exporter in and to the region. This had to do with Kenya's more advanced manufacturing sector and patterns of trade established and entrenched during the colonial era.

As much as one may want to discuss the successes of the former EAC, eventually the EAC boils down to a story about its demise. Explaining the reasons for the fall of the EAC is like explaining why a couple divorced; it is rarely due to just one or two clear, specific reasons. The EAC collapsed due to a confluence of factors including unrealistic expectations, external factors, the Ugandan dictator Idi Amin, and ideological differences.

Unrealistic Expectations

Hindsight is 20/20. But it is not as if there were no warnings from the very beginning. The EAC was built on unrealistic expectations in what was disguised as a workable compromise. Sooner or later, someone, if not everyone, was going to be disappointed. The treaty to establish the EAC placed undue attention on the economic disparity between Kenya, on the one hand, and Tanzania and Uganda, on the other. Tanzania and Uganda saw every head start that Kenya seemed to have had as a disadvantage for them, in need of correction. The result was a treaty that supported trade barriers and suppressed competition, instead of promoting trade between the three countries. Transfer taxes (tariffs) were allowed, supposedly to address industrial inequality.

The industrial inequality argument for transfer taxes was linked to the infant industry argument for protection. The basis for the infant industry

Table 4.2 *Intra-regional Trade in the EAC, 1968–1999*

	Exports as Percent of Total EAC Exports			Exports to EAC as a Percent of Total Exports to Africa			Intra-regional Exports as a Percent of Total Exports
	Kenya	Tanzania	Uganda	Kenya	Tanzania	Uganda	
1968	64	11	25	77	31	79	17
1969	66	12	22	72	40	78	16
1970	62	14	24	72	46	77	17
1971	64	17	17	71	49	77	17
1972	71	13	16	70	25	73	14
1973	75	16	9	68	38	53	13
1974	76	18	6	63	40	54	12
1975	82	15	3	62	39	22	13
1976	83	16	1	64	59	18	11
1977	96	2	2	61	12	16	7
1978	95	0	5	47	0	26	6
1979	87	11	2	45	18	10	6
1980	91	7	2	63	17	11	9
1981	92	7	1	38	14	28	7
1982	96	2	2	43	5	31	6
1983	93	3	4	43	8	85	7
1984	84	6	10	45	20	91	7
1985	94	3	3	45	19	82	6
1986	97	2	1	45	14	87	6
1987	97	2	1	42	15	91	7
1988	99	0	1	46	0	81	8
1989	96	3	1	46	36	20	7
1990	93	7	0	60	45	11	14
1991	86	12	2	47	25	50	6
1992	86	10	4	50	18	83	7
1993	91	6	3	54	18	67	11
1994	93	6	1	64	31	50	16
1995	93	6	1	64	30	71	17
1996	96	4	0	66	20	14	17
1997	92	6	2	65	36	63	17
1998	93	6	1	69	43	25	18
1999	90	9	1	63	35	30	16

Source: Various issues of IMF, *Direction of Trade Statistics.*

argument is that comparative advantage is dynamic. Comparative advantage refers to lower relative opportunity costs. Producers in one country have a comparative advantage in a given product if their opportunity cost in producing that product is lower, for whatever reason, than that of producers in another country. The infant industry argument for limiting imports is based, in part, on the assertion that temporary protection will allow the domestic industry to learn and acquire comparative advantage. Accordingly, transfer taxes were supposed to be temporary – at most eight years for any individual tax, with the whole transfer taxes system coming to an end in 15 years.

The transfer taxes element was accompanied by certain conditions. A transfer tax could be applied only to those goods that the country had a capacity to produce in the amount of at least 15 percent of the domestic market or output with the minimum value of £100,000. In addition, a transfer tax on a given product could not exceed 50 percent of the external tariff on that product. For example, if Tanzania had a tariff rate of 20 percent on ploughs imported from Zambia, the tariff rate ceiling on imports of ploughs from Kenya was 10 percent.

While at its core the infant industry argument is not against trade, a few caveats must be kept in mind; these played out in the EAC. First, it is difficult, for economic and political reasons, to identify viable infant industries, when each one of them is an "infant." The requirement that a minimum domestic production capacity had to be met was intended to help Tanzania and Uganda choose viable industries. However, the minimum domestic production capacity is tied to the transfer tax rate. The higher the transfer tax rate, the higher the domestic price, the lower the domestic quantity demanded and, thus, the higher the likelihood of meeting the 15 percent production threshold.

Second, trade barriers implemented to protect infant industries are difficult to remove, whether the industry remains an "infant" or it matures. In either case, it becomes politically very risky (for politicians) to remove protection. In addition, transfer taxes are not the only (or best) method to nurture infant industries. A "transfer tax" (tariff) is equivalent to a simultaneous tax on domestic consumers and a subsidy for domestic producers. If the objective is to support domestic producers, a direct production subsidy is more efficient than a tariff. Of course, fiscally, tariffs are easier to apply to support domestic production because they do not involve direct government spending. Moreover, it was an achievement for the Philip Commission to establish a transfer tax system which was less restrictive than the overreaching quota system negotiated in the Kampala Agreement. Of course, the treaty did not eliminate the use of quotas altogether.

It is important to note that transfer taxes created an interesting situation where the source of imports could be diverted from Kenya to a country outside the regional bloc. Tanzania, for example, might have been importing ploughs from Kenya instead of Zambia, not because Kenya was the lower cost producer, but only because imports from Zambia faced a tariff and imports from Kenya did not. In other words, economic integration in East Africa might have diverted Tanzania's external source for ploughs from Zambia to Kenya. Trade diversion may cause a net welfare loss to the importing country (Tanzania, in this example). A new tariff imposed by Tanzania on ploughs from Kenya, even if it was less than the tariff on ploughs from Zambia, could reverse trade diversion, where now Tanzania would import ploughs from Zambia instead of Kenya. For Tanzania and Uganda, while such reversal would not have reflected the true spirit of the treaty, it might have actually been a benefit to them because they would be importing from a cheaper producer, thus improving their terms of trade.

Figure 4.1 illustrates what could have happened. Suppose Tanzania is the domestic country. DD and SS are Tanzania's demand and supply lines for ploughs, respectively. P_Z and P_K are the free trade prices of ploughs from Zambia and Kenya, respectively. $P_Z + t$ is the tariff-inclusive domestic price of ploughs imported from Zambia. $P_K + .5t$ is the tariff inclusive domestic price of ploughs imported from Kenya. The ".5" suggests that Tanzania would not impose a tariff rate on Kenyan ploughs that exceeds 50 percent of the tariff on Zambian ploughs. Initially, there is no tariff on ploughs imported from Kenya. Because of the discriminatory application of the tariff, Tanzania imports ploughs from Kenya, even though Zambia is the lower cost producer. (That is what is referred to as trade diversion.) The volume of imports is given by the horizontal distance between Q_1 and Q_4. However, when Tanzania is allowed to impose a tariff on Kenyan ploughs, Tanzania would import ploughs from Zambia, reversing trade diversion. The volume of imports shrinks to the horizontal distance between $Q_2 - Q_3$. Consumer surplus decreases by areas A + B + C + D. Producer surplus increases by area A. Tariff revenue increases by area C + E. If area E exceeds the sum of areas B + D, Tanzania would realize a net welfare gain.

There were no clear measures to prevent such a reversal of trade diversion, something that, obviously, Kenya was not happy about. However, it is unlikely that Tanzania and Uganda were sympathetic regarding Kenya's potential losses. Losses to Kenya were generally seen as unavoidable steps towards regional industrial equality.

The point here is not to suggest that the economic disparity should or could have been ignored. However, a regional economic bloc that is

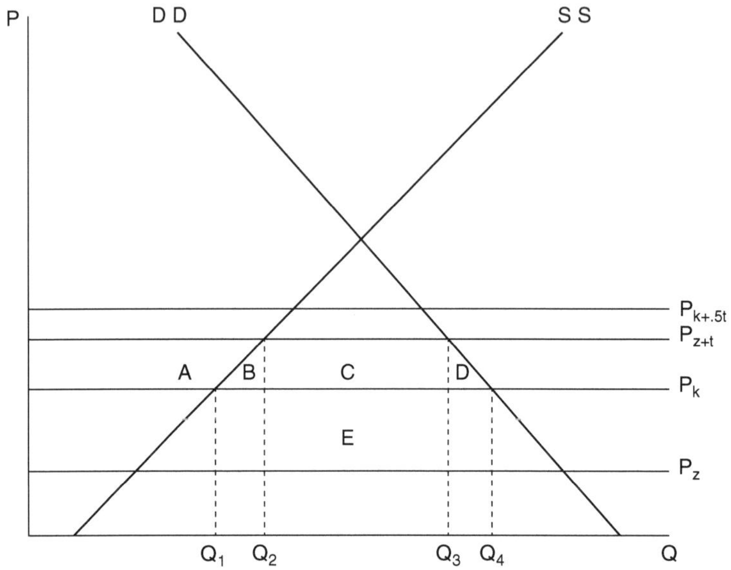

Figure 4.1 Trade Diversion Reversal

obsessed with the inequality of its members sets itself up for incessant grumbling. The relatively poor countries will not cease to ask for preferential treatment, and the relatively more advanced ones are bound to resent constant complaints and what they may consider as unfair costs to them. Worse still, there was an implicit assumption that those trade barriers, together with the initiatives of the EADB, would produce the intended results rather quickly. That did not happen. Instead, Kenya's dominance in exports to the region continued to grow.

Notwithstanding its earnest efforts, the EADB, which was established to promote balanced industrial development in the EAC, could not rectify the imbalance. It was a task too large for an infant bank with very little autonomy. As the bank acknowledged in its ten-year report, very little progress was made to balance industrial development in the three countries. The bank did not provide an explanation for the lack of progress, except to say that it was due to a "range of unresolved and divisive issues" (The East African Development Bank, 1977, i). In actuality, the bank's resources were too small to make a real difference. Moreover, even the little that was available was not distributed according to the formula that had been agreed upon – 22.5 percent to Kenya and 38.75 percent each to Tanzania and Uganda.

Table 4.3 *EADB Disbursement of Loans, 1969–1977 (in thousands)*

	Kenya	Tanzania	Uganda	Total
1969	1,935	nil	2,000	3,935
1970	11,255	nil	7,480	18,735
1971	23,800	20,100	14,170	58,070
1972	28,840	37,360	17,320	83,520
1973	45,820	62,900	19,860	128,580
1974	55,380	78,630	39,620	173,630
1975	84,900	108,110	46,740	239,770
1976	111,901	129,859	67,516	309,276
1977	118,956	135,529	90,971	345,456
Total	482,787	572,488	305,677	1,360,952

Source: The East African Development Bank, 1977.

Table 4.3 shows the disbursement of loans by the EADB to Kenya, Tanzania, and Uganda from 1969 to 1977. No disbursements were made in 1967 and 1968. Aggregating all disbursements up to 1977, Kenya, Tanzania, and Uganda received, respectively, 35.5 percent, 42 percent, and 22.5 percent. It is not surprising that the bank became another source of conflict, given its failure to conform to the specified formula. Incidentally, the relatively low disbursement to Uganda was most likely due to the chaotic environment created by Idi Amin's brutal dictatorship. Idi Amin seized power in Uganda in 1971. The trade imbalance reflected in Table 4.2 was the main barometer Tanzania and Uganda used to conclude that the EAC was not working to their advantage.

External Factors

Trade barriers of many forms, including exchange rate controls, were used in Tanzania to reduce the trade deficit, but to no avail. Negative external factors contributed to the trade deficits and further discontent. The price of oil quadrupled in 1974, causing severe trade balance hardship for oil-importing countries like those in the EAC. In Tanzania, almost half of its export revenues were spent on oil imports. To make things worse, the East African region suffered an extended drought in 1973–74 which caused a decrease in the traditional export commodities such as coffee, tea, cotton, and tobacco. At the same time, the drought made it necessary to increase imports of food.

The dramatic increase in the trade imbalance overall and, in particular, with Kenya, regardless of its primary causes, made Tanzania even more disgruntled. (Uganda had its hands full with Idi Amin.) However, perhaps the trade deficit with Kenya alone would not have caused the former EAC to collapse. An additional trigger was Idi Amin. Tanzania was unequivocally disgusted with Idi Amin.

Idi Amin

Idi Amin seized power in Uganda in 1971 by overthrowing Milton Obote. Amin ruled like a mad man, killing tens of thousands of innocent people. He deported all Asians (including Ugandan citizens) in his blatantly racist, "Ugandanization" program. During his reign, Uganda's economy deteriorated. Uganda's real GDP, which had grown by an annual average of 5.9 percent in 1960–70, declined by an annual average of 0.4 percent during the Idi Amin era, from 1971 to 1979 (World Bank, 1981).

Idi Amin disturbed the political equilibrium that existed between the three African leaders, Jomo Kenyatta of Kenya, Julius Nyerere of Tanzania, and Milton Obote of Uganda. These three leaders respected each other. Moreover, Obote was Nyerere's protégé. When Amin seized power, Nyerere declared outright that he would not sit at the same table with him. The East African Authority, whose members were the presidents of the three countries, now lacked coherence. Hostility between Tanzania and Uganda escalated to the point that each one blocked the EAC employees of the other country from working in its territory. Eventually the border between Tanzania and Uganda was closed (Sircar, 1990). Kenya tried to play the role of mediator to the extent that it could. However, in 1976 Amin upset Kenya as well, when he claimed parts of Western Kenya for Uganda. Moreover, Kenya and Tanzania were growing far apart in their economic philosophies.

Ideological Differences

To appreciate the ideological differences between Kenya and Tanzania, it is important to understand how socialism was operationalized in Tanzania. Despite the signing of the treaty to establish the EAC, these two countries aggressively pursued two ideologically divergent economic systems. Barkan (1994) labeled the economic systems of the 1960s and 1970s in Kenya and Tanzania, respectively, as patron-client capitalism and one-party socialism. Uganda was somewhere in the middle.

Kenya's economic system was a continuation of the system developed and entrenched by the British colonial powers. It promoted economic growth by giving the private sector a pivotal role to play and by attracting foreign direct investment from Britain and other Western countries. In the Cold War era, Kenya embraced the economic system of the West, that is, the market economy. While on aggregate, Kenya's economy prospered, the benefits accrued mostly to just a few.

Inequality in income and resource distribution did not seem to bother the conscience of the Kenyatta administration. (Jomo Kenyatta was the first President of Kenya.) If anything, the Kenyatta administration seemed to encourage it, with favoritism for his fellow Kikuyu and key interest groups. Political and economic corruption became the lubricant of the system. As Barkan (1994, 7) remarked, "In Kenya, patron-client capitalism was also corrupted – literally and figuratively, in respect to politics and economics." There were various sets of exchanges within the patron-client networks – for example, exchanges between the political elites and business owners. Political elites (patrons) provided license favors and monopoly protection to business owners (clients) in return for political alliance, financial contributions, and job offers for the patrons' friends and relatives. The patrons discriminately provided scholarships for studying abroad to members of their tribes for political support and dominance.

If Kenyatta was satisfied with the economic system inherited from the British, Nyerere (the first President of Tanzania) was utterly appalled by it. Julius Nyerere, who was keen on equality, viewed capitalism as a sure way of creating the haves and the have-nots. To him, maintaining capitalism meant extending the colonial economic system. In 1967, the same year that the former EAC came into existence, Nyerere committed Tanzania to the path of socialism, *ujamaa*, in a manifesto called the *Arusha Declaration* (TANU, 1967). The Tanganyika African National Union (TANU), the only legal political party at the time, set the country on a course to "socialism and self-reliance." The objective was to achieve quick economic growth with equitable distribution of income and better provision for basic needs.

On the road to *ujamaa*, key sectors and social and economic activities in Tanzania, such as the financial system, external and internal trade, large and medium manufacturing enterprises, private schools, and estate farms, were nationalized and placed under direct state control. A number of public sector agencies were created, and they attained a position of dominance in the economy. As an additional step towards *ujamaa*, a "villagization" program – compulsory grouping of the scattered rural population into designated villages – was initiated. About five million people, almost half of the rural population, were uprooted from their homes and farms and placed in 8,000 designated villages of about 250 to 600 families between 1973 and 1976. This operation happened at the worst of times, as it coincided with the skyrocketing of oil prices and severe drought (Hyden, 1980).

In aspiring to establish socialism, the Tanzanian leadership ignored the important role played by private entrepreneurs in combining labor, capital, and land to produce goods and services. Entrepreneurship was regarded with disdain. The *Arusha Declaration* proclaimed Tanzania to be "a state of peasants and workers." According to the conventional rhetoric at the time, private entrepreneurs were neither workers nor peasants. They were considered people who made unethical use of others and others' properties for their own advantage and profit.

In 1971, the government nationalized private rental houses whose prevailing unit value was 100,000 Tanzanian shillings ($14,000) or above. In mid-2016 prices, that is equivalent to 105 million shillings ($48,000). The owners were considered exploiters. It was argued that all they did to acquire those houses was to borrow money from the bank, buy some material, and employ some people to build the houses for them. Then they simply rented them out, collected the rental income, used part of it to pay the loan, and pocketed the rest. They did not actually "work." That was TANU's notion of exploitation, a notion that mistakenly underestimated the critical value of entrepreneurs and their risk-taking to the economy.

Although the *Arusha Declaration* did not and could not eliminate all private enterprises, there was strong propaganda and real action to ridicule and discourage them. A private entrepreneur was regarded as a capitalist (*bepari* in Swahili) and a capitalist was synonymous with an exploiter, a tick that sucked people's blood, or a thief.

The rapid growth of the public sector and the attack on private enterprise suppressed the private sector. The state took control of wholesale businesses. Regional trading companies were formed to distribute goods to retailers, and they also participated in retail business. The purchasing of all major crops fell under government monopsonies (single buyers). For each major crop (cashew nuts, coffee, cotton, tea, tobacco, and grains), there was a government authority. For example, the Coffee Authority of Tanzania was the sole legal buyer of coffee from farmers. These authorities were marked with unnecessary bureaucracy, inefficiency, and high marketing costs. They resulted in low producer prices. Worse still, farmers often received promissory notes in lieu of actual payments. These "pieces of paper" had to be held until a day when money, a cashier, and transport for the cashier were available. Since it was not always clear when money would be available, farmers would go to the payment stations every day with the hope of being paid. Sometimes the waiting period was more than a month.[2]

An institution to regulate prices, the Price Commission, was established in 1967 and came into operation in 1973. The Commission set price ceilings, purportedly taking into account production and transportation costs and all overhead expenses. By 1974, 602 groups of goods and services produced domestically and 464 groups of imported items were under the Price Commissioner's decree (Rice, 1979). Standard theory and evidence show that price ceilings lead to perpetual shortages, black markets, and high search costs.

Both Tanzania and Kenya maintained a fixed exchange rate system under the former EAC. However, in Tanzania, the government had a pure monopoly on banking services. Buying and selling foreign currency was only legally possible through government banks. The government set an exchange rate ceiling that grossly overvalued the Tanzanian shilling. In the mid-1970s, the official (legal) price of the US dollar in Tanzanian shillings was set at less than 50 percent of the market value of the dollar. The exchange rate ceiling led to a shortage of foreign currency, and it became necessary for the Bank of Tanzania (BoT) to use non-market factors to ration it. Needless to say, the system was both highly inefficient and notoriously corrupt.

The irony is that many of the "infant" factories that were built in the name of import substitution (to reduce imports from Kenya and elsewhere) were highly dependent on imported inputs. Because of the shortage of foreign exchange, factories were underutilized as they lacked adequate supplies of imported inputs and spare parts. This is partly why Kenya continued to be a dominant exporter of manufactured goods to Tanzania.

Gradually, Tanzania became a country of price ceilings and widespread severe shortages, where permits, road blocks, and corruption became the norm. (Of course, capitalism in Kenya produced its own version of corruption.) The author remembers his family having to go through many hoops over a period of several months just to be able to buy $30 from the Bank of Tanzania to purchase AA batteries in Kenya for his younger brother's hearing aid. AA batteries were not available in Tanzania. The author also remembers people having to go to their local government offices to beg or give a bribe for a permit to bring a gift of a bag (20 kilograms) of beans to a relative who lived in a different town. Without such a permit, one could be harassed by the militia at road blocks and even lose the gift to the militia and their supervisors.

The shortage of goods and services turned many government departments into allocation agencies. At the national level, ministers and principal secretaries were engaged in allocating goods to the regions. At the regional level, Regional Commissioners and Regional Development Directors became actively involved in determining allocation quotas for their districts and local governments. At the local government level, goods were allocated for various shops, restaurants, schools, and individuals who had special requests. To buy a few crates of soda and beer or a bag of rice and a gallon of cooking oil for a wedding celebration, for example, one needed a special allocation from the local government.

The divergent economic systems that Kenya and Tanzania embarked on not only produced different economic outcomes; they also became a source of disdain for each other. Tanzania accused Kenya of being a "man-eat-man society" and Kenya described Tanzania as a "man-eat-nothing society." Furthermore, as Tulya-Muhika (1995, 33) remarks, Tanzania's socialism demanded certain political allegiance, like attending political rallies and *ujamaa* meetings, often disrupting the EAC functions and, as to be expected, annoying other countries. None of these was helping to sustain the EAC.

The Ultimate Collapse

By the early 1970s, a number of divisions as well as reductions in areas of cooperation beleaguered the EAC. As could be expected, every country was complaining about something. In 1972, the East African monetary union was dissolved, preceded and precipitated by exchange controls and trade barriers on intra-regional trade. In 1973, intra-regional transfers of funds were restricted, thus hampering the functions of regional corporations. In 1974, The East Africa Income Tax Department was disbanded, with Kenya complaining that it had been carrying a heavy burden, subsidizing Tanzania and Uganda. Tanzania and Uganda complained that even though the headquarters of the EAC were in Arusha, Tanzania, a disproportionately large number of EAC employees were still located in Kenya. In 1974, Kenya had 54 percent of the EAC employees, Tanzania had 33 percent, and Uganda had 13 percent (Sircar, 1990, 127). Tanzania complained that Kenya's heavy trucks hauling goods between Kenya and Zambia were damaging Tanzania's roads. Uganda's dictator Idi Amin complained that Kenya aided Israel in rescuing hostages held by Uganda. Tension was mounting from all directions. However, according to Sircar (1990, 128):

> the climax in inter-state tension came in January 1977, when Tanzania was celebrating the creation of its new single party, the Chama cha Mapinduzi (The Revolutionary Party) in the presence of a distinguished international

gathering. Having made certain that all the aircraft had returned to Kenya, the Kenya authorities grounded the Community-owned East African Airways, thus stranding the guests of Tanzania, and launched the new Kenya Airways.

Whether the timing of Kenya's unilateral decision was relevant or not, is hard to tell. However, by then, the collapse of the EAC was imminent and Kenya was simply grabbing what it could.[3] Tanzania responded with harsh words and on February 4, 1977, closed the border with Kenya, leaving the EAC in a very precarious situation. After failing to pass the budget for the new fiscal year, the EAC collapsed officially on July 1, 1977. In short, it was the confluence of many factors, including colonialism, that brought the former EAC to life, as well as to its grave.

The EAC died without a will and, therefore, without an executor. That created an interesting challenge, to put it mildly, particularly because these countries were no longer on speaking terms. The situation got worse in 1978 when Ugandan troops invaded Tanzania, provoking a war that lasted eight months. Not only did Tanzania fight back to regain its territory; it also pushed into Uganda and removed the dictator Idi Amin from power.[4]

It took the World Bank's intervention for the three states to get a mediator, Victor Umbricht, a very able, patient, and dedicated diplomat who, at the time, was with the United Nations. Umbricht and his staff started their work in November of 1977 and completed it at the end of 1986. It took nine years. The agreement on how to divide the assets and liabilities was signed on May 14, 1984, though later Umbricht had to deal with the issue of pensions for the former EAC employees (Umbricht, 1989; World Bank, 1987).

Assets were divided using a combination of two criteria, geography and equality, with a 50:50 proportion. That is, 50 percent of the assets were allocated based on geographical location and the remaining 50 percent were divided equally. For an asset worth $600,000 located in Uganda, for example, Uganda would get $400,000, and Kenya and Tanzania would get $100,000 each. Using this criteria, Kenya, Tanzania, and Uganda were entitled to, respectively, 42 percent, 32 percent, and 26 percent of all assets. The percentages derived for dividing the assets were used to divide the long-term liabilities, as shown in Table 4.4. Kenya and Tanzania had extra shares of assets. They were required to compensate Uganda $191 million plus an annual interest rate of 7 percent from the date of signing the agreement. The compensation could be paid in hard currency or by some other method agreed upon by Uganda and the compensating country (Umbricht, 1989). Following the agreement on the division of assets and

Table 4.4 *Division of Assets and Long-term Liabilities*

			Kenya		Tanzania		Uganda	
		Total $ (000)	$ (000)	%	$ (000)	%	$ (000)	%
Assets	Held	1,432,640	746,450	52	504,845	35	181,350	13
	Assigned share	1,432,640	601,709	42	458,445	32	372,486	26
	Excess	0	144,736	10	46,400	3	(191,136)	(13)
Liabilities		344,396	144,646	42	110,207	32	89,543	26

Source: Kenya National Council for Law Reporting (2012).

liabilities, the border between Kenya and Tanzania was reopened and, cautiously, relations between the three countries started to normalize again.

INTRA-REGIONAL TRADE AFTER THE COLLAPSE OF THE FORMER EAC

It is important to remember that trade among East Africans predates colonialism and, most certainly, the former EAC. The three countries are divided by arbitrary borders drawn by Europeans. The land boundaries between the three countries are almost 2,000 kilometers long. The borders are porous and usually disregarded by the people living in the border regions. Some of these borders divide people of the same ethnic group, as is the case with the Maasai, a semi-nomadic tribe in northeastern Tanzania and southern Kenya. Even when East African countries had special trade relations with each other, informal and underground trade between the peoples of East Africa was part of the economic dynamic of the region. Some of it was benign, as neighbors traded small items at their borders, but some involved an elaborate smuggling scheme to avoid taxes and restrictions. With the closure of the border, severe shortages in Tanzania, and relatively low producer prices for farmers in Tanzania, smuggling became almost a necessary way to survive (Lofchie, 1989).

It is not surprising that the pattern of smuggling involved Tanzania exporting livestock, hides, cash crops, and food grains to Kenya and other neighboring countries and importing manufactured goods such as soap, batteries, toilet paper, spare parts, butter, shoes, and clothing. Of all the products that were smuggled, it is likely that the smuggling of coffee from Tanzania into Kenya was the most prominent. Mshomba (1993) estimated that an annual average of 15 percent of coffee produced in northern Tanzania between 1976 and 1985 was smuggled into Kenya. That is a total of 47,000 metric tons generating (at most) a total of 1.6 billion Kenyan shillings.[5] Most likely the export revenue from smuggled coffee was spent to buy goods in Kenya which were in short supply, if available at all, in Tanzania. These goods were, in turn, smuggled into Tanzania.

The smuggling of coffee from Tanzania into Kenya was a direct result of the difference in producer prices in those countries. Table 4.5 shows producer prices of Arabica coffee in Kenya and Tanzania between 1976 and 1986.[6] Farmers in Tanzania could sell their coffee to a monopsony – the Coffee Authority of Tanzania (CAT) – which would, in turn, export it and

Table 4.5 *Producer Prices of Arabica Coffee in Kenya and Tanzania*

Year	PCOFK (Kshs.)	OEXR	PEXR	PCOFKT (Tshs.)	PCOFT (Tshs.)	PRATIO
1976	2,524	0.86	2.11	5,326	800	.15
1977	3,975	0.82	1.57	6,241	1,500	.24
1978	2,818	0.77	1.21	3,410	1,089	.32
1979	2,835	0.85	1.40	3,969	907	.23
1980	2,635	0.77	2.50	6,588	1,142	.17
1981	2.258	0.69	2.02	4,561	1,236	.27
1982	2,780	0.67	2.05	5,699	1,490	.26
1983	3,488	0.84	3.40	11,859	1,517	.13
1984	3,844	1.08	10.93	42,015	2,287	.05
1985	3,872	0.93	9.45	36,590	2,330	.06
1986	5,020	1.88	7.51	37,700	3,820	.10

PCOFK – producer price of Arabica coffee in Kenya (Kenyan shillings per 100 kilograms).
OEXR – official market exchange rate, Tanzanian shilling per Kenyan shilling.
PEXR – parallel market exchange rate, Tanzanian shilling per Kenyan shilling.
PCOFKT – producer price of Arabica coffee in Kenya (Tanzanian shillings per 100 kilograms – PCOFK x PEXR)[7].
PCOFT – producer price of Arabica coffee in Tanzania (Tanzanian shillings per 100 kilograms).
PRATIO – PCOFT/PCOFKT.
Sources: Calculated using data from Lofchie (1988), various issues of International Monetary Fund's *International Financial Statistics*, Marketing Development Bureau, Ministry of Agriculture, Tanzania (1986), and Ministry of Finance and Planning, Kenya (1987).

accept the price set by the government, or they could export it directly by engaging in smuggling and avoid any export tax.

The CAT paid farmers in local currency. Since the local currency was overvalued, in effect, farmers were implicitly being taxed. To illustrate this point, suppose the official exchange rate was one Tanzanian shilling per one Kenyan shilling, and the parallel market exchange rate was 10 Tanzanian shillings per Kenyan shilling. (This was the reality in 1984.) Now suppose the world price of coffee, in Kenyan shillings, was 10 shillings per kilogram and that 30 percent of it was passed along to the farmers. Using the official exchange rate, the farmer received only 3 Tanzanian shillings per kilogram, whereas through the free market, the farmer could have received 30 Tanzanian shillings (30 percent of 100 Tanzanian shillings).

In border regions in East Africa, smuggling and the parallel market for currencies became the lifeblood of the economy. Even governments seemed resigned to this fact. In Tanzania, by 1983, the shortage of manufactured goods had reached a critical state. The government, in despair, allowed and encouraged anyone able to import to do so with no questions asked about the source of the foreign currency. At the time, Tanzanians living in Tanzania were not allowed to hold foreign currency, and the Bank of Tanzania was the only legal source of foreign currency for them. Tanzanians responded overwhelmingly with their hidden foreign currency; by 1988 almost 20 percent of all imports were imported with foreign currency which was not obtained through the Bank of Tanzania.

The official collapse of the former EAC was a clear setback in trade relations, but the ingenuity of East Africans and market factors sustained some of the trade flows within the region. Moreover, unrecorded trade activities within East Africa (and other parts of Africa) have always been and will continue to be part of the economy, with or without formal economic integration. An extensive study by Ackello-Ogutu and Echessah (1998) suggested that in 1995 Tanzania's informal cross-border trade with all her neighbors amounted to US$277 million. Tanzania's official trade with her neighbors in that year was only US$204 million. This suggests that almost 60 percent of Tanzania's trade with her neighbors was conducted through informal commercial channels.

The former EAC was a product of colonialism, as demonstrated in Chapter 3 and this chapter. At the same time, the former EAC was strangled by the residual impact of colonialism. In other words, a major reason for its collapse was the economic inequality between the three countries, which itself was largely a product of colonialism.

The economic cooperation between Kenya, Tanganyika, and Uganda during the colonial era was primarily fashioned for the convenience of, and the benefit of, the British. Britain benefited from the economies of scale associated with governing. It even wanted to form a federation of the East African colonies, so as to rule a single entity and reduce its administrative costs even further. While the Conference of Governors and the EAHC deepened and widened economic cooperation, the system remained exploitative. Most of the economic gains of economic cooperation accrued directly to the British entrepreneurs in East Africa and their associates. In addition, the dynamics of economic cooperation widened the inequality between the countries, already a product of colonialism.

When Kenya, Tanganyika, and Uganda were about to gain their independence, the ambivalence about economic cooperation became even more apparent. While Nyerere called for forming a federation, at the same time he threatened to pull Tanganyika out of East African cooperation if inequalities were not satisfactorily addressed. In the end, a half-hearted compromise was reached to replace the EAHC with the EACSO. The EACSO was later replaced by the Treaty for East African Cooperation which was signed in June 1967, giving rise to the former EAC. The former EAC was greeted with enthusiasm and hope, as it was finally an agreement reached by independent states based on their own will and judgment.

Yet the EAC came with ample space for trade barriers, supposedly meant to correct the inequalities created by colonialism. The EAC was on a rough path from the start. It was like a runner tied to a stretchy rope. The resistance exerted by the rope increased the farther the runner sprinted. On top of that, Idi Amin's brutality and the ideological divide between Kenya and Tanzania were like headwinds through which the EAC was trying to run. With an uncompromising "rope" tied around its waist and the "headwinds" blowing into its face, it was only a matter of time before the EAC fell to the ground. It collapsed in 1977 when it was only ten years old.

Of course, the collapse of the EAC did not stop trade between the three countries altogether. Trade among East Africans was not started by colonialists or the EAC. In fact, some trade in the region continued in spite of the formal trade barriers before the establishment of the former EAC and throughout its existence. Trade relations between people of neighboring countries, with artificial borders no less, happen naturally. This is not to suggest that official trade arrangements, bilateral, regional, or multilateral, are irrelevant. Those arrangements are critical for enhancing formal and transparent trade where rules and standards can be enforced and governments can collect revenues. They also provide the context within which countries can negotiate agreements for mutual benefits. Moreover, having experienced the benefits of regional economic integration, though shared disproportionately, and in the less than ideal environment of colonialism and subsequent antagonism, East African countries could not resist for too long another attempt to integrate.

Notes

1. One was Sudan, which had been ruled jointly by Britain and Egypt since 1899.
2. The author's parents were among thousands of small coffee farmers who experienced this.
3. East African Airways had 17 airplanes. When the former EAC officially collapsed in 1977, 14 were in Kenya, 3 were in Tanzania, and none were in Uganda (World Bank, 1987, 7–8).

4. Idi Amin fled to Libya and then to Saudi Arabia where he died in 2003. For analysis of the war between Tanzania and Uganda, see Acheson-Brown (2001).
5. The amount of Kenyan shillings generated was calculated using producer prices that prevailed in Kenya. However, the full amount did not go to Tanzanians because coffee was being smuggled through intermediaries. It is important to note that each coffee producer in Kenya was a registered member of a cooperative society to which he could sell his coffee. Those societies paid Kenyan farmers free trade prices which were significantly higher than producer prices in Tanzania. Not everyone could sell coffee to those societies. A Tanzanian farmer, for instance, could not sell his coffee directly to any of the Kenyan cooperative societies unless he was also a producer of coffee in Kenya. However, he could sell directly to a Kenyan farmer who had access to a cooperative society.
6. For a comprehensive study of agricultural policies pursued by Kenya and Tanzania from the 1960s to the 1980s, see Lofchie (1989).
7. Kenyan shillings were converted into Tanzanian shillings using the parallel market exchange rate. People who successfully smuggled their output were paid in Kenyan shillings which were exchanged readily without any substantial risk in the parallel market.

5

The Birth and Growth of the Current East African Community: The Customs Union

East African countries could not resist for too long another attempt to integrate. They had experienced the benefits of regional economic integration, though distributed disproportionately and, for the most part, under the exploitative and repressive British colonial environment. Moreover, Idi Amin was forced out of Uganda in 1979, allowing discussion on the division of assets and liabilities and contemplation about the future to proceed with less antagonism.

On May 14, 1984, a mediated agreement was reached on how to divide the assets and liabilities of the former EAC. The agreement was clearly forward-looking in that it left the door wide open for future cooperation. The agreement established that the Soroti Civil Flying School and the Inter-University Council would operate as common services and that the East African Development Bank would remain a joint institution. More importantly, Article 14.02 of the agreement stated that, "the States [Kenya, Tanzania, and Uganda] agree to explore and identify further areas for future cooperation and to work out concrete arrangements for such cooperation" (Kenya National Council for Law Reporting, 2012, 17). At the same time, as discussed in Chapter 2, the Organization of African Unity (OAU) was appealing for African unity which was to come through regional economic integration.

The first clear step towards exploration to revive the EAC took place in November 1991 when Presidents Daniel Arap Moi, Ali Hassan Mwinyi, and Yoweri Museveni, of Kenya, Tanzania, and Uganda, respectively, had a side meeting in Harare, Zimbabwe, during the Commonwealth Heads of Government summit. While the summit provided a convenient opportunity and neutral location for the three presidents to meet, a number of new circumstances made their meeting promising. By then, Uganda was relatively stable under its strong leader, President Museveni. In addition, the "cookie-cutter" structural adjustment programs, which the International Monetary Fund and World Bank had urged these countries to adopt in the 1980s, had brought the economic policies of Kenya and Tanzania (and Uganda, for that matter) more in line with each other. Structural adjustment programs included liberalizing trade and the foreign exchange market, agricultural reforms that allowed the private sector to buy and export crops, removing price controls, and reforming the public sector (World Bank, 1994). At the same time, signs of political reforms towards multiparty democracy were getting stronger in Kenya and Tanzania.

In 1992, Tanzania's economy took an altogether different direction from its former socialist policies, allowing and encouraging the growth of the private sector and, essentially, adopting the market system. In the same year, Kenya and Tanzania amended their constitutions and allowed for a multiparty system, bringing competition to politics and a good measure of freedom of speech. These changes gave these countries respect for each other and a common economic and political language with which to speak with each other. While there were still no formal trade agreements between the three countries, formal intra-regional trade began to increase steadily in the early 1990s. Formal negotiations were also in high gear.

In 1993, the three countries established a Permanent Tripartite Commission for East African Cooperation, and a permanent secretariat for the Commission was established in 1996 in Arusha, Tanzania. The Treaty to establish the current EAC was signed in November 1999 and came into force on July 7, 2000 (East African Community, 2002).

Like people who feel the need to make up for lost time, the EAC wanted to sprint towards deeper integration this time around. It envisioned a full-fledged customs union by July 2010 and the launch of a common market in 2010, a monetary union by 2012, and ultimately a federation by 2015. It was very ambitious.

CUSTOMS UNION

The EAC Customs Union Agreement

In a customs union, member countries maintain common external trade barriers. The EAC entered into a customs union in 2005 with a transitional period of five years. Since Kenya, Tanzania, and Uganda were members of the World Trade Organization (WTO) and had all been members of COMESA until 2000 before Tanzania pulled out, their external trade barriers were already, generally speaking, in sync with each other.

There is a Swahili proverb that says, "*aliyeumwa na nyoka huogopa gamba lake*," which means, "one who has been bitten by a snake is afraid of a snake's skin." Aware that the former EAC collapsed due in part to Kenya's dominance in intra-regional exports, the current EAC was sensitive to Kenya's competitive advantage. The five-year transitional period was to give Tanzania and Uganda some special treatment. Goods could flow between Tanzania and Uganda, duty-free. Likewise, goods from Tanzania and Uganda could flow into Kenya duty-free. However, not all goods from Kenya could flow into Tanzania and Uganda duty-free.

Kenya's exports to Tanzania and Uganda were divided into two categories, A and B. Goods in category A were eligible for immediate duty-free. Tanzania had 880 products in category B that had tariff rates ranging from 3 to 25 percent. Uganda had 443 products in category B, all of them with a tariff rate of 10 percent (East African Community, 2004). Kenya did not have much say in the creation of these lists by Tanzania and Uganda. Tanzania and Uganda were to reduce those tariffs by equal percentage points so that they would be zero by 2010. A 25 percent tariff rate on Tanzania's imports of lubricating oils from Kenya, for example, was to be reduced yearly by 5 percentage points starting in 2005. That was set as the lowest rate of reduction. Tanzania and Uganda had the prerogative to make those reductions at a faster rate.

In setting the common external tariffs (CETs), products were divided into four broad groups – three-band CETs and a fourth group of sensitive products. The three-band CETs reflected a typical tariff escalation scheme seen in many countries. They were set at 0 percent for raw materials, inputs, capital goods, and medical equipment; 10 percent for semi-finished products; 25 percent for finished products; and higher than 25 percent for sensitive products (East African Community, 2004a). The rationale for tariff escalation was to protect and encourage processing in East Africa. Fifty-seven products (at 8-digit HS code) were classified as sensitive products, including sugar (100 percent), rice (75 percent), milk, baby formula, and wheat flour (60 percent), cement (55 percent), corn flour (50 percent), and khangas, vitenge, bed linen, and used clothes (50 percent). The numbers in parentheses are the CETs set for those products.

EAC's CETs Compared to Pre-customs Union Tariffs

Stahl (2005) has a detailed description of how the EAC's CETs compared to the pre-customs union tariffs in each country. (Remember that the EAC entered into a customs union in 2005.) The numbers in Table 5.1 are taken

Table 5.1 *Pre-EAC Customs Union Tariffs and Tariffs Agreed to Be in Place by 2010*

			2003	2010
Kenya	Simple average tariff rate	Intra-EAC	1.9	0.0
		Non-EAC imports	19.0	11.2
	Weighted average tariff rate	Intra-EAC	1.9	0.0
		Non-EAC imports	17.6	5.9
Tanzania	Simple average tariff rate	Intra-EAC	3.3	0.0
		Non-EAC imports	12.6	11.2
	Weighted average tariff rate	Intra-EAC	3.4	0.0
		Non-EAC imports	8.5	5.9
Uganda	Simple average tariff rate	Intra-EAC	3.2	0.0
		Non-EAC imports	7.8	11.2
	Weighted average tariff rate	Intra-EAC	3.6	0.0
		Non-EAC imports	6.3	9.2
EAC	Simple average tariff rate	Intra-EAC	5.8	0.0
		Non-EAC imports	12.4	11.2
	Weighted average tariff rate	Intra-EAC	3.4	0.0
		Non-EAC imports	10.2	6.5

Source: Stahl (2005).

from his study. Since most of Kenya's imports originating from outside the EAC were inputs or intermediate products, the EAC's CETs lowered the overall Kenyan protection level. The simple average tariff rate was reduced by 7.8 percentage points (from 19 to 11.2 percent) and the weighted average tariff rate (using trade volumes that prevailed in 2003) was reduced by 11.7 percentage points from 17.6 to 5.9 percent – a 66 percent reduction.[1]

For Tanzania, the CETs were substantially higher than its pre-customs union tariffs for important imports such as wheat, palm oil, motor vehicles, and used clothes. Nonetheless, overall, the EAC's CETs lowered Tanzania's average tariff rate by 1.4 percentage points (from 12.6 to 11.2 percent) and the weighted average tariff rate (using trade volumes that prevailed in 2003) by 3.2 percentage points, from 9.1 to 5.9 percent – a 35 percent reduction.

Uganda's most important import was petroleum. According to the Ugandan Bureau of Statistics (2006), in 2003–2005, imports of petroleum accounted for 15 percent of its total imports. The tariff rate on petroleum was zero before and after the establishment of the EAC customs union. For all the other important Ugandan imports, the EAC's CETs were higher than the pre-customs union tariffs for imports from non-EAC member countries. Contrary to the situation with Kenya and Tanzania, Uganda was projected to become more protective against non-EAC imports. The EAC's CETs increased Uganda's average tariff rate by 3.4 percentage points (from 7.8 to 11.2 percent) and the weighted average tariff rate (using trade volumes that prevailed in 2003) by 2.9 percentage points, from 6.3 to 9.2 percent – a 46 percent increase. Even with the elimination of tariffs on intra-EAC trade, Uganda's projected overall weighted tariff rate increased by 0.8 percentage points, from 5.9 to 6.7 percent, a 14 percent increase.

Stay Applications and Duty Remissions

In reality, the commonality of the tariff rates was only on paper. In practice, the CETs were used as tariff ceilings. The established CETs reduced the divergence of the external tariffs of member countries, but they did not make applied tariffs on imports from third parties "common." As was typical of similar negotiations, the CETs were set with a provision to allow exceptions and flexibility by member countries. It was a way to reach a compromise after nine years of arduous negotiations and to move forward, in the hope that those exceptions would be eliminated over time.

Countries were allowed "stay applications" and duty remissions.[2] A stay of application allows a country to disregard a given CET and apply a different tariff rate. A duty remission allows a company to pay lower import duties or be exempted from paying duties altogether. A duty remission lists specific items and amounts. In 2007, Burundi and Rwanda acceded to the EAC, and they were also allowed to take advantage of stay applications and duty remissions.

No country has been bashful in using these loopholes. The EAC *Gazette* publishes stay applications and duty remissions and their extensions on a regular basis. Table 5.2 gives only a small sample of what is contained in the June 19, 2015 issue of the *Gazette*. In that issue alone, over 50 products (at 8-digit HS code) were listed that received stay applications or duty remissions. For most of these products, these exemptions have simply been a matter of renewing them every year.

The Complexity of CETs, Stay Applications, and Duty Remissions

Some CETs were set to satisfy some lobbying groups but were not practical. Consider a 75 percent CET on rice which did not make much sense for Kenya. It was too high, considering Kenya's interests. Before the customs union came into effect, the tariff on rice was 37.75 percent in Kenya, 27.75 percent in Tanzania, and 25 percent in Uganda (Ahmed, 2012). Rice is the third most important food staple in Kenya after corn

Table 5.2 *Sample of Stay Applications and Duty Remissions*

Product	CET	Stay Application or Duty Remission
Aluminum alloy in sheets	25	Kenya to stay application of EAC CET and apply import duty of 10% for one year.
Rice	75	(a) Kenya to stay application of EAC CET and apply import duty of 35% for one year. (b) Rwanda to stay application of EAC CET and apply import duty of 45% for one year.
Sugar	100	(a) Tanzania to import 100,000 metric tons at import duty of 50% between April–June 2015. (b) Rwanda to import 70,000 metric tons at import duty of 25% for one year.
Motor vehicles for transport of goods with gross vehicle weight 5–20 tons	25	Burundi, Rwanda, and Uganda to stay application of the EAC CET and apply import duty of 10% for one year.
Motor vehicles for the transport of more than 25 persons	25	(a) Burundi, Rwanda, and Uganda to stay application of the EAC CET and apply import duty of 10% for one year. (b) Tanzania to stay application of the EAC CET on heavy duty buses for the "Dar Fast Bus Project" for one year.
Motor vehicles for the transport of 50 or more persons	25	Rwanda and Uganda to stay application of the EAC CET and apply import duty of 0% for one year.
Road tractors for semi-trailers	10	Burundi, Rwanda, and Uganda to stay application of EAC CET and apply a duty rate of 0%.
Wheat grain	35	(a) Rwanda granted a duty remission of 0% for one year. (b) Kenya, Tanzania and Uganda granted a duty remission of 10% for one year.

Source: East African Community (2015a).

and wheat. On average, 85 percent of rice consumed in Kenya is imported, as shown in Table 5.3. Almost all of Kenya's imports of rice come from outside the EAC region, with over 70 percent of it coming from Pakistan, as shown in Table 5.4. Apparently, the pressure to have a high CET on rice came from lobbyists in Uganda who wanted protection, claiming that they could increase production to meet the EAC's demand for rice. However, Uganda's production could not meet Kenya's demand for rice.

Table 5.3 *Metric Tons of Milled Rice Production, Imports, and Apparent Consumption in Kenya, 2005–2010 (in thousands)*

	2005	2006	2007	2008	2009	2010
Production	58	65	47	22	42	45
Imports	228	232	262	299	308	284
Exports	n.a.	0.8	0.6	1.5	2.3	1.6
Apparent consumption	286	296	308	320	348	327
Import dependency (%)	80	78	85	93	89	87

Source: Short et al., 2012.

Table 5.4 *Kenya's Imports of Rice by Source, 2006–2010*

Country	Percent of Imports
Pakistan	74
Vietnam	9
Thailand	4
Egypt	4
India	4
Tanzania	2
US	1
Other	2

Source: Short et al., 2012.

When Kenya attempted to apply a 75 percent tariff on imported rice, Pakistan threatened to retaliate by imposing trade barriers on Kenyan tea. Kenya is the largest exporter of tea in the world, with a world market share of about 15 percent. On average, from 2000 to 2015, tea contributed about 18 percent of Kenya's export revenue. While Kenya's tea is exported to more than 50 countries, Pakistan imports about 20 percent of Kenyan tea (World Bank, 2013, 77). Pakistan has been the top or the second top importer of Kenyan tea, swapping those leading positions back and forth with Egypt. Fear of retaliation by Pakistan forced Kenya to take advantage of a stay application and to keep the tariff rate at 35 percent. However, Pakistan and Kenya continued to be on the verge of a true trade dispute because every year Kenya hinted at using the CET of 75 percent.

As Ochieng and Majanja (2010) explain, this case illustrates some of the challenges inherent in harmonizing an economic bloc's trade barriers when, in all likelihood, member countries have different import needs.

Kenya was in a precarious situation because it could not please Pakistan and its fellow EAC members at the same time. Kenya and its EAC partners, especially Uganda, were very much at odds with each other – Kenya claiming Uganda was charging a 100 percent tariff rate on rice grown in Kenya, and Uganda arguing that rice from Pakistan was being transshipped into Uganda from Kenya. At the same time, seemingly in retaliation, Kenya restricted imports of sugar from Uganda, saying that Uganda was simply repackaging sugar that it had imported from outside the EAC (Otage, 2013). This specific dispute was eventually resolved in 2014 when both countries relaxed their restrictions (Wahome, 2014).

Each country has utilized stay applications, and hundreds of manufacturers in the EAC have received duty remissions on inputs or intermediate products. These loopholes were supposed to be closed by 2010, when the EAC was to become a full-fledged customs union. Nonetheless, the EAC continues to function in many ways as an advanced free trade area, not even as a true customs union. Stay applications and duty remissions continue to be a feature of the EAC, as reported in each new issue of the EAC *Gazette*. "Temporary" benefits or protection have a way of getting entrenched, no matter how strong the intention to remove them might be. It is similar to the well-experienced dilemma regarding temporary protection for infant industries. Either domestic manufacturers remain infant and thus dependent, or they become strong and thus politically powerful. Either way, it is hard to remove the temporary protection or loopholes.

In the EAC, as the duty remission window was approaching its supposed closure date, December 31, 2009, domestic manufacturers successfully lobbied for the extension of special waivers. The Ugandan Manufacturers Association was particularly influential, to the point where in late 2010, the EAC Council of Ministers allowed Uganda to continue to exempt its importers of inputs from paying import taxes, seemingly indefinitely. It was reported that, "[t]he agreement with Uganda government is that it will continue to retain this list [of 138 inputs] as long as its industries can prove to the council that the schemes removal will cause injuries to them" (Omondi, 2010). That was a very nebulous criterion for ending the duty remission program.

In addition to manufacturers' self-interest, bureaucracies also have a tendency to be biased in favor of extending special programs. Special programs create jobs and some personal benefits such as per diem allowances. For example, duty remission applications involve meetings and even travel benefits. Verification of the applications often entails visiting the facilities of the applicants.

Applications for duty remissions are sent to respective national Duty Remission Committees for consideration. Each national Duty Remission Committee has representatives from various ministries and manufacturers' associations. Each national Duty Remission Committee forwards its list of approved manufacturers (applications) and the respective quantities to the EAC Secretariat, for announcement in the EAC *Gazette*.

A manual detailing the procedure for applications for duty remission is meant to provide uniform and objective criteria in considering applications for duty remission, but each country has autonomy in dealing with its applications. Applications approved by a national Duty Remission Committee can undergo some procedural scrutiny at the Secretariat level but, in effect, they are generally taken at face value and published in the EAC *Gazette*. While the decentralization of power to individual countries may be more efficient than a centralized system, it creates unhealthy silent competition between countries. Each one is likely to be more indulgent in favor of its applicants, as a way of responding to approved applications by other countries for their manufacturers. The duty remission scheme is implemented with a very strong nationalistic spirit, no matter how strong the aspirations for deeper integration might be.

To the credit of those who prepared the Protocol on the Establishment of the East African Customs Union, duty remissions come with some restrictions. According to Article 25 of the protocol:

> The Partner States agree that goods benefiting from export promotion schemes shall primarily be for export. In the event that such goods are sold in the Customs territory, such goods shall attract full duties, levies and other charges provided in the Common External Tariff. The sale of goods in the Customs territory shall be subject to authorisation by a competent authority and such sale shall be limited to 20 per centum of the annual production of a company. (East African Community, 2004b, Article 25)

These conditions were put in place with the clear intention of promoting exports and preventing unfair competition within the customs territory. From 2005 to 2009, the period established for transitioning into the customs union, sales of products between two countries in the EAC were considered to be exports (imports). As such, 100 percent of goods produced using inputs imported with duty remission could be sold in East Africa. Of course, in accordance with Article 25, those goods faced full duties, as they were treated as coming from outside the EAC.

In 2010, when the EAC was supposed to start functioning as a full-fledged customs union, only 20 percent of the goods produced using duty-free inputs were allowed to be sold in the EAC region. Goods shipped from one country to another in the EAC were no longer considered exports. One caveat was that firms could use the rules of origin provision to circumvent this restriction. Goods are qualified as originating from a member state if they have been transported directly from a member nation and

> have been produced in a Partner State wholly or partially from materials imported from outside the Partner State or of undetermined origin by a process of production which effects a substantial transformation of those materials such that:
> (i) the c.i.f. value of those materials does not exceed sixty per centum of the total cost of the materials used in the production of the goods [and]
> (ii) the value added resulting from the process of production accounts for at least thirty five per centum of the ex-factory cost of the goods. (East African Community, 2004d, 5)

Like most other economic blocs, for the purpose of determining the origin of the finished products, the EAC applies the cumulative principle. Raw materials or intermediate goods originating from any member of the EAC are considered to have originated from the EAC country where the final processing or manufacturing took place. The rules of origin provision retained the possibility that a company in the EAC that used inputs imported with duty remission could still sell more than 20 percent of its output to partner states. Those would be goods that did not meet the "rules of origin" threshold. Full duty would be applied to those goods.

The change in the definition of exports that took effect in 2010 seemed to have affected Kenya's manufacturing sector the most because of its reliance on the East African market. Kenyan manufacturers had to scramble to find new markets, but also petitioned to have Article 25 of the Protocol on the Establishment of the East African Customs Union suspended. Their request was not granted.

Needless to say, the whole issue of duty remissions is rather complex for various reasons, including: (a) the lack of uniformity in granting duty remissions, and (b) an inability to verify which inputs were actually used to produce the final product. The Kenyan Association of Manufacturers found it unfair that Uganda was allowed by the EAC Council of Ministers to retain stays of application with duty remissions on the full list of inputs and intermediate products that had been created since 1994. The so-called "Uganda list," which had 138 inputs, became a source of contention. The Uganda Manufacturers Association had argued that their manufacturing sector was at an infancy stage and could not compete fairly with Kenya's manufacturing sector, which was much more advanced. However, with mounting criticism from Kenya, Uganda eventually agreed to reduce the number of duty-free inputs from 138 to 49, effective July 2013 (Omondi, 2013). Inputs that were dropped from the protection list faced an import duty of 10 percent. It is interesting that while Burundi and Rwanda had similar lists of inputs imported duty-free, there were no complaints against them. This may have to do with their economies being small and thus, particularly in the case of Burundi, inconsequential. In other words, Burundi could legitimately claim that its manufacturing sector was indeed still an "infant."

Another complication regarding the provision of duty remissions has to do with how the duty-free inputs are actually used. There are different scenarios, but two will suffice for illustration. A company might import some inputs under duty remission and at the same time use similar inputs (perfect substitutes) acquired from the domestic market or from a partner state. Both imported and domestic inputs are used to produce the same final product. Suppose the share of the product produced using imported inputs is exported and the share of product produced using local inputs is sold to other countries in the customs union. Should there still be a full duty imposed on the amount sold within the customs union? This is not an implausible scenario.

There was a claim that some companies such as British American Tobacco Kenya Ltd. manufactured goods for the EAC market using local inputs. That is, while British American Tobacco Kenya Ltd. imported some inputs under the duty remission scheme, those specific inputs were used only for the production of cigarettes and other tobacco products exported outside of the EAC. Tanzania did not buy that argument, saying that it could not verify which cigarettes were produced using imported inputs and which ones were produced using local inputs (Ligami, 2013). Tanzania applied a full duty on products produced by British American Tobacco Kenya Ltd., irrespective of the source of inputs.

Here is another situation. Suppose a company uses just a small amount of inputs imported under duty remission (relative to other inputs) to produce products sold in the EAC. Should a full duty be applied to those products? That was the dispute between Kenya and Tanzania with respect to beef and pork produced by Kenya Farmers Choice. Tanzania applied a 25 percent duty on beef and pork produced by Kenya Farmers Choice. However, Kenya complained that Tanzania's strict interpretation of Article 25 of the Protocol on the Establishment of the East African Customs Union was a form of a non-tariff barrier. In 2012, it was decided "that a Regional Committee be constituted to propose how to treat products which use small proportions of imported inputs under the EAC duty remission scheme" (East African Community, 2012a, 34). It is not clear whether or not a committee was ever formed, but there was no mention of this dispute, as resolved or unresolved, in subsequent reports.

In the case of British American Tobacco Kenya Ltd., even if it could be verified that cigarettes from Kenya did not contain imported duty-free inputs, it would still have been reasonable for Tanzania (and Kenya on Tanzanian products, if the situation was reversed) to apply a full duty. The point is that British American Tobacco Kenya Ltd. would not have been able to produce the amount it produced without the duty-free inputs, and its overall cost would have been higher without the duty remission. The attempt to separate identical inputs purely by the destination of the final product is only a tactic to circumvent Article 25 of the protocol and should not be accepted. Kenya Farmers Choice has even less of a case to make, and it is surprising that a Regional Committee had to be assembled to look into it.

It is not clear when the EAC will do away completely with duty remissions and stay of application provisions and function as a true customs union (let alone the common market it claims to be, as discussed in Chapter 6). Moreover, these provisions are only part of the complication. In addition, policies and standards are not adequately harmonized, and all EAC partners are guilty, though to varying degrees, of imposing unlawful non-tariff barriers.

NON-TARIFF BARRIERS

The EAC defines non-tariff barriers as "quantitative restrictions and specific limitations that act as obstacles to trade and which appear in the form of rules, regulations and laws that have a negative impact [on] trade" (East African Community and East African Business Council, 2008, 3). Lately, non-tariff barriers have taken a prominent position in discussions about trade constraints in East Africa. Ironically, this may actually suggest greater openness exists, in the sense that the attention given to non-tariff barriers reflects significant reductions in explicit tariffs. What is clearly promising is the fact that a monitoring mechanism has been put in place, aimed at identifying, reporting, and eliminating non-tariff barriers within the EAC (East African Community and East African Business Council, 2008). However, what is disconcerting is that non-tariff barriers in the EAC are entrenched, and while some are being eliminated, new ones are also being introduced. While EAC leaders seem to be publicly against them, they have allowed them.

Non-tariff barriers infiltrate all trade and supply chain processes and comprise a wide range of measures, including customs and administrative procedures, business hours, traffic laws, inspection requirements, import or export bans, product classifications, export and import licenses, packaging and labeling requirements, police roadblocks, weight limits, rules of origin, sanitary and phytosanitary measures, and trade regulations. Surveys by the East African Business Council suggest that customs procedures, administrative requirements, and police roadblocks are the most severe forms of non-tariff barriers (East African Community and East African Business Council, 2012). (Immigration procedures could also be included on the list, but they are a special category, discussed in Chapter 6.) Multiply these and other measures by the number of countries involved and one can see why non-tariff barriers are a real challenge. Here are a few examples.

The major complaint from all associations of manufacturers with which the author consulted was a lack of harmonization of policies and standards. For example, in the horticultural sector, Kenya seems to have more stringent standards for cut flowers than those applied by Tanzania. In May of 2011, Kenya imposed a ban on flowers from Tanzania that passed through Nairobi (Kenya) to Europe and other markets. Kenya claimed that Tanzanian cut flowers did not meet the standards necessary to assure that Kenyan cut flowers were protected from the risks of pests and diseases. With concerted efforts by the Tanzania Horticultural Association, the ban was eventually lifted in March of 2013 when the two countries signed a Memorandum of Understanding. However, the ban created an element of uncertainty, and as of 2016 Tanzania had not yet fully recovered from that ban, as some importers switched to other suppliers during the ban. About 80 percent of Tanzania's cut flower exports went through Kenya.

Tanzania also seems to have different and, apparently, lower standards for the packaging of onions. According to the Tanzania Chamber of Commerce, Industry and Agriculture (TCCIA), the low packaging standards reduce producer prices for farmers and subject exports of onions to Kenya to extensive scrutiny and delays at the border. At the same time, this situation brings a windfall to Kenyan traders. They buy onions in Tanzania that are unpackaged or packaged in a substandard way, bring them to Kenya, repackage the onions using international packaging standards, and re-export them as a Kenyan product. In fact, there were allegations that Kenyan traders formed a cartel to create monopsony power which lead to unfair producer prices for

Tanzanian farmers. This led some local governments in Tanzania to ban Kenyan traders from buying onions directly from farmers (McAdams, 2010).

Members of the EAC also lack uniform sanitary and phytosanitary certification procedures. Staying with onions as an example, Kenya does not recognize phytosanitary certification issued by Tanzanian authorities. Someone importing onions from Tanzania into Kenya will first need a certificate of quality assurance in Tanzania. However, upon entering Kenya, the phytosanitary and country of origin certificate issued by Tanzanian authorities is surrendered to the Kenya Plant Health Inspection Service. The onions are re-inspected and a new certificate is issued. Each inspection takes time (a great concern with respect to a perishable product like onions) and each time one must pay inspection fees, which can be as high as $100 per consignment, often depending on how quickly one wants the inspection to be done.

Two other examples that highlight challenges caused by the lack of common standards are Uganda's rejection of Tanzania's mosquito nets and Kenya's beef and beef products. Uganda claimed that mosquito nets from Tanzania did not meet the requirements set by the Uganda Bureau of Standards. However, they were certified by the Tanzania Bureau of Standards and the International Organization of Standardization. In 1997, Uganda, fearing the spread of mad cow disease, restricted imports of cattle products from Kenya, which by the way was never found in Kenya. Sixteen years later, Uganda was still restricting beef products from Kenya, claiming that Kenya's meat standards were below those required in Uganda (Odeke, 2012, East African Community, 2013, 7).

The Ripple Effect of Non-tariff Barriers

As can be expected, these forms of trade bottlenecks have a ripple effect. Since the rules and procedures guiding trade facilitation are often amorphous and lack transparency, countries are able to retaliate silently with various forms of non-tariff barriers. For example, during Kenya's ban on Tanzanian flowers, Tanzania became less hospitable to Kenyan traders. Tanzania introduced non-tariff barriers that targeted Kenya in retaliation: Kenyan trucks entering Tanzania were charged a levy of US$200 each, tourist vans registered in Kenya were not allowed to enter Tanzania (they were required to transfer their passengers into vans registered in Tanzania), and Tanzania made it difficult for Kenyans to get simplified certificate of origin forms needed by Kenyan exporters of products to Tanzania. Once the ban on Tanzanian flowers was lifted, some of these and other non-tariff barriers were relaxed, but the damage was already done.

Kenya and Tanzania have often demonstrated their discontent with each other by enforcing restrictions in the tourism industry. In 1985, when these countries were barely talking to each other, they decided that tourist vehicles registered in one country would not be allowed to enter the other country's national parks. One would think that the Protocol on the Establishment of the East African Customs Union, reached in 2005, would have nullified such decisions, but both countries have enforced them, on and off, depending on the political sentiment they felt for or against each other. In mid-2014, Kenya's Tourist Regulatory Authority banned Tanzania's tour operators from entering Kenyan game reserves, supposedly in retaliation for Tanzania's similar action against Kenyan tour operators (Mtulya, 2014).

To put more pressure on Tanzania, in December of 2014, Kenyan authorities banned Tanzanian-registered vehicles from dropping off or picking up passengers at the Jomo Kenyatta International Airport (JKIA) in Nairobi. About 40 percent of international tourists that visit Tanzania go through Kenya. The ban on Tanzanian-registered vehicles to JKIA was lifted within a month and Kenya and Tanzania agreed to review their bilateral relationship as it applied to tourism, but clearly they were flexing their muscles more than negotiating with earnest.

The review process did not go well because Kenya imposed that ban again in February of 2015. This time, Tanzania retaliated by cutting back Kenya Airlines' flights to Tanzania from 42 to 16 per week (Mugarula, 2015). These actions were hurting the tourism industry in both Kenya and Tanzania, as some tourists treat these two countries as complementary destinations. From 2011 to 2013, the total number of international tourists to Kenya and Tanzania was 4.52 million and 2.86 million, respectively (United Nations World Tourism Organization, 2015). In both countries, export revenues generated from international tourism, as a ratio of the value of exports of all goods and services, is about 20 percent.

Tensions were high, and the rhetoric and name-calling from the general public was reminiscent of the period just before and after the collapse of the former EAC in the late 1970s. It is not clear which side blinked first, but Presidents Kenyatta and Kikwete of Kenya and Tanzania, respectively, reached an agreement in March of 2015 to immediately remove the ban on Tanzanian-registered vehicles to JKIA and to restore Kenya Airlines flights to 42 per week while negotiations continued (*The Citizen*, 2015a). The executive orders from the two presidents were a welcome relief to many, but the underlying tension and mistrust between these countries remained. These bans build mistrust and create uncertainty, which can only hurt both countries and slow down the pace of integration in the East African Community.

An immigration officer confided to the author that during Kenya's ban on Tanzanian flowers, Tanzania became stricter with illegal immigrants from Kenya. Retaliation is a reflexive reaction and is used to exert pressure on the trading partners to remove their trade barriers. The danger is that retaliation and counter-retaliation can cause an upward spiral effect on trade barriers.

The Pervasiveness of Non-tariff Barriers

Table 5.5 provides the number of non-tariff barriers reported between 2011 and 2014. They include non-tariff barriers related to labor mobility in the region. Note that the number of non-tariff barriers that are resolved is given in aggregate; that is, by December 2014, a total of 78 cases had been resolved.

Many non-tariff barriers have persisted. Among the most enduring or seemingly "chronic" non-tariff barriers according to various issues of the EAC's *Status of Elimination of Non-Tariff Barriers in the East African Community* are: "numerous institutions involved in testing goods," "Ugandan restriction of beef & beef products from Kenya," "non-recognition by Kenya for [Sanitary and Phytosanitary] SPS certificates issued by Uganda for tea destined for Mombasa auction," "lack of interface within the customs' systems in the Revenue Authorities in Partner States,"

Table 5.5 *Number of Non-tariff Barriers as Reported*[3]

Status of Elimination of Non-tariff Barriers in the East African Community	Non-tariff Barriers		
	Unresolved	New	Resolved
Volume 1 – August 2011	30	–	19
Volume 2 – March 2012	23	16	26
Volume 3 – June 2012	31	5	36
Volume 4 – November 2012	35	10	36
Volume 5 – December 2012	37	4	40
Volume 6 – May 2014	23	9	62
Volume 7 – September 2014	21	8	69
Volume 8 – December 2014	18	4	78

Source: East African Community, *Status of Elimination of Non-Tariff Barriers in the East African Community* (various issues).

"border management institutions' working hours are not harmonized," "corruption along the Northern and Central Corridors (police roadblocks, weighbridge and border gates)," "no movements of Cargo Trucks beyond 6:00 pm within Tanzania," and "several Police roadblocks along Northern and Central Corridors, estimated at 36 between Mombasa- Kigali and 30 between Dar-es-Salaam to Rusumo border." It is important to note that most of these roadblocks are not official checkpoints.

The number of roadblocks is overwhelming, making some ask if all these checkpoints are necessary (Eyakuze and Salim, 2012). The distance from Mombasa (Kenya) to Kigali (Rwanda) via Uganda is 1,700 kilometers; thus, on average, there is a roadblock every 47 kilometers. The distance from Dar-es-Salaam to Rusumo (Rwanda-Tanzania border) is 1,320 kilometers; thus, on average, there is a roadblock every 44 kilometers. It should be noted some of those roadblocks are well-established checkpoints and others are random, where police officers simply decide to stop vehicles at their own discretion and without probable cause. Truckers breathed a sigh of relief when in 2016, President Magufuli of Tanzania ordered the closure of four official checkpoints (out of seven) on the Dar-es-Salaam-Rusumo route (*The Citizen*, 2016). Of course, truckers still have to contend with the many unofficial checkpoints (roadblocks).

Because of the many non-tariff barriers such as the large number of roadblocks, bribery is a salient feature of intra-regional trade in the EAC. In 2011, Transparency International, Kenya, conducted an extensive survey on bribery incidences associated with trade in the EAC (Transparency International, Kenya, 2012). It was found that bribery was prevalent in all trade-related authorities – customs, regulatory authorities, revenue authorities, and police. According to the study, bribes were triggered by the slow pace of service (unnecessary delays), excessive amount of documentation requirements, poor understanding of clearing procedures, and high tax rates. In summary, the survey concluded that "bribes were mainly demanded and offered to speed up the service at various points, avoid full verification of goods and to avoid paying full tax and other charges payable" (p. 8). A similar conclusion was reached in a previous study by Regional Strategic Analysis and Knowledge Support Systems, which had focused on the maize and beef trade in Kenya, Tanzania, and Uganda (Karugia et al., 2009).

However, it is not clear why both studies categorized bribery purely as a non-tariff barrier. In fact, Transparency International, Kenya, titled its study, *Bribery as a Non-Tariff Barrier to Trade: A Case Study of East African Trade Corridors.* The bribery discussed in both studies is mostly used to facilitate trade, that is, to overcome official non-tariff barriers. The point here is not to condone bribery or corruption, but there is no denying that most of the bribery is a result of costly trade barriers. Needless to say, bribes are a cost to private actors, but as rational, profit-maximizers, private actors are aware that the cost of bureaucracy-induced delays are even greater. They determine that the marginal cost of giving a bribe is less than the additional cost of delay. Incidentally, both the person who gives a bribe and the one who receives it are aware of the cost of delays; that is why there are, often, explicit negotiations about the amount of a bribe. The reference here is to delays that would occur if one were to go through the full length of the labyrinth created by cumbersome procedures and processes. In this regard, bribery is an informal way of reducing trade barriers.

Of course, bribes are also extorted by various officials by harassing people, even those who have paid all the fees and complied with all other requirements. Those bribes are indeed an additional non-tariff barrier. But even those bribes are, partly, a function of official trade barriers. Official trade barriers promote bribery to the point where demanding and giving bribes become a "normal" and "acceptable" practice, whether one has complied with the export and import requirements or not. The standard cue from a police officer at a roadblock is that he or she "greets" the truck driver by announcing that he or she has not had breakfast or lunch yet, depending on the time of the day.

It is important to note those roads blocks are not limited to trucks carrying merchandise goods. Shuttle buses face similar intimidation, and if the drivers don't "cooperate," their schedules can be thrown off completely. The author has traveled many times between Nairobi (Kenya) and Arusha (Tanzania) on shuttle buses and has witnessed police corruption on just about every trip. While the following example is not unique, it illustrates the point. In July 2013, while on a shuttle bus from Nairobi to Arusha, just about 20 kilometers before arriving in Namanga (a border town between Kenya and Tanzania), two police officers stopped the shuttle bus. One got on the bus and the other went to talk with the driver. The one on the bus pointed at a number clipped on her collar and said in broken Swahili: "hii ndiyo kitambulisho yangu; ya wewe iko wapi?" [Here is my identification; where is yours?]. Everyone pulled out his/her passport, obediently. She took one from the person sitting by the entrance, opened a random page, and pretended to be studying it. However, her eyes were on the other police officer. Once the driver gave something to the other police officer, the one on the bus suddenly handed the passport back and announced, again in broken Swahili, "mimi naona wote nyie iko sawa"

[I see that you are all okay]. She got off the bus, and the bus was permitted to leave. At the Namanga border itself, everything went smoothly.

About five kilometers past the border (now in Tanzania), the bus was stopped by a police officer who, as if to be transparent, asked the driver in an obnoxiously loud voice to follow him as he inspected the luggage. The bus was about one-third empty so the driver had put the luggage in the back seats. The police officer walked with the driver behind the bus and somehow the inspection was completed without the police officer inspecting even a single suitcase. But, of course, why would he have inspected suitcases anyway? The passengers had just gone through customs, and Kenya and Tanzania are supposed to be a customs union.

When drivers know they will be extorted to pay a bribe regardless, they may not strive for full compliance. Instead, they will try to figure out an optimal combination of non-compliance and bribery that would maximize their profits. A truck driver who worked for many years transporting goods between Arusha (Tanzania) and Bujumbura (Burundi) revealed to the author that often times the way to speed things up at check points was to have at least one conspicuous innocuous violation such as a little crack on the side mirror. If you took responsibility for it, apologized, demonstrated some humility, and gave the police officer a little something for breakfast or lunch, normally you would not be checked for other potential violations.

Measuring Non-tariff Barriers

The welfare impact of non-tariff barriers can be analyzed by evaluating their impact on consumer surplus and producer surplus.[4] Non-tariff barriers decrease consumer surplus and increase producer surplus in the importing country and vice versa in the exporting country. The net welfare impact is usually negative, although if the non-tariff barriers were introduced to correct market imperfections, it is possible for the net welfare impact to be positive.

There are several ways to quantify non-tariff barriers and estimate their impact, but no single method or even a combination of methods is without its limitations. This is especially true when a number of non-tariff barriers are applied to a single product and when they are not applied consistently.

Deardorff and Stern (1997), Bora et al. (2002), and Fugazza (2013) summarize a few ways to quantify non-tariff barriers, including the frequency index, coverage ratio, price-comparison measures, quantity-impact measures, and the gravity model of trade. The frequency index involves calculating the percentage of import lines subject to at least one non-tariff

Table 5.6 *Illustration of Covered Ratio*

Product	Value of Imports (Vi)	Non-tariff Barriers	$Di^* Vi$
Oranges	\$4,000	no	0
Orange juice	\$1,000	yes	\$1,000
Grapes	\$2,000	no	0
Wine	\$5,000	yes	\$5,000

barrier. An obvious weakness of this measure is that it does not take into account the value of imports. The frequency index also does not capture the restrictive nature of non-tariff barriers. It treats all of them as equal, and at the same time it does not differentiate between products protected by one non-tariff barrier and those protected by more than one. It also treats all products the same, whether they are inputs or finished products.

The covered ratio measures the share of imports, in value, on which non-tariff barriers are applied. It is calculated using the following formula: $Cj = \sum(Di * Vi)/\sum Vi$, where Cj is coverage ratio, j is the importing country, Di is a dummy variable for product i (it takes the value of 1 if one or more non-tariff barriers is applied to the product or zero otherwise), and Vi is the value of imports of product i. Suppose Table 5.6 represents total imports into Kenya from Tanzania. In this example, $\sum(Di * Vi) =$ \$6,000; $\sum Vi =$ \$12,000; therefore, Cj is 0.5.

Similar to the frequency index, the coverage ratio does not take into account the stringency of the trade barriers. In addition, similar to the frequency index, the coverage ratio can be misleading because it does not differentiate between different types of products. In this hypothetical numerical example, Kenya has trade barriers on processed (finished) products from Tanzania but not on unprocessed products. If the non-tariff barriers were removed from orange juice and wine and applied to oranges and grapes, the coverage ratio would remain the same. However, their impacts would be very different. Non-tariff barriers on processed products would limit Tanzania's efforts to add value to its primary products, whereas trade barriers on unprocessed products (only) could actually stimulate Tanzania's processing industry.

Another problem with the coverage ratio measure (and the frequency index, for that matter) is that it is downward biased. To continue with the same example, if non-tariff barriers on wine became so extensive as to eliminate imports of wine from Tanzania altogether, the coverage ratio would actually decrease. That would suggest, incorrectly, that Kenya has reduced non-tariff barriers, when in fact those barriers had instead caused wine imports to stop altogether. The coverage ratio would decrease from 0.5 to 0.143.

The price-comparison measure (price wedge) is used to estimate the scope of non-tariff barriers by calculating what the price of a given product would have been under free trade and comparing it with the actual price. The same approach is used, respectively, with the quantity-impact measure. The "price wedge" and the "quantity gap" give some indication of how restrictive the non-tariff measures are. Note that the "price wedge" and "quantity gap" are both measures of the scope of non-tariff barriers, and at the same time, they serve as estimates of the impact of non-tariff barriers. The price and quantity effects are often calculated using the gravity model of trade pioneered by Tinbergen (1962). The gravity model estimates bilateral trade using GDP, geographical distance, population, non-tariff barriers and other explanatory variables. When data limitations prevent inclusion of non-tariff barriers as determinants, the residual errors can be considered the residual effect of non-tariff barriers, depending on the exact specification of the model.

Some studies on the impact of non-tariff barriers have incorporated extensive surveys on the impediments of trade. Such is the study by Karugia et al. (2009) which focused on the maize (corn) and beef cattle trade in Kenya, Tanzania, and Uganda. The study suggests that the elimination of all non-tariff barriers on maize and beef cattle trade would result in net welfare gains for all three countries, albeit by the minute percentages of 0.09, 0.11, and 0.56, for Kenya, Tanzania, and Uganda, respectively. According to the study, the combined baseline consumer surplus and producer surplus for the maize and beef cattle markets in Kenya, Tanzania, and Uganda were, respectively, \$2.3 billion, \$1.8 billion, and \$800 million. The negligible positive impact of eliminating non-tariff barriers estimated by Karugia et al. (2009) may have to do with two main factors: (a) maize and beef cattle production are mostly for domestic consumption, and (b) most of the maize and beef cattle trade in East Africa is done in the informal market. Exports and imports of maize in East Africa constitute less than 10 percent of total maize trade in the region (Barreiro-Hurle, 2012; Short et al., 2012a; Ahmed, 2012a). Lesser and Moisé-Leeman (2009) estimate that 83 percent of maize exported from Uganda to Kenya is through informal channels. Informal cross-border trade in cattle in East Africa is about 85 percent of the total trade (FEWSNET, FAO, and WFP, 2012).

Export Bans

Non-tariff barriers are not limited to those that are imposed to limit imports. Export taxes and export bans are also forms of non-tariff barriers. A good example is Tanzania's periodic export ban on maize and other grains, even to its EAC partner countries. An export ban is an example of the many inconsistencies common in the EAC and other African regional economic blocs. When the EAC was supposed to start functioning as a full-fledged customs union in 2010, goods from one country to another in the EAC were no longer to be considered exports. In other words, technically, there could not be an export ban on goods from one country to another in the customs union. Yet export bans to member countries have occurred even since 2010. Again, this illustrates that the EAC is not yet a full-fledged customs union.

The maize export ban in Tanzania has been on and off depending on domestic production. However, even when bans are lifted, securing an export license is a long, bewildering, and costly process. It involves someone completing an application form at the regional office and waiting for the final approval, which is given by the Ministry of Agriculture, Livestock, and Fisheries (previously, Ministry of Agriculture, Food Security, and Cooperatives) in Dar-es-Salaam. Unlike trade barriers on imports which tend to support domestic producers of those products, restrictions on exports hurt domestic producers.

Figure 5.1 illustrates the potential impact of an unanticipated export ban, using Tanzania's ban on exports of maize to Kenya as an example. Panel (T) represents Tanzania, the exporting country. SS and DD are domestic supply and demand lines of maize, respectively. Panel (W) represents the "world" maize market. Assume that Kenya and Tanzania trade maize only with each other. EX and IM are export supply and import demand lines, respectively. Panel (K) represents Kenya, the importing country.

Under free trade, the world price of maize is Pw. Tanzania exports a-b and Kenya imports e-f. Note that the horizontal distances a-b, c-d, and e-f are equal. An unanticipated export ban on maize in Tanzania causes the price of maize in Tanzania to fall from Pw to Pt and the price in Kenya to increase from Pw to Pk. In Tanzania, consumer surplus increases by areas G and I. Producer surplus decreases by areas G and H. In addition, producers lose areas J and I. The net welfare loss to Tanzania is given by areas H and J. In Kenya, the export ban causes consumer surplus to decrease by areas K, L, and M. Producer surplus increases by area K. The net welfare loss in

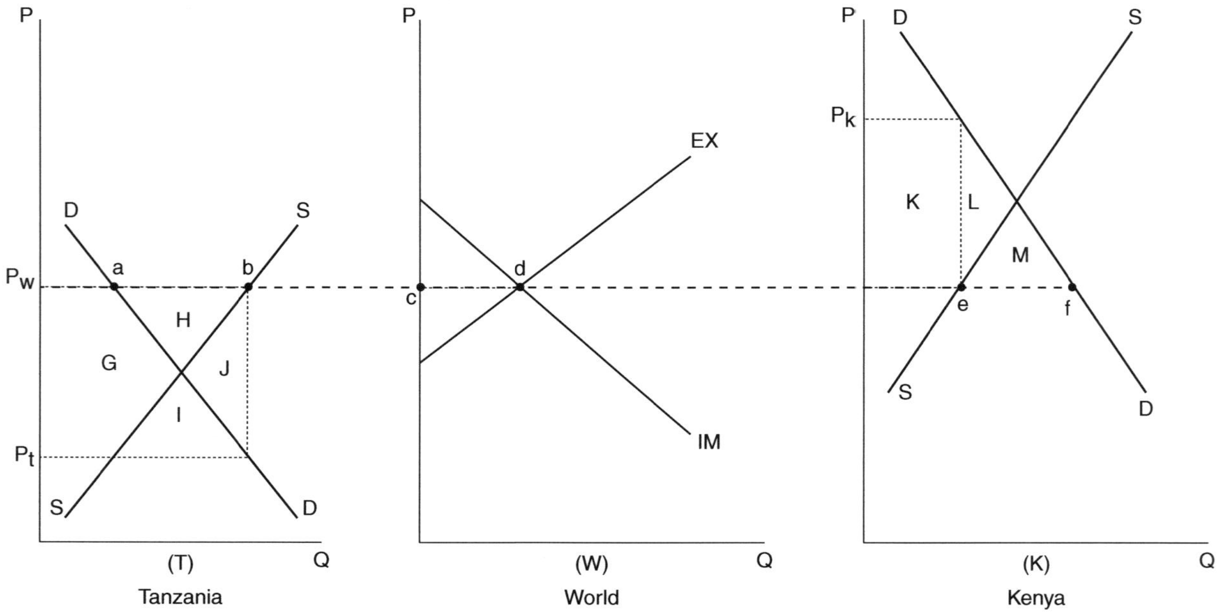

Figure 5.1 Impact of an Unanticipated Export Ban

Kenya is given by areas L and M. While the presentation in Figure 5.1 exaggerates the net welfare losses, it leaves no doubt that farmers in Tanzania would suffer major losses.[5]

It is interesting that African leaders often proclaim the importance of agriculture and the need to support farmers only when prices are low. They even "fight" for small farmers at international meetings and demand elimination of agricultural subsidies in developed countries that reduce producer prices for African farmers. Yet, each time food prices go up, the political pendulum shifts from a concern for low incomes for subsistence farmers to the plight of urban residents. Of course, much of this has to do with small farmers lacking political power. The agricultural sector in the United States employs less than 2 percent of the labor force. However, US farmers are well-organized and have a lot of political power, which explains, in part, why they receive subsidies. The agricultural sector in East Africa employs 80 percent of the labor force.

Non-tariff barriers are not unique to the EAC – they are common in other regional economic blocs in Africa (Brenton and Gözde, 2012). Ngo-Eyok (2013) explains how some countries in ECOWAS impose export bans on grain even to other ECOWAS countries, blatantly disregarding their own agreement to allow the free movement of goods and persons within the region.

THE COMPLEXITY OF NON-TARIFF BARRIERS

Not all non-tariff barriers are bad. In fact, some non-tariff barriers can improve the social welfare of a nation. In other words, some non-tariff barriers can be justified. Non-tariff barriers can be introduced to correct market imperfections such as asymmetrical information and externalities. Extensive food labeling requirements can be considered a non-tariff barrier, but they are also a way to enable consumers to make informed decisions. For example, non-tariff barriers can be used, legitimately, to limit imports and consumption of cigarettes and other tobacco products due to health hazards associated with consumption of such products. The same can be said about hard liquor. Likewise, non-tariff barriers can be used to safeguard public health and prevent the spread of plant and animal diseases.

Needless to say, even "good" non-tariff barriers can be abused, and that is why standards need to be harmonized and the means of verification must be agreed upon and respected. Of course, it is important for the EAC and other regional blocs to avoid the minimalist approach and, instead, strive to adhere to international standards so as to be able to sell their products in many markets. It is promising that in 2015, the EAC and the United States signed an agreement under which the United States will assist the EAC countries in streamlining their customs procedure to meet the WTO's Trade Facilitation Agreement. The United States will also provide technical assistance to the EAC to build and standardize capacity in sanitary and phytosanitary measures (ICTSD, 2015).

Whatever the standard and whatever the justification for a non-tariff barrier might be, it is imperative to evaluate carefully the impact of non-tariff barriers. It seems reasonable, for example, to justify an export ban on maize and other grains based on a concern for food security. From a political point of view, it is also a way to please urban residents; they are net buyers of food. However, as demonstrated in Figure 5.1, export bans hurt domestic producers, and in the case of maize, it hurts millions of small farmers. In fact, an export ban on maize can create food insecurity for farmers who may depend on maize revenue to buy complementary food items. Moreover, an export ban may not even achieve its objective. It depresses producer prices and can lead to reduced production in the future. It also increases uncertainty, thus slowing investment in the agricultural sector. Furthermore, an export ban often leads to increased smuggling of maize out of the country (Otieno, 2009; Ubwani, 2011).

Some ECOWAS countries have defended bans on grain exports with the argument that they subsidize supplies of fertilizers and seeds to their farmers (Ngo-Eyok, 2013). They contend that exporting grain produced using subsidized inputs is tantamount to subsidizing consumers in other countries. It is not clear whether farmers are told that a condition to accepting subsidized inputs is a ban on exports produced using those inputs. Moreover, there has not been consistency in setting these export bans. In most cases, the decision to ban exports is made for myopic political reasons and not based on carefully considered economic factors. As already suggested, it is not actually clear that those subsidies benefit farmers at all when in the end, producer prices are depressed by export bans. Moreover, if it is determined that subsidized inputs are a legitimate reason for export bans, ECOWAS members should find an equitable way to share the cost of subsidies to prevent bans on exports within the region.

Yet another complication with non-tariff barriers is that administrative processes, trade rules, and taxation requirements between the central and local governments are not fully harmonized. For example, levies on trucks can be imposed independently and concurrently by the central government and local authorities. When Tanzania and Kenya thought they had resolved their dispute over the ban on Tanzanian flowers into Kenya and Tanzania's levy of $200 on Kenya's trucks, a new challenge surfaced, as local authorities in Tanzania imposed their own levies on Kenyan trucks (Ihucha, 2013). What was ironic about this was that the Kenyan trucks being taxed were rented to carry Tanzanian products to Kenya, so the levies were a form of an export tax. However, levies imposed by local authorities are usually not part of trade policy; they are primarily for generating revenue. In fact, the levies administered by the local authorities were not limited to foreign trucks, though foreign trucks were charged a higher levy than local trucks.

Here then is another complexity regarding non-tariff barriers. Some of the non-tariff barriers involve domestic policies and bureaucracies which affect trade, but are neither specifically targeting trade nor necessarily trying to give an unfair advantage to domestic producers. Trade is just an incidental casualty. For example, while police officers may try to intimidate transporters of foreign goods, roadblocks are everywhere in East Africa and do not necessarily target international trade activities. In East Africa (as in many other parts of Africa), police officers can stop a vehicle without any probable cause whatsoever. They then ostensibly conduct a vehicle inspection, but usually they are really just soliciting a bribe from the driver. This can take place while they are totally oblivious to the most blatant and dangerous traffic violations occurring before their very eyes. This is very common in the center of cities where international traders are not the target. This is to say that the trade barrier feature of roadblocks is an extension of the general culture of inefficiency, abuse of power, and police corruption.

The same can be said with respect to unwieldy administrative procedures. They are not unique to trade. They are common even in processes that are 100 percent domestic. Take, for example, the process of getting a title deed for your property in Tanzania. The process involves tens of officials and a number of offices – the hamlet (kitongoji), the sub-ward (mtaa), the ward (kata), the Municipal Council, the Regional Land Office, the Ministry of Land, and the Land Registrar. What is so bewildering and frustrating is that each civil servant involved (sometimes more than one from the same office) can give a different version of what the process is and what the fees are. A question as to how long the whole process will take (after providing all the documents) is usually met with a condescending look, suggesting you are truly naïve to ask such a question. The typical voiced response is usually, "*inategemea bahati yako*" (it depends on your luck) or "*inakutegemea wewe*" (it depends on you). It is left for you to decode those responses.[6] This same type of administrative bureaucracy is found in trade facilitation processes, but it is only a manifestation of the overall domestic administrative culture.

There have been instances in Tanzania where farmers were not allowed to sell their own crops even in local domestic markets because that would be "inviting hunger" (Mwananchi, 2008). Of course, such paternalism was a salient feature of Tanzania during the socialist era, but apparently it has not gone away completely. In 2006, the author observed how farmers in Arusha were not allowed to sell corn on the cob (*mahindi mabichi*), with the assertion that it would invite hunger. Members of the militia were instructed to apprehend violators.[7] Thus, even the maize export ban in Tanzania, which is an explicit trade barrier, is, in some ways, an extension of domestic policies and interventions that have little to do with trade.

REMOVING NON-TARIFF BARRIERS: THE DISPUTE SETTLEMENT PROCEDURE

Characterizing some non-tariff barriers as being incidental is not to suggest that they are benign. Their impact on trade and the overall economic welfare of the EAC economies can be just as harmful as those that are imposed deliberately to limit imports or exports. It is appropriate and important, therefore, that all non-tariff barriers are reported regardless of the underlying reasons for them. It is encouraging that pressure is increasing to reduce or remove them.

One of the major benefits of economic integration is that it challenges inefficient and burdensome domestic policies and regulations. Regional economic integration promotes economic efficiency in trade-related operations that can spill over into other areas of the economy. This is an important positive externality of economic integration. For example, any success in streamlining the application process for export licenses will spillover to other application processes that may have little or nothing to do with trade.

To challenge non-tariff barriers and address other disputes, the EAC has, on paper, a dispute settlement procedure, as stipulated by Article 24 of the Protocol on the Establishment of the East African Customs Union. The dispute settlement process emulates that of the World Trade Organization (WTO).[8] It consists of a maximum of seven stages with a timetable as follows: the *consultation stage*, up to two months; the *good offices, conciliation, and mediation* stage, up to two months; the *panel* stage, up to four months; the *EAC Committee on Trade Remedies* stage, up to two

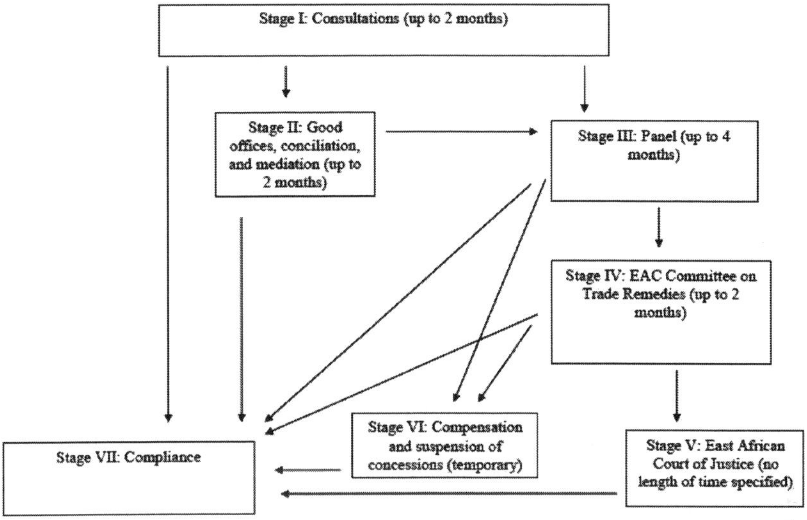

Figure 5.2 EAC Dispute Settlement Mechanism

months; the *East African Court of Justice* (*EACJ*) stage, indeterminate; the *compensation and suspension of concessions* stage, indeterminate; and finally the *compliance* stage. The time periods for various stages are shorter for urgent cases, such as those involving perishable products. The settlement procedure can leap to the compliance stage from any juncture, as indicated in Figure 5.2. That is, a stage or stages may be skipped. For example, after consultations (Stage I), the defending country may decide to comply and move directly to State VII, skipping all the stages in between.

At the first stage, the *consultation* stage, a complainant submits a written request for consultations with a partner state who is detected to have breached an obligation and whose infringement causes an adverse effect. The request for consultation is also forwarded to the EAC Committee on Trade Remedies. The defending country has the burden to rebut the charge and is required to reply and enter into consultations within 10 days and 30 days, respectively, after receiving the request for consultations.

During the *consultation* stage, the parties involved can pursue the *good offices, conciliation, and mediation* process. This is a voluntary stage. The parties involved will only move into this stage if they believe there is a chance of resolving their dispute without engaging a panel. Otherwise, the case moves directly to the *panel* stage. The main role of good offices is to provide logistical support to the parties involved so they can carry on their consultations efficiently. Conciliation involves the participation of an outside neutral person in the negotiations, but that person may not necessarily suggest any solution. In mediation, the outside person would propose a solution, but, of course, the parties involved do not have to accept it.

The *panel* stage involves establishing a panel and terms of reference, determining a timetable for the panel process, including the submission of written reports to the dispute, assessing the facts of the case, and submitting a report to the EAC Committee on Trade Remedies. There is no set number of panelists. The panel is expected to issue its report within three months (and no more than four months) from the time a panel is requested.

If the panel's report is not accepted by either of the parties involved, the dispute settlement process moves on to the *EAC Committee on Trade Remedies* stage. The Committee has to render its final decision within two months of receiving the panel's report.

The *EACJ* stage can be seen as an "appellate" stage, although it is not clear how much jurisdiction the EACJ would have in this process. The decision by the EAC Committee on Trade Remedies is supposed to be final (East African Community, 2004b, 30). A party to a dispute can only appeal to the EACJ "on grounds of fraud, lack of jurisdiction or other illegalities." The Registrar of the EACJ has, in his personal capacity, interpreted that as the EACJ being left out of the process and thus denied the opportunity to play its fundamental role (Ruhangisa, 2011). However, the EACJ itself, as an institution, seems unruffled by the dispute process that has been put in place.

The *compensation and suspension of concessions* stage is meant for restitution and to induce compliance. In plain language, "suspension of concessions" means the complainant can be allowed to retaliate, for example, by placing trade barriers on goods from the country determined to be in infringement. To the extent that it is effective, suspension of concessions is supposed to be temporary.

In 2011, the East African Law Society filed a case against the establishment of the EAC Committee on Trade Remedies, contending that it took away the "jurisdiction of the East African Court of Justice in matters relating to East African Community Regional Integration processes" (East African Community, 2013a, 3). However, in 2013, the EACJ ruled that:

> The dispute settlement mechanisms created under the Customs Union and Common Market Protocols do not exclude, oust or infringe upon the

> interpretative jurisdiction of this Court. Further, the impugned provisions of both protocols are not in contravention of or in contradiction with the relevant provisions of the Treaty ... [A]ny submission that this Court lacks jurisdiction over disputes arising out of the interpretation and application and implementation of the protocols cannot be sustained. (East African Community, 2013a, 40)

This has been a rather curious case because as of 2017 (thirteen years since the signing of the Protocol to establish the EAC customs union), the EAC Committee on Trade Remedies had not operated. Perhaps this should not be too surprising. As ambitious as the EAC might be, it is highly unlikely that non-tariff barriers will be removed through legal pressure any time soon. It is, therefore, no wonder that the EAC Committee on Trade Remedies is mostly a project on paper.

To the extent some progress has been made regarding non-tariff barriers, it has little to do with the legal framework outlined above. Rather, credit is due to the monitoring mechanism for the elimination of non-tariff barriers initiated by the East African Business Council and the EAC Secretariat. That mechanism has led to more awareness and some pressure from the media and business groups to remove non-tariff barriers. It is worth mentioning that many business associations have been providing recommendations, and increasingly there has been a good consultative relationship between business associations and the EAC Secretariat. In fact, this is one important difference between the current EAC and the previous one. So far, most of the interests represented are those of businesses, as opposed to those of consumers, but this is only because consumer-advocacy groups are not yet well established. Eventually, however, noticeable removal of non-tariff barriers will be determined by the political will of the EAC leaders and a clear understanding of the long-run benefits of freer trade. For the foreseeable future, non-tariff barriers will continue to be a real challenge to integration in Africa, even more so as the regional blocs commit themselves to higher levels of integration and admit more members.

INTRA-EAC MERCHANDISE TRADE

Notwithstanding the prevalence of non-tariff barriers, intra-EAC merchandise trade, at least in absolute terms, has been increasing, from about \$5 billion in 2004 to about \$15.4 billion in 2014. Intra-EAC merchandise exports increased by an annual average rate of 14.5 percent between 2004 and 2014. However, total EAC exports to the rest of the world during that period have also increased rapidly, by almost 13 percent. Total EAC imports from the rest of the world increased by an annual average of 17.5 percent during that period. Intra-EAC merchandise trade (exports and imports) as a percent of the region's total merchandise trade has remained more or less constant at around 11 percent, as shown in Table 5.7.

Other economic blocs in Africa have not been successful either in increasing the share of official intra-regional trade, as shown in Table 5.8. It is important to note that informal intra-regional trade in Africa is substantial and is not included in the official figures.[9] For example, it is estimated that informal intra-regional trade in SADC might be as high as 40 percent of the total intra-SADC trade (UNCTAD, 2013). If informal trade was included, the share of intra-regional trade in SADC would be shown to be at least 22 percent instead of just 13 percent. Nonetheless, the existence of unofficial intra-regional trade does not explain why the official intra-regional trade has not been growing. Moreover, if trade barriers are actually decreasing as the levels of integration increase, one would expect informal trade to decline, since traders engage in informal trade in part to circumvent trade barriers.

As the discussion in this chapter suggests, one reason why the share of intra-regional trade in Africa has not shown any noticeable upward trend is that non-tariff barriers are still a hindrance. Reducing tariffs alone has not been sufficient. Moreover, while tariffs on intra-regional trade have been falling, efforts by the World Trade Organization (WTO) have also led to a reduction in worldwide tariffs in general. Since 1995, openness has increased for all WTO members, albeit to varying degrees. In addition, preferential trade arrangements such as the US African Growth and Opportunity Act (AGOA), the EU Everything But Arms (EBA), and the Generalized System of Preferences (GSP) continue to make developed countries Africa's most important trade partners. At the same time, trade between China and African countries has grown very quickly in the last two decades. The share of Africa-China trade as part of Africa's total trade increased from 4 percent in 2000 to 16 percent in 2012 (Global Times, 2013). Sub-Saharan African exports to China contributed about 30 percent of Sub-Saharan African's total export growth in 2005–2012 (Drummond and Liu, 2013). Therefore, it is not surprising that an empirical study by Musila (2005) found no evidence of trade diversion in COMESA, ECCAS, and ECOWAS. Likewise, Shinyekwa and Othieno (2013) concluded that the implementation and deepening of integration in EAC have not produced trade diversion.

While the overall intra-regional trade in Africa has been relatively low, it is important to remember that increasing intra-regional trade is not in itself good. If it were, it could be achieved quite easily by shutting off trade with

Table 5.7 *Intra-regional Trade in the EAC, 2004–2014*

	Exports of Goods to Partner States as a Percent of Total Exports					Imports of Goods from Partner States as a Percent of Total Imports							
	BURUNDI	KENYA	RWANDA	TANZANIA	UGANDA*	BURUNDI	KENYA	RWANDA	TANZANIA	UGANDA[a]	Intra-EAC Exports as a Percent of Total EAC Exports	Intra-EAC Imports as a Percent of Total EAC Imports	Overall Intra-EAC Trade as a Percent of Total Trade
2004	11	30	31	9	20	31	1	5	6	24	22	7	12
2005	6	28	30	8	18	20	1	21	5	27	21	8	13
2006	9	21	25	8	31	14	1	31	5	15	18	7	11
2007	9	23	26	10	33	26	2	25	2	11	20	5	10
2008	9	24	54	8	35	21	2	35	3	11	20	6	11
2009	9	26	20	11	39	32	2	28	5	11	21	7	12
2010	12	25	19	10	38	18	2	31	4	11	20	6	11
2011	20	27	17	9	30	35	2	25	3	12	20	6	10
2012	12	26	58	10	32	20	2	24	6	11	22	6	11
2013	36	25	17	22	35	42	2	22	3	12	24	6	11
2014	20	23	19	10	29	16	2	27	6	13	19	6	11

Source: East African Community (2014 and 2015).
[a] Since 2006, Uganda's data include the informal sector.

Table 5.8 *Share of Intra-regional Merchandise Trade*

		Percent	
		2001–2006	2007–2011
Africa	Fuel exporters	4.9	5.7
	Non-fuel exporters	15.7	16.3
Regional Economic Blocs	CEN-SAD	6.9	6.6
	COMEA	5.8	6.4
	EAC	13.1	12.0
	ECCAS	1.5	1.9
	ECOWAS	10.9	9.4
	IGAD	7.7	5.8
	SADC	13.8	12.9
	UMA	2.6	3.0

Source: UNCTAD (2013).

other parts of the world. Such induced trade diversion, which would blatantly neglect the dictates of comparative advantage, would make African countries worse off.

Intra-regional trade in Sub-Saharan Africa is limited due to the high costs associated with trade in Africa, including transportation costs, inefficiencies of border procedures, corruption, a lack of transparency and predictability, and other non-tariff barriers. It is by addressing these impediments that African countries will be able to take full advantage of their geographical proximity to each other. Members of each regional economic bloc need to reach binding commitments to reduce trade barriers. Countries must devise realistic mechanisms to hold violators of such agreements accountable. It is more effective to agree on a few commitments that will be implemented, than to create an ambitious wish list that ends up simply becoming a source of tension between member countries. It is imperative that producer and consumer advocate groups have a real voice in the process of devising policies and drawing up agreements. It is also important to develop and empower regional dispute settlement bodies such as the EAC Committee on Trade Remedies.

Notes

1. The simple average tariff is calculated by adding all the tariff rates and dividing by the number of tariff lines. For example, suppose products A, B, and C are charged tariff rates of 5 percent, 12 percent, and 13 percent, respectively. The average tariff rate is

10 percent. The average tariff rate does not take into account how much of each product is actually imported. The trade-weighted tariff rate is calculated by dividing the total tariff revenue by the total value of imports.

2. See Articles 12 (3) and 39 of the Protocol on the Establishment of the East African Community Customs Union (East African Community, 2004b), Section 140 of the EAC Customs Management Act 2004 (East African Community, 2004c), and the 2008 East African Community Customs Management (Duty Remission) Regulations (East African Community, 2008).
3. There is an apparent discrepancy in how the cases were reported, because the three columns are not entirely in sync with each other. If, for example, the report on new and resolved cases is correct, then the December 2014 report should have indicated 27 unresolved cases, not 18. Taking the initial number of unresolved cases, adding all new cases up to the December 2014 report, and subtracting the increase in the number of cases resolved equals 27.
4. Consumer surplus is the difference between the maximum amount a consumer is willing and able to pay for a product and the actual price of the product. Producer surplus is the difference between the actual price of a product and the minimum payment a supplier is willing to accept.
5. The actual net welfare losses would be less than those suggested in Figure 5.1 for various reasons. The export ban may not have been completely unanticipated and some farmers in Tanzania may hold a portion of their maize to wait for better prices. In addition, maize can be smuggled into Kenya, and both countries in fact trade with other countries.
6. This discussion is based on the experience of the author who, with some relatives and friends, was engaged in the process of obtaining a title deed for a plot on which they built a free library for the community. In 2016, Tanzania's Minister of Lands, Housing, and Human Settlements announced that the government is preparing to carry out a nationwide land registration. He said that the responsibility for issuing title deeds will rest upon local governments and that a title deed will be issued within a month from the time an application is filed. He further said that any land officer who gives an applicant the runaround for more than three months can consider him/herself as having terminated his or her employment. Notwithstanding the tough language, local governments do not have adequate resources to conduct basic land surveys to demarcate property boundaries and prepare accurate land drawings expeditiously.
7. To avoid being caught, farmers transported their own produce to the market in the middle of the night as if they were thieves. What was surprising was that local leaders knew the advantages of selling corn on the cob. For example, it allowed some farmers to have two harvests in a year instead of just one. In addition, it reduced security costs in the farms against monkeys and thieves. Of course, some farmers make poor decisions about their output and incomes. But that observation can be made about people in all walks of life. Government leaders are not warned, for example, that they will be prosecuted if they don't spend their salaries wisely.
8. Some of the description regarding the stages involved in dispute settlement is taken from Mshomba (2009).
9. Uganda started to include them in 2006.

6

The Common Market

The protocol to establish an EAC common market was signed in 2009 and came into force on July 1, 2010. At this level of integration, not only does the regional bloc agree to have common external tariffs and free movement of goods within the region, it also agrees to allow free movement of capital and labor. The focus here is on labor mobility because it is in that area of the common market agreement that implementation has been problematic.

The protocol calls for a common standard travel document that is verifiable by immigration officers. The procedure is that a foreign worker with a contract of employment and other required documents is initially given a special pass to enter the territory of the host partner state. Upon entry, the worker must apply for a work permit within 15 business days. If approved, the permit must be issued within one month of receipt of the application. The initial work permit is good for up to two years and may be renewed.

Trade is an indirect way of exporting and importing labor (and other resources) used to produce the goods being traded. In other words, trade policy is an indirect labor or immigration policy. In the simple Heckscher-Ohlin world where free trade causes factor-price equalization, there would be no wage-incentive for labor to move from one country to another. The simple Heckscher-Ohlin model assumes a world with two countries, two goods, and two factors of production, labor, and capital. The two countries are alike in every respect except for the relative availability of the two resources. One is labor abundant and the other is capital abundant. The two goods can be unambiguously ranked in terms of factor intensity. One is labor intensive and the other is capital intensive. Other assumptions include perfect competition, full employment, constant returns to scale, perfect mobility of resources within each country, and zero mobility of resources between countries. Free trade results in factor-price equalization.

In such a world, wages of similar workers will be equal among the trading partners. However, in the real world, while trade reduces the wage differential of similar workers, it does not eliminate the difference altogether. This is due to many factors, including imperfect competition, transportation costs, trade barriers, the use of different technologies by different producers, imperfect labor mobility within a nation, wage rigidity, the existence of unemployment, and the existence of non-traded goods and services.

THE WELFARE EFFECTS OF INTERNATIONAL LABOR MOBILITY

The benefits, or "welfare effects," of international labor mobility can be analyzed using a simple, two nation, partial equilibrium diagram. This will show that there would be a net increase in output in the region. Suppose English teachers are moving from Uganda to Rwanda.[1] In Figure 6.1, there are two marginal revenue product lines, MRP_U and MRP_R, for Uganda and Rwanda, respectively. The marginal revenue product of labor is given by the marginal product of labor multiplied by the price of the product produced by that labor. Marginal product is the additional output associated with each additional unit of labor. The marginal revenue product lines are downward sloping, reflecting the law of diminishing marginal returns.

The net welfare impact is clearly positive. The region would see an increase in education output given by area KDEJ. In this example, which is very limited, the full net welfare is generated in Rwanda. However, note that Uganda also benefits because the emigration of English teachers eliminates the unemployment problem. In addition, Ugandan teachers who were

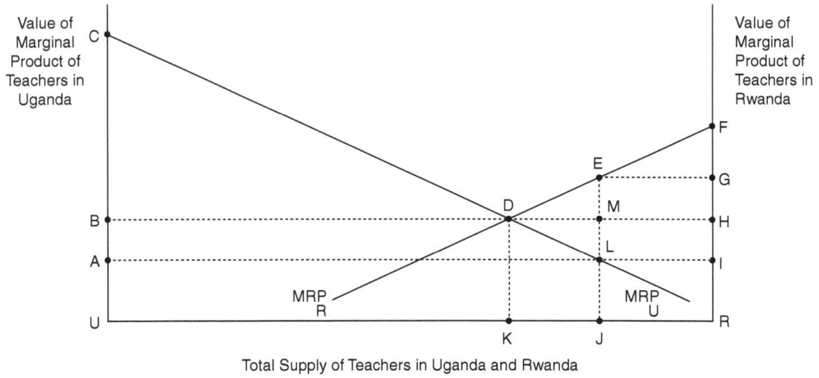

Figure 6.1 The Effects of International Labor Mobility

Welfare Effects of Labor Mobility Using Figure 6.1

Situation before labor was mobile between the two countries

Uganda:

UK	English teachers that are employed
KJ	English teachers that are unemployed
UJ	the total supply of English teachers
UB	the wage rate
UCDK	total output, for example, the number of students that are taught English to a certain level. Technically, this is the value of total output.

Rwanda:

RJ	the supply of English teachers
RG	the wage rate
RFEJ	the value of total output

Situation with labor mobility – the unemployed labor in Uganda immigrate to Rwanda

Uganda:

UK	English teachers employed
KJ	Ugandan teachers who immigrate to Rwanda
UB	the wage rate
UCDK	the value of total output

Rwanda:

RK	the supply of English teachers; KJ are those who emigrated from Uganda
RH	the wage rate
RFDK	the value of total output

were unemployed now earn a total of KDMJ in wages in Rwanda. They will no doubt send remittances to their home country, which will in turn boost Uganda's economy. It is important to note that even if all English teachers in Uganda are initially employed, migration of English teachers to Rwanda would still produce a positive net outcome to the region. The region would see a net gain of output given by area DLE.

Yet if the whole region benefits, what is holding the EAC back from transitioning quickly into a full-fledged common market? Even in this simple example, it is clear that some people lose. English teachers in Rwanda will feel threatened and, in this case, they will see their wages going down from RG to RH. It is also possible that the number of teaching jobs is limited and that Ugandan English teachers (supposedly better than Rwandan English teachers) would simply displace Rwandan teachers. One can, therefore, understand why Rwandan English teachers would not be in favor of an influx of English teachers from Uganda. However, the potential losses in Rwanda described here are, in part, due to the use of a partial equilibrium model. Presumably, in a general equilibrium model, Rwanda may have a comparative advantage in French teachers (or in any number of other skills) who would gain when they have access to teaching jobs in Uganda.[2]

Just as is the case with the trade of goods, where a country would export certain products and import other products, allowing international labor mobility means that a country would "export" certain types of labor (brain drain) and import other types of labor (brain gain). Tanzania, for example, can "export" Swahili teachers to its EAC partners and import English teachers from Kenya and Uganda. Burundi and Rwanda can export French teachers. The whole point is that a common market allows countries to take advantage of their differences in the relative availability of various types of professionals through labor mobility. Both economic theory and practice show that, in general, initiating freer labor mobility policies would produce net welfare gains. Moreover, a true East African common market could actually limit brain drain out of the region, which is often a concern.[3]

That said, introducing labor mobility does inevitably produce losers, at least in the short run. People who are displaced by more efficient workers flowing in from other countries may not find new jobs immediately. Even those who may not necessarily lose their jobs may find their wages falling, as demonstrated in Figure 6.1. And while one might argue that in the long run everyone will be better off and that shifts in labor supply and demand are a natural phenomenon in a market economy, the politics involved are not that simple. This may explain why even though some EAC countries have removed work permit fees for EAC citizens, all EAC countries still have lengthy (and different) procedures for issuing work permits and continue to introduce new barriers.

In 2012, Kenya made a major policy change that prohibited the issuance of work and residence permits to foreign workers who were not at least 36 years old and whose assured gross monthly salary was not at least $2,000. This was supposedly one way Kenya was dealing with the rising youth unemployment. However, as Ogalo (2012, 7) remarked, "most of the workers who usually move to other countries are in the age bracket restricted by Kenya" and "more than 60 percent of the [labor force in the] EAC is youth below 35 years of age."

BARRIERS TO LABOR MOBILITY IN THE EAC

There are many barriers to labor mobility in the EAC, leaving aside the procedure for and the cost of getting a work permit. These include (not in any particular order) poor infrastructure, tribalism and nepotism, language concerns, a mistrust of foreigners, inadequate awareness of the Common Market Protocol, a lack of harmonization, and a lack of political commitment.

Poor Infrastructure

One of the major impediments to intra-regional trade in Africa is poor infrastructure. Good and reliable infrastructure is important for trade as well as labor mobility. The likelihood of workers seeking jobs in neighboring countries depends, in part, on the ease with which they can go back and forth to their home country for vacations and various occasions. A few major cities in the EAC are well connected by road and air, but traveling to smaller towns can be a real challenge. It is no wonder, therefore, that foreign workers are concentrated in or near major cities, even though there is a shortage of skilled labor in small towns and rural areas. Moreover, major cities are more culturally diverse. The infrastructure challenge is declining over time as countries invest in roads, railway, and air transportation.

Tribalism and Nepotism

The labor market is imperfect even in the most market-oriented economies. To get a job, who you know is a major factor. The imperfection of the labor market in East Africa is accentuated by tribalism. Ironically, this problem is connected to a very important and admirable social system in Africa – extended family. An extended family can literally comprise hundreds of people. Offering jobs to people of your extended family or of your own tribe is seen as a sign of loyalty to "your own people." It is a way one shows that he or she has not forgotten his or her roots. In addition, this is one way a boss protects himself or herself; it is a form of job security and insurance. Even in Kenya, where profit motives in business have been dominant for decades, tribalism in the workplace (and tribalism in general) is still a common phenomenon. National labor laws and Article 10 of the Common Market Protocol prohibit discrimination (East Africa Community, 2009), but it is an endemic problem. Moreover, the laws against discrimination in the workplace are not enforced nearly enough.

Language Concerns

Three international languages are spoken in East Africa – Swahili, English, and French, with the latter spoken almost exclusively in Burundi and

Rwanda. The degrees to which the populations of the EAC countries are fluent in these languages vary, with Kenya and Uganda, followed by Tanzania, having an advantage in the use of English. According to Walusimbi-Mpanga and Bakunda (2012, 19–20), a major concern of employers and workers in Burundi is the language barrier. "Most of the EAC workers [in] Burundi cannot speak French yet the general population and the employers largely speak French. The majority of workers from Uganda can neither speak French nor Swahili. As a result, language barriers have failed the smooth transition of workers."

Language is also a concern in Tanzania, but in a different way. Unlike in Burundi where the language difference is a barrier, in Tanzania, it is the language similarity that seems to be a concern. English is widely spoken in Tanzania. However, Tanzanians are worried that they will lose jobs, especially those created by foreign investors, to Kenyans and Ugandans who, on average, have a better command of English. But the fear is not only that of potentially being shut out of jobs connected to foreign investors. A few people who operate private schools in Tanzania have told the author that they try to hire teachers mostly from Kenya and Uganda because their English is better. Rugemalira (2005, 80) also notes that, "[dissatisfaction] with teacher English proficiency levels in Tanzania has prompted some schools to recruit teachers from other countries, notably Kenya and Uganda."

In Tanzania, Swahili is the language of instruction in all public primary schools and English is taught as a subject. When students get to secondary school, this is switched around, with English the language of instruction and Swahili taught as a subject. However, almost all private primary schools in Tanzania are English medium schools.[4] The number of private schools has been growing very rapidly, creating a high demand for teachers proficient in English. Given an increasing demand in Tanzania for teachers who are proficient in English, one would think that Tanzania would welcome an inflow of foreign teachers with open arms. However, the great demand for foreign teachers is tempered by the fear that nationals will be displaced and also by the general uneasiness with foreigners, something that is not unique to Tanzania.

Mistrust of Foreigners

East Africans are regionalists and internationalists, but they are also very nationalistic (and some are even tribalistic) in ways that are both positive and, at the same time, negative when it comes to close neighbors. While one must be cautious in interpreting news reports and commentaries, every time a controversial issue is debated in East Africa, many highly antagonistic commentaries are exchanged between "neighbors." This has been particularly evident between Kenyans and Tanzanians, and Rwandans and Tanzanians, but it has not been limited to them. Some leaders in Tanzania suspect that the neighbors are pushing for integration with the ultimate goal of "grabbing" land in Tanzania. "Land is out of the EAC 'empire'" is the message Tanzania's Minister for East African Cooperation, Samwel Sitta, gave to the newly elected Tanzanian members of the East African Legislative Assembly in 2012. He did not mince words. He warned them that "there are all sorts of dirty tricks being applied in order to drag the land issue into the East African cooperation treaty" (Tambwe, 2012). Whether these concerns are well founded or not, is actually irrelevant. Regardless, they slow down the pace of integration.

While the EAC nations have been at peace with each other, it does not mean that these countries have always maintained cozy relationships. The relationship between Burundi and Rwanda, for example, has been tense since the President of Burundi, Pierre Nkurunziza, was re elected in July of 2016 for a third term, which opponents said was unconstitutional. Burundi has accused Rwanda of training rebels to remove Nkurunziza from power. The United Nations made similar accusations about Rwanda (Gettleman, 2016).

Rwanda was also clearly agitated by Tanzania in 2013 when (a) Tanzania sent troops to the Democratic Republic of Congo as part of the UN force to neutralize the M23 rebel group that Rwanda was allegedly helping; and (b) at an African Union summit, President Kikwete of Tanzania suggested that Rwanda should negotiate with the Congo-based Democratic Forces for the Liberation of Rwanda (FDLR) rebels. The relationship between these two countries deteriorated to the point where the "peace talks" that ensued were between Presidents Kikwete and Kagame, rather than between Rwanda and the FDLR. Eventually, the tensions were reduced, but an element of mistrust between these two countries remained, notwithstanding a closer working relationship between President Magufuli of Tanzania (who came to power in October of 2015) and President Kagame. Moreover, Tanzania was clearly irritated by the isolation from the so-called "coalition of the willing," that comprised Kenya, Rwanda, and Uganda.[5] In 2013, Tanzania deported almost seven thousand "illegal immigrants" from Rwanda (BBC News, 2013). These types of friction have an implicit negative impact on the implementation of the Common Market Protocol, especially when the implementation is often at the discretion of the attending officers and many people are not fully aware of the provisions of the protocol.

Inadequate Awareness of the Common Market Protocol

A study sponsored by the East African Business Council and the East African Employers' Organization reveals that neither employers nor workers are adequately informed about the provisions of the Common Market Protocol (Walusimbi-Mpanga and Bakunda, 2012). Given the advocacy provided by the East African Business Council and other business associations, a lack of awareness of the Common Market Protocol may be less of a problem over time. Nonetheless, the rules continue to change in each country and without uniformity.

One way to increase awareness of the protocol, in a sustainable way, is for each college and university in East Africa to establish a well-administered career services center. A career services center would maintain a list of job and internship openings in all EAC states. It would familiarize itself with the rules and procedures for applying for jobs in each of the EAC countries and assist students with applications for internships and jobs in the whole regional bloc. Career services centers could also be a force behind a harmonization of education standards in the region. In addition, the Ministry of Labor in each member state should maintain a website that provides relevant information for those interested in seeking jobs in an EAC country other than their own.

Lack of Harmonization

A lack of harmonization in the EAC will be a challenge for a long time. This is due in part to the inherent complexities involved in harmonizing different countries' rules and standards that have been in place for decades. It takes time, for example, to harmonize in orderly fashion education standards, professional credentials, labor laws, and social security benefits. Moreover, standardizing education, for example, may require reforms that are not welcome by teachers' unions or suppliers of textbooks. Many stakeholders are involved in public policy making, so no one should expect a quick harmonization process. The costs of implementing the reforms could also be very high and the benefits may take years to accrue. But the lack of harmonization is also a reflection of a lack of true commitment to the Common Market Protocol.

Lack of Political Commitment to the Common Market Protocol

If there was one challenge that seems to bring all the other challenges together, it is a lack of sustained political commitment. True political commitment must not be confused with overzealous ambitions of leaders who are seeking power. The Common Market Protocol was agreed upon prematurely: (a) the common market in East Africa seems to be a case of putting the cart before the horse; (b) the Common Market Protocol lacks sufficient specificity; (c) the EAC does not even function fully as a customs union yet; and (d) there is no uniformity in the categories of workers that are to benefit from the Common Market Protocol.

(a) Cart before the horse

Tanzania and Uganda have yet to distribute national identification cards to all their citizens. How can a region have free movement of people when the nationality of its people cannot be ascertained? It is analogous to instituting a policy of different privileges based on age, when people do not have an authoritative document stating their date of birth. The identification card exercises in Tanzania and Uganda are far from being complete, and so far the few who have gotten them are people who needed them the least. They are government and political officials who already have passports.

(b) Lack of sufficient specificity

The Common Market Protocol lacks sufficient specificity regarding its implementation. An example of this is the lack of uniformity in the procedure for and the cost of getting a work permit. One would think that even if the member countries could not agree on charging the same fees for work permits, at least they would have agreed on "ceilings" on those fees before they signed a protocol to establish a common market. By not doing so, they left room for wide variation in work permit fees.

After starting with a bilateral agreement to remove work permit fees between them in 2011, Kenya and Rwanda had removed such fees for all EAC workers by 2014. In 2014, Uganda removed work permit fees for Kenyan and Rwandan citizens. However, at the same time, this member of the so-called "coalition of the willing" also made it more difficult to get a special pass for people applying for work permits for the first time. Uganda required that most foreign workers, including those from the EAC partner states, obtain work permits before entry. The application process was already complicated when one was applying while in Uganda; the change just made the process that much more complicated.

Meanwhile, Burundi and Tanzania stood steadfast with their fees. Burundi work permit fees are set at 3 percent of the foreign worker's gross annual salary, paid annually. Walusimbi-Mpanga and Bakunda (2012) highlight a complexity caused by Burundi belonging to another regional bloc, the Economic Community of the Great Lakes Countries (ECGLC). The ECGLC has three members: Burundi, Democratic Republic of Congo, and Rwanda. While the ECGLC is not nearly as coherent as the EAC, it has some features of a regional economic bloc that has led Burundi to give preferential treatment to workers from Rwanda and the Democratic Republic of Congo. As pointed out by Walusimbi-Mpanga and Bakunda (2012, 21), this violates the non-discrimination principle and the *most favored nation* principle enshrined in Article 3.2 (a) and (b) of the Common Market Protocol, respectively. Article 3.2 (a) and (b) of the Common Market Protocol requires EAC members "to observe the principle of non-discrimination of nationals of other Partner States on grounds of nationality" and "to accord treatment to nationals of other Partner States, not less favorable than the treatment accorded to third parties," respectively (East African Community, 2009). Rwanda seems to have avoided the brunt of this problem by removing work permit fees for all EAC workers.

In 2012, mainland Tanzania increased work permit fees by 33 percent for workers from the other EAC states (Omondi, 2012). When Uganda announced that it was going to remove work permit fees for Kenyan and Rwandan citizens effective January 1, 2014, Tanzania was quick to brush it off, saying "it will not rush to waive work permit fees for East Africans seeking jobs in Tanzania because such a move not only needs legal review but also a thorough assessment of its advantages and disadvantages" (Kisanga, 2013).

(c) EAC not even a full-fledged customs union yet

The EAC does not yet function fully as a customs union. For example, in the World Trade Organization, the EAC does not negotiate as a bloc. One would think that as an economic bloc, supposedly with a common external trade policy, the EAC would negotiate as a bloc. Instead, each country individually belongs to a number of coalitions. Additionally, member countries still have many non-tariff barriers to trade, as discussed in Chapter 5. The EAC Committee on Trade Remedies, which was supposed to handle trade disputes, has not become operational as of this writing in 2017. Yet it is also to handle cases arising from the implementation of the Common Market Protocol.

The point here is not to suggest that the implementation of the agreement establishing the customs union had to be achieved to the fullest before signing the common market agreement, nor to advocate hasty implementation. However, things could and should have been spelled out more clearly before agreeing on the Common Market Protocol. The political will to implement the Common Market Protocol would have been tested better by considering the gaps that existed in the implementation of the previous agreements and also by setting clear parameters to guide and harmonize the implementation of the protocol.

As of 2013, according to a Regional Immigration Officer in Tanzania with whom the author spoke, there had not been a single written directive from the Ministry of Home Affairs that the citizens of the EAC partner states should be treated differently as a result of the protocol to establish a common market. The officer said that when they decided to treat leniently a Kenyan, for example, who violated immigration laws, compared to how they would treat someone from outside the EAC region, it was at their own discretion and purely because of *ujirani mwema* (good-neighborliness). To make sure the author understood that *ujirani mwema* was not simply a geographical phenomenon, the officer added that it also depended on the political undertones. Of course, that is not a unique sentiment. However, it leaves the suspicion that the crackdown by Tanzania of illegal immigrants, most of them teachers from the EAC partner states, in 2013 was, at least, in part its retaliation for being excluded from the so-called "coalition of the willing" (Mwalimu and Mbashiru, 2013; The Citizen Reporter, 2013).

It should be noted that the lengthy procedures for obtaining a work permit lead to thousands of foreigners working in host countries without employment-authorization documents. It also leads to the use of bribery as a way to facilitate the administrative process for getting a work permit. Ogalo (2012) writes about how undue delays in processing work permit applications in Kenya has led to "the old habit of rent-seeking [bribery] . . . Why would it take 6–9 months to process work permit applications when the same can be processed in 2–3 weeks where one goes through 'Immigration Consultants'?"

(d) Lack of uniformity in the categories of workers

There is no uniformity in the categories of workers that are to benefit from the Common Market Protocol. In Annex II of the protocol, each country has its own list of the category of workers and its implementation dates (East Africa Community, 2009a). Even more revealing about the lack of true commitment is that the lists (Kenya's list to a lesser extent) include only highly qualified workers. This is not only inconsistent with the spirit of articles 76 and 104 of the EAC Treaty, which call for free movement of labor in general, but it also leaves out semi-skilled workers, who form a large proportion of workers in the EAC. Ironically, at the same time, the EAC countries give work permits to semi-skilled workers from China and other Asian countries. In fact, the Common Market Protocol should have been more favorable to the region's semi-skilled labor. Highly qualified workers were already in a better position to obtain work permits in the EAC partner states without the protocol.

THE SERVICE SECTOR

While the focus has been on labor mobility, it is important to note that the Protocol on the Establishment of the East African Community Common Market covers the movement of services as well. When the WTO was established in 1995, one of the new multilateral agreements that came into effect was the General Agreement on Trade in Services (GATS). Emulating the GATS, EAC members agreed that they would allow free movement of services within the region. The relative size of the service sector and the growth in exports of services in the five EAC countries is shown in Table 6.1.

The sheer size of the service sector makes it an important area of cooperation. In addition, there is a direct link between trade in goods and trade in services. Removing trade barriers on merchandise goods, for example, would be of little relevance, if there were trade barriers

Table 6.1 *Value of Services as Percent of GDP and the Growth of Exports of Services*

		Exports of Services		Imports of Services	
	Services as Percent of GDP 2014	Value (million $) 2014	Average Annual Percentage Growth Rate (2009–2014)	Value (million $) 2014	Average Annual Percentage Growth Rate (2009–2014)
Burundi	42	91	25	11	8
Kenya	50	4,258	14	2,320	11
Rwanda	53	442	1	52	10
Tanzania	44	2,592	12	2,222	7
Uganda	51	1,789	12	2,270	12

Sources: Various issues of World Bank, *World Development Indicators* and International Trade Centre, *International Trade Statistics.*

prohibiting entry of vehicles transporting those goods from other member countries. All EAC members have made commitments to liberalize a number of areas, including professional services, retail services, communication, distribution, education, financial services, tourism, and transport (East African Community, 2012b). However, a joint study by the World Bank and the East African Community (2014) found that telecommunications and retail were the only sub-sectors (among those studied) in which member countries did not have nonconforming measures, that is, laws or regulations that were contrary to the liberalization commitments. Nonconforming measures were found in all other studied sectors at varying degrees, depending on the sub-sector and country.

It can be appreciated that the implementation of the Common Market Protocol only started in 2010 and that it will take a long time for a genuine common market actually to be achieved. Hasty and impulsive implementation can be disastrous. Even in the best of circumstances, creating a full-fledged East African common market will be a long process with bumps along the way. However, given that the EAC leaders have agreed to allow free labor movement, and East African workers appear to be ready for it, serious efforts should be undertaken to remove impediments to labor mobility. So far, mixed signals and a mishmash of ad hoc policies and regulations from different countries have only led to inconsistencies, confusion, uncertainty, and suspicion about motives. As the EAC moves forward, it is imperative that the Common Market Protocol not simply be masked by a commitment to a higher level of integration, as might happen if the regional bloc were to be pushed into a monetary union prematurely.

Notes

1. The author was inspired to use this example after reading various news articles about a shortage of English teachers in Rwanda, including one titled, "Exodus of Ugandan teachers to Rwanda" (Schenkel, 2012).
2. A partial equilibrium model considers how a market for a single good or service clears without taking into account prices and quantities of other goods and services. A general equilibrium model considers market clearance for the whole economy. A supply and demand diagram is a typical partial equilibrium model. A production possibilities curve is a typical general equilibrium model.
3. For the costs and benefits of the brain drain from Africa, see Easterly and Nyarko (2008).
4. In 2015, the President of Tanzania unveiled a new education and training policy for Tanzania (Ministry of Education and Vocational Training, Tanzania, 2014). It was not clear when it would start to be implemented. In fact, before it could be

implemented clarification was needed, partly because of contradictory statements in the policy document (Mshomba, 2015). For example, section 3.2.19 of the new education policy declares that Kiswahili will be used as the medium of instruction at all levels of education in Tanzania. In the subsequent section (3.2.20), it is affirmed that the government will continue with the structure that strengthens the use of English as a medium of instruction "*katika ngazi zote za elimu na mafunzo*" [at all levels of education and training].

5. The leaders of Kenya, Rwanda, and Uganda came to be referred to as such for their apparent eagerness to speed up the integration process.

7

The Road to a Monetary Union

The East African Community (EAC) Treaty called for the establishment of "a Customs Union, a Common Market, subsequently a Monetary Union, and ultimately a Political Federation" (East African Community, 2002, 13). The hallmark of a monetary union is the use of a common currency by all member countries of the union and the consolidation of monetary policies. The EAC leaders anticipated that a monetary union and a political federation would be achieved in 2012 and 2015, respectively. One could say that was optimism running amok. Nonetheless, these are stages of integration which are envisioned and may, one day, actually be achieved. Moreover, Kenya, Tanganyika (mainland Tanzania), Uganda, and Zanzibar shared a common currency during the colonial era and up until 1965.

Towards the end of 2013, the five leaders of the EAC met in Uganda and signed a protocol to establish an East African Monetary Union (EAMU) within ten years, following the schedule shown in Table 7.1. The potential benefits of a single regional currency include reduced transaction costs, increased trade and job creation, and presumed macroeconomic discipline. Of course, creating and maintaining a monetary union involve many challenges, as will be discussed in this chapter.

If and when the EAC becomes a monetary union, it will be the fourth one in Africa. The other three are the Common Monetary Area (CMA), comprised of Lesotho, Namibia, South Africa, and Swaziland; the Economic and Monetary Community of Central Africa (CEMAC), comprised of Cameroon, Central African Republic, Chad, Congo, Equatorial Guinea, and Gabon; and the West African Customs and Economic Union (UEMOA), comprised of Benin, Burkina Faso, Côte d'Ivoire, Guinea Bissau, Mali, Niger, Senegal, and Togo.

The EAC monetary union will be different from the other three in some fundamental ways. The CMA is, in effect, a quasi-monetary union. Each country has its own currency, but the South African rand circulates freely

Table 7.1 *Schedule for the Realization of an East African Monetary Union*

Step	Activity	Timeline
1	Implementation of the Customs Union and Common Market Protocols.	By 2015
2	Establishment of the East African Monetary Institute.	By 2015
3	Establishment of institutions responsible for: (a) surveillance, compliance, and enforcement; (b) statistics; and (c) financial services.	By 2018
4	Coordination and harmonization of fiscal policies.	By 2018
5	Coordination and harmonization of monetary and exchange rate policies during the transition to the monetary union.	By 2018
6	Harmonization of payments and settlement systems. (a) Develop a payment and settlement system framework for harmonization and integration of payment and settlement system infrastructure. (b) Create a framework for integration of trading, a securities depository, and infrastructure for a payments and settlement system.	By 2018
7	Harmonization of policies, standards, and laws relating to production, analysis, and dissemination of statistical information. (a) Develop a framework for production, analysis, and dissemination of statistical information. (b) Develop national statistical systems while observing the requirements of the EAC statistical system and internationally accepted best practices. (c) Harmonize statistical methods, concepts, definitions, and classifications for compiling statistics while observing internationally accepted best practices.	By 2018
8	Integration of financial systems and adoption of common principles and rules for the regulation and supervision of the financial system.	By 2018
9	Harmonization of relevant national laws and frameworks to facilitate the establishment of the monetary union.	By 2020
10	Phasing out of any outstanding central bank lending to public entities. (a) Prepare a timetable for progressively phasing out overdraft facility. (b) Establish a mechanism to bridge temporary liquidity gaps.	By 2021
11	Attainment of the macroeconomic convergence criteria.	By 2021
12	Strict adherence to the macroeconomic convergence criteria.	From 2021
13	Establishment of East African Community stabilization facility.	By 2022

(continued)

Table 7.1 *(continued)*

Step	Activity	Timeline
14	Design and implementation of a common exchange rate mechanism.	By 2022
15	Determination of conversion rates and design of a single currency.	By 2024
16	Conversion and re-denomination of existing legal instruments.	By 2024
17	Enactment of the legal instrument establishing the EACB.	By 2024
18	Introduction of a single currency.	2024

Source: EAC Secretariat (2014).

in all four countries. The three other national currencies are pegged to the rand. As for the CEMAC and UEMOA, each has a common currency (historically known as the CFA franc). The two currencies were initially pegged to the French franc; now they are pegged to the euro and are at parity with each other. Nonetheless, the French Treasury guarantees the convertibility of the two currencies. As can be expected, the fixed exchange rate system limits the monetary policy space of the two monetary unions. The EAC monetary union plan is to have a single currency that will float against other currencies. As such, the EAC is limited as to how much it can emulate the CEMAC and UEMOA.

A fifth monetary union is also in the works, so to speak. The West African Monetary Zone (WAMZ), comprised of Gambia, Ghana, Guinea, Liberia, Nigeria, and Sierra Leone, plans to establish a common currency called the eco. The WAMZ has already set and missed four target dates for the eco – 2003, 2005, 2009, and 2015. The latest target date is 2020, but it is safe to predict that the target date will be moved again. It is unlikely that the prerequisite macroeconomic convergence will have been achieved by 2020. A study by Asongu (2014) suggests that the WAMZ has a long way to go to achieve the convergence necessary for a viable monetary union. Given its relatively vast economic size, Nigeria was expected to be an obvious leader of this group of six countries. Nigeria's economy is about nine times the combined size of the other five members of the WAMZ. However, corruption and the havoc caused by Boko Haram attacks on civilians and Niger Delta Avengers on oil infrastructure have distracted Nigeria from this initiative.[1]

THE BENEFITS AND COSTS OF A MONETARY UNION[2]

The potential benefits of a single regional currency include (a) reduced transaction costs; (b) the establishment of an autonomous regional monetary policy authority[3]; and (c) macroeconomic stability. Intra-regional exports in the EAC in 2014 were $3 billion (and growing), about 19 percent of the EAC total exports. Hundreds of citizens of EAC countries cross each other's borders every day for business, leisure, education, and medical services. Every year, thousands of tourists from the rest of the world visit multiple countries in the EAC on the same trip. A monetary union would reduce the transaction costs associated with exchanging currencies. It would also eliminate uncertainties associated with exchange rate fluctuations within the EAC. It would be equivalent to reducing a trade barrier, and thus one would expect adjustments in supply and demand that would increase trade in goods and services.

While it would require a careful empirical study to estimate the actual reduction in transaction costs in foreign exchange, it is safe to say that those transactions costs are much lower today than they were in the early 1990s when exchange rate controls were in place. Today, businesses hold their financial assets in multiple currencies and can exchange them freely. For tourists and ordinary people, bureaus de change can be found in all cities and towns in East Africa; currencies can easily be exchanged at market rates without any hassle. The bureaus de change in Tanzania, at least through 2016, did not even bother to ask for identification or give a receipt. In addition, tourists are also increasingly using credit cards (at major hotels), thus reducing transaction costs. Nonetheless, transaction costs are real. This is partly because the selling price and buying price of a currency are different.

Table 7.2 shows exchange rates at a bureau de change in Arusha, Tanzania, on April 2, 2016. Using those rates, suppose someone used Tanzanian shillings to buy Ugandan shillings, and subsequently sold back whatever Ugandan shillings were not spent after a trip to Uganda. For every Tanzanian shilling that the person converted into Ugandan shillings and later converted back into Tanzanian shillings, he or she would lose 33 percent. A Tanzanian shilling would buy 1.67 (i.e., $\frac{1}{.6}$) Ugandan shillings. Converting the Ugandan shillings back into Tanzanian shillings, one would get only 0.67 (i.e., 1.67 *.4) Tanzanian shillings. A common currency in the EAC would eliminate such losses, thereby reducing transaction costs.

A second potential benefit of a monetary union is that a regional central bank would be established, and that bank would be relatively more independent than national central banks. The main function of a central bank is to control the supply of money and maintain price stability. While on paper central banks are supposed to be autonomous (yet accountable) in devising monetary policy, in many developing countries the national central banks tend to be more or less appendages to the Ministry of Finance, serving the

Table 7.2 *Tanzanian Shillings per Unit of Foreign Currency, April 2, 2016, in Arusha, Tanzania*

	Buying by Bureau de Change	Selling by Bureau de Change
US dollar: 50, 100	2,180	2,195
US dollar: 5, 10, 20	2,140	2,185
Euro	2,430	2,485
British pound	3,060	3,150
South African rand	130	150
Swiss franc	2,030	2,250
Kenyan shillings	21.2	21.8
Ugandan shillings	0.4	0.6
Japanese yen	16	19
Canadian dollar	1,450	1,650
Australian dollar	1,450	1,650
Saudi riyal	530	580
Indian rupee	26	32
Danish kroner	280	330
Norway kroner	220	260
Swedish kroner	230	268
UAE durham	560	600
Hong Kong dollars	235	270

Source: A bureau de change in Arusha, Tanzania.

politics of the party in power. Through this ministry, the government can order an increase in the supply of money to finance budget deficits, and the leadership of the central bank may not have the power to refuse. It is assumed that a monetary union would ensure the autonomy of its central bank and, thus, make monetary policy independent.

However, a monetary union is not a necessary condition for monetary policy to be independent. In fact, in the last few years, all EAC countries have made strides towards giving their central banks the space to pursue monetary policy without too much interference. This development can be attributed, in part, to the level of integration already achieved in the EAC, IMF guidance, increased awareness of the key role of the central bank, and the high caliber of the EAC's central bankers.

Finally, the macroeconomic stability envisaged by having a monetary union goes beyond what an independent central bank can achieve alone. The fiscal criteria established for membership in the monetary union are meant to restrain politicians from excessive deficit spending. While fiscal discipline does not necessarily require outside intervention, the political aspect of fiscal policy suggests that being accountable to other member states may encourage that discipline. A less optimistic view regarding fiscal discipline is discussed below under "some additional challenges."

If and when the EAMU is in fact established, the new regional currency will enhance the mobile money transactions which are already widespread in all countries in the EAC. According to the United Nations Conference on Trade and Development (UNCTAD, 2012a, iii):

> [the] EAC has been ahead of other parts of the world in electronic money transfers, with M-PESA which started operating in Kenya in 2007, having taken the lead in terms of innovation for providing more inclusive access to finance to a large part of the population who hitherto had been without a bank account.

A single regional currency will allow East Africans to take full advantage of mobile money transactions and allow quick and easy capital flows within the region. However, to make sure this relative ease of transferring money is not abused, for money laundering, for example, the EAC governments and central banks must be ahead of the game, devising regulations and directives regarding customer services and protection, taxation rules, transaction limits, transparency of transactions, and inter-operability of different mobile money platforms (UNCTAD, 2012a).

Of course, a monetary union does not come without costs. They include (a) losing control of monetary policy; and (b) tensions due to misalignments of business cycles (Beetsma and Giuliodori, 2010). Article 20 (4) of the Protocol to establish the EAMU stipulates that "[i]n the performance of its functions, the East African Central Bank shall be independent and shall not be influenced by a Partner State." By joining the EAMU, a country loses a key policy instrument, and as Buiter (2010) put it, joining a "[m]onetary union represents a surrender of national sovereignty to a supranational entity." It is a decision that some countries would only make through a referendum (Jonung, 2004). The timetable towards an EAMU does not include a call for a referendum, but this does not prevent any country from holding one. Holding a referendum may be a mechanism through which the public can be informed about, and debate, the advantages and disadvantages of joining a monetary union.

The loss of control over monetary policy is significant, but it must not be exaggerated. The national central banks, though stripped of key decision making, will be an integral part of the structure of the EAMU, as stated in Article 20 (2) of the Protocol to establish the EAMU: "The East African Central Bank shall, together with national central banks of the Partner

States in the single currency area, form a functionally integrated system of central banks." The EACB will not be like some institution thousands of miles away, say, in Washington, DC, making decisions about what is going on in East Africa. The EACB will be right there, in the midst of macroeconomic activities. Moreover, notwithstanding its autonomy, the EACB will be accountable to the elected and appointed leaders of the EAC.

While this seems reassuring, a "one-size-fits-all" monetary policy will not work agreeably all the time. Inevitably asymmetric or country-specific shocks and misalignments of business cycles will, understandably, cause tensions, and different countries may call for different monetary policies. These tensions may exacerbate old conflicts, such as those related to non-tariff barriers and work permits, and can also feed off those old conflicts. A monetary union represents not only a deeper level of cooperation; it can also be a more potent source of conflict.

The oil and gas discoveries in East Africa can also exacerbate the impact of asymmetric shocks (Masson, 2012). Large reserves of oil and gas have been discovered in Kenya, Tanzania, and Uganda. Fluctuations of oil and gas prices will affect them one way and Burundi and Rwanda the opposite way, thus requiring different fiscal policy responses. If production of these resources becomes sizable in these countries, there is potential for the *Dutch disease* to occur, and its impact will spill over to Burundi and Rwanda. The *Dutch disease* refers to a situation where a country loses international competitiveness in its traditional sectors such as agriculture and tourism, as the country's currency appreciates due to an increase in exports of domestic natural resources. If this were to happen, Burundi and Rwanda would suffer from the "disease" as well, and they would not be able to do anything to neutralize the situation on their own. There are other challenges as well, discussed towards the end of the chapter.

CREATING A MONETARY UNION

As with monetary unions elsewhere in Africa and around the world, many steps must be taken before the EAMU can become a reality. The Protocol to establish the EAMU outlines those steps and specifies, among other things: (a) the objectives of the monetary union; (b) the prerequisites for the monetary union; (c) the adoption of a single currency; and (d) establishment of an East African Central Bank (EACB) (East African Community, 2013b).

The objectives of the monetary union are to promote and maintain monetary stability, facilitate economic integration, and enhance equitable economic growth and development in the EAC countries. In other words, the ultimate goal of the protocol, as of the other protocols, is to increase the standard of living and quality of life of the people of East Africa.

The prerequisites for establishing the monetary union include full implementation of the protocols to establish a customs union and a common market, harmonization and coordination of monetary and exchange rate policies, and the introduction of exchange rate bands. An exchange rate band is a combination of a floor and ceiling on an exchange rate. For example, after agreeing on a base period, member countries could decide that the EAC currencies must not depreciate or appreciate by more than 5 percent against each other.

In addition, to join the EAMU a country must, for at least three consecutive years, meet certain macroeconomic convergence criteria. These criteria are discussed at length later in this chapter. Each country vying for membership in the monetary union would also need to build economic resilience to external shocks that could arise.

To form the EAMU, at least three countries must adopt a single currency. The "Summit," that is, the heads of state or government of the EAC countries, will determine the name of the single currency. Before the single currency becomes the legal tender of the single currency area, binding conversion rates will be set at which the single currency will replace the currencies of the member states of the monetary union.

Finally, an East African Central Bank will be established that will work with the national central banks. Although the EACB will collaborate with the national central banks, it will make the final decisions regarding monetary policy.

A CLOSER LOOK AT THE PREREQUISITES FOR A MONETARY UNION

Establishing a monetary union can be compared to painting a house that has valuable pictures hanging on the walls. The preparation can be more work than the actual painting itself. This is to say that good and complete preparation for a monetary union is critical. Since the macroeconomic convergence criteria require special attention, they are discussed in their own section below.

Full Implementation of the Protocols to Establish a Customs Union and a Common Market

It is stipulated that member states shall fully implement the EAC's customs union and common market protocols as a prerequisite for the establishment of the EAMU. The discussion in Chapters 5 and 6 suggests that if this prerequisite is to be taken seriously, it will be a long time before there is an EAMU. Still, this prerequisite is important. The implementation of the earlier protocols is vital, not only because it will demonstrate the commitment of the member countries to integration, but also because it will enhance the economic resilience of the region. Exogenous shocks (factors outside a country's control) such as drought or economic crises in the global economy would typically affect EAC countries differently. Those are what are called asymmetric shocks. Free trade, as well as regional labor and capital mobility, would soften the blow of an asymmetric economic shock (Mundell, 1961). For example, the severity of the impact of a drought in Kenya would be lessened by the ease with which Kenya could import food from other EAC countries. By indirectly sharing the impact of external shocks, the EAC countries would have a better chance of staying within the macroeconomic ceilings they have set for themselves.

Harmonization and Coordination of Monetary and Exchange Rate Policies, and the Introduction of Exchange Rate Bands

Harmonizing and coordinating monetary and exchange rate policies, and the introduction of exchange rate bands, are logical transitional steps towards a single currency. Tables 7.3 and 7.4 and Figure 7.1 show how the currencies of the EAC countries have depreciated or appreciated with respect to the US dollar, from 2002–2016. The numbers in Table 7.4 are percentage changes in the values of the respective currencies. A positive number indicates depreciation, and a negative number indicates an appreciation. For example, in 2002, the Burundian franc depreciated by 13.4 percent and the Kenyan shilling appreciated by 1.9 percent, compared to the US dollar.

Figure 7.1 plots exchange rate indices (from Table 7.3), with 2001 as the base year. While the overall picture that emerges from Tables 7.3 and 7.4 and Figure 7.1 is that East African currencies have been depreciating with respect to the US dollar, noticeable variations make any hasty convergence of these currencies ill-advised. Between 2001 and July 2016, the US dollar appreciated against the Kenyan shilling by only 29 percent, while it appreciated against the Tanzanian shilling by 239 percent.[4] For a gradual transition, the EAC would need "crawling" exchange rate bands which are wide in the beginning. As the economic fundamentals such as employment and economic growth are strengthened, economic resilience will be enhanced. The bands could then be tightened accordingly, to bring the exchange rate

Table 7.3 *Exchange Rate Index, Domestic Currency per US Dollar (with 2001 as the base year)*

	Burundian Franc	Kenyan Shilling	Rwandan Franc	Tanzanian Shilling	Ugandan Shilling
2001	100.0	100.0	100.0	100.0	100.0
2002	113.4	98.1	110.5	106.6	107.2
2003	131.4	96.8	125.3	116.1	112.0
2004	133.4	98.3	123.7	113.8	100.6
2005	120.0	92.1	120.7	127.2	105.2
2006	120.6	88.3	119.8	137.7	100.8
2007	134.6	79.7	118.6	123.6	93.3
2008	148.5	98.9	121.8	139.7	112.8
2009	148.0	96.4	124.5	143.3	110.2
2010	148.3	102.7	129.5	158.6	133.6
2011	163.7	108.2	131.6	171.0	144.2
2012	184.5	109.5	137.6	172.2	155.6
2013	186.4	109.8	147.7	174.6	147.0
2014	185.2	115.2	151.7	187.4	160.2
2015	189.7	124.7	156.2	229.2	192.5
2016 (July)	200.8	128.9	169.5	239.0	197.1

Sources: East African Community Statistics Portal (www.eac.int/statistics/index.php?option=com_content&view=article&id=141&Itemid=111) and websites of the respective central banks.

floors and ceilings closer to each other. Convergence criteria will take different lengths of time to be achieved. As similar as these countries may appear to be from a distance, on closer look, one can appreciate that they will be moving to convergence from different starting lines (Gupta and McHugh, 2012).

The differences among the EAC countries are in, among other areas, trade orientation, economic development (as highlighted by the GDP per capita and inflation), and reliance on grants. Trade orientation is the extent to which a country is integrated into the world economy, as measured by *trade ratios.* Trade ratios are a country's exports and imports as a percentage of GDP. As with most developing countries where major commodities are produced primarily for export and most machinery and other industrial inputs are imported, merchandise trade ratios are high in all EAC countries. Nonetheless, there is variation between countries, as shown in Table 7.5, indicating that an equal change in exchange rates would affect them to different degrees. They are also different in their export structures and export concentration.[6] Their export concentration

Table 7.4 *Depreciation and Appreciation of EAC Countries' Currencies Against the US Dollar*[5] *(percentage changes in the value of the currencies)*

	Burundian Franc	Kenyan Shilling	Rwandan Franc	Tanzanian Shilling	Ugandan Shilling
2002	13.4	−1.9	10.5	6.6	7.2
2003	15.9	−1.3	13.4	8.9	4.5
2004	1.5	1.6	−1.3	−1.9	−10.2
2005	−10.1	−6.4	−2.4	11.8	4.5
2006	0.5	−4.1	0.8	8.2	−4.2
2007	11.7	−9.7	−1.0	−10.3	−2.5
2008	10.3	24.0	2.7	13.1	14.8
2009	−0.4	−2.5	2.2	2.6	−2.3
2010	0.2	6.5	4.1	10.7	21.3
2011	10.4	5.3	1.6	7.8	7.9
2012	12.7	1.1	4.5	0.7	7.9
2013	1.0	0.3	7.4	1.4	−5.5
2014	−0.6	5.0	4.2	9.6	9.7
2015	2.4	8.3	3.0	22.3	20.1
2016 (July)	5.9	3.4	8.5	4.3	2.4

Sources: East African Community Statistics Portal and websites of the respective central banks.

ratios for 2013 were as follows: Burundi, 0.36; Kenya, 0.19; Rwanda, 0.36; Tanzania, 0.2; and Uganda, 0.18 (UNCTAD, 2015). The larger the concentration ratio, the less diverse the export sector is. These numbers suggest that these countries are exposed to different levels of risks related to exchange rates and the terms of trade.

ADDITIONAL PREREQUISITES: THE MACROECONOMIC CONVERGENCE CRITERIA[7]

In addition to the criteria already discussed in this chapter, certain macroeconomic convergence criteria must also be met as a necessary condition before a monetary union can be established. The EAC countries have agreed on the following macroeconomic convergence criteria, as shown in Table 7.6. The macroeconomic convergence criteria for other monetary unions are included only for a casual comparison. The EAMU is not a monetary union yet, while the other three are already monetary unions.

(a) A ceiling of 8 percent and 5 percent on headline inflation rate and core inflation rate, respectively

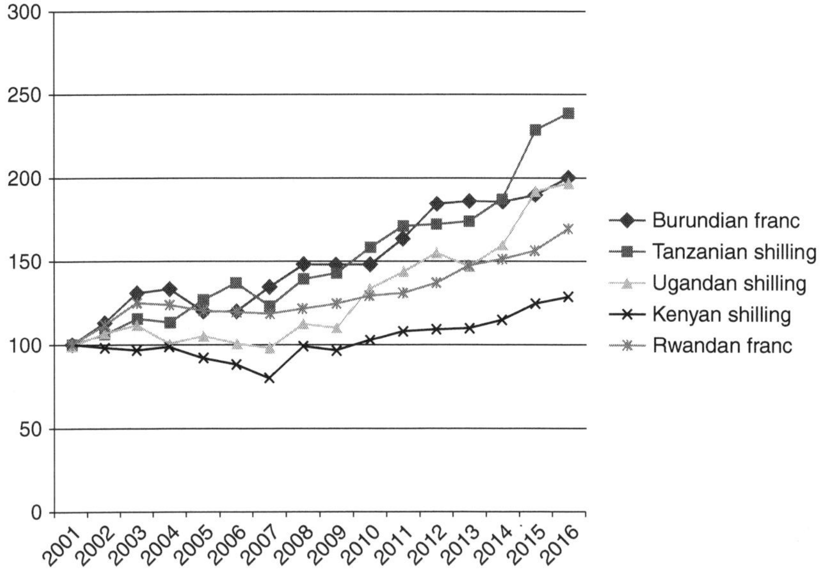

Figure 7.1 Exchange Rate Index, Domestic Currency per US Dollar (with 2001 as the base year)
Sources: East African Community Statistics Portal and websites of the respective central banks.

When inflation runs wild, the real value of money decreases and people have a harder time paying for the basic necessities of life. The headline inflation rate measures the rise in the general level of prices based on the prices of all goods and services. The core inflation rate (also known as the *underlying* inflation rate) also measures the rise in prices, but it does not include food and energy prices. It is true that overall, the headline inflation rate may not be a good basis for a change in monetary policy because food and energy prices can be quite volatile. Nonetheless, because East Africans, on average, spend almost 50 percent of their income on food (Muhammad et al., 2011), the headline inflation rate is the one that is more relevant to them. In general, the headline inflation rate has been higher than the core inflation rate in the EAC countries, which explains why the core inflation rate criterion is lower (5 percent).

As Ben Ltaifa (2014) suggests, achieving the inflation convergence criterion is rather demanding, considering EAC countries are exposed to large exogenous shocks such as droughts and recessions in developed countries. Actually CEMAC and UEMOA have an even more demanding

Table 7.5 *Merchandise Trade (X) and Service Trade (Y) as a Percent of GDP*[8]

	Burundi		Kenya		Rwanda		Tanzania		Uganda	
	$\frac{Y}{GDP}$	$\frac{Y}{GDP}$	$\frac{X}{GDP}$	$\frac{Y}{GDP}$	$\frac{X}{GDP}$	$\frac{Y}{GDP}$	$\frac{X}{GDP}$	$\frac{Y}{GDP}$	$\frac{X}{GDP}$	$\frac{Y}{GDP}$
2009	27	13	40	13	29	17	33	13	33	14
2010	30	12	43	15	30	16	38	13	31	15
2011	37	14	49	15	39	17	46	13	38	21
2012	36	13	45	15	40	13	43	13	36	20
2013	33	14	40	14	40	16	37	13	33	21
2014	29	n. a.	40	13	41	n. a.	35	n. a.	30	n. a.

n. a.– not available.
Source: World Bank, various issues of *World Development Indicators.*

inflation convergence criterion, but at the same time members of CEMAC and UEMOA have not been able to meet this criterion on a consistent basis (IMF 2012, 2013). Nonetheless, full-fledged monetary unions are able to insulate themselves better from shocks, given the high mobility of capital, goods, and resources within the region.

Note that the European Union expresses the inflation convergence criterion relative to the best performing members – inflation should not exceed 1.5 percentage points of the average inflation rate for the three best-performing EU member states. When the number of members in a monetary union is large, that might be a more relevant way of expressing the inflation criterion. Nonetheless, given the experience of the Euro zone, where some countries have been threatened by deflation, there must be a clear understanding of what it means to say a country is "best performing."

The average annual headline inflation rates since 2013 have been within the ceiling of 8 percent. While this is promising, the challenge would be to sustain such low inflation rates. A low inflation rate is desirable. However, if the experience of the last 13 years, as shown in Table 7.7, is the basis on which to predict the future, it would take extraordinary discipline to maintain a ceiling of 8 percent for the headline inflation rate and 5 percent for the core (underlying) inflation rate.

(b) A ceiling on budget deficits: deficits equivalent to a maximum of 3 percent and 6 percent of GDP, including and excluding grants, respectively

Table 7.6 *Macroeconomic Convergence Criteria*

	Proposed East African Monetary Union (EAMU)	European Monetary Union	Economic and Monetary Community of Central Africa (CEMAC)	West African Customs and Economic Union (UEMOA)
Headline inflation rate	≤ 8 percent	≤ 1.5 percentage points higher than the average for the three best-performing EU member states	≤ 3 percent	≤ 3 percent
Core inflation rate	≤ 5 percent	n. a.	n. a.	n. a.
Budget deficit including grants	≤ 3 percent of GDP	≤ 3 percent of GDP	≥ 0	≥ 0
Budget deficit excluding grants	≤ 6 percent of GDP	n. a.	n. a.	n. a.
Gross public debt (in net present value terms)	≤ 50 percent of GDP	≤ 60 percent of GDP	≤ 70 percent of GDP (external debt only)	≤ 70 percent of GDP (external debt only)
Tax revenue as a percent of GDP	≥ of 25 percent of GDP	n. a.	≥ of 17 percent of GDP	≥ of 17 percent of GDP
Foreign exchange reserves	Enough to cover at least 4.5 months of imports	n. a.	n. a.	n. a.

n. a. – not applicable.
Sources: East African Community (2013b) for information on EAMU and Ben Ltaifa et al. (2014) for the rest.

Table 7.7 *Annual Headline Inflation Rate*

	Burundi	Kenya	Rwanda	Tanzania	Uganda
2003	10.7	9.8	7.5	3.5	8.7
2004	8.3	11.6	12.0	4.2	3.7
2005	13.2	10.8	9.1	4.4	8.6
2006	2.7	6.0	8.8	7.3	7.2
2007	8.3	4.3	9.1	7.0	6.1
2008	24.5	16.2	15.4	10.3	12.0
2009	10.5	10.6	10.3	12.1	13.0
2010	6.5	4.1	2.3	7.2	4.0
2011	9.6	14.0	5.7	12.7	18.7
2012	18.1	9.4	6.3	16.1	14.0
2013	8.0	5.8	4.2	7.9	5.5
2014	4.4	6.8	1.8	6.2	4.3
2015	5.5	6.5	2.5	5.9	8.7

Sources: East African Community Statistics Portal and websites of the respective central banks.

Just like people, when governments spend more money than they have, they can run into problems. A budget deficit occurs when government spending exceeds government revenues.

Excessive budget deficits can lead to macroeconomic instability and hurt the real economy. An expansionary deficit spending fiscal policy can lead to inflation if the government resorts to financing the deficit by printing money.[9] But even if the government financed the fiscal deficit through internal borrowing, it could lead to high interest rates and crowd out the private sector and, in turn, prompt an increase in the money supply. Fiscal spending may also lead to increases in sales taxes and value added taxes, again leading to inflation (Hilbers, 2005).

The budget deficit ceilings are also meant to prevent too much reliance on external sources to finance government spending. However, with the exception of Kenya, the EAC countries are already highly dependent on grants. All members of the EAC, except Kenya, are officially categorized as least developed countries (LDCs), and Burundi, Rwanda, and Uganda are also landlocked. Burundi, the poorest country in the EAC, has a GDP per capita that is only one-fifth that of Kenya.

The difference in economic development can be a stumbling block to policy convergence and can also create a division in how these countries network with the rest of the world.

Still, it should be noted that there are some advantages to being an LDC. The LDCs in the EAC receive preferential treatment that is not necessarily available to Kenya. This is both with respect to market access for their products in developed countries and direct assistance from developed countries and international organizations such as the IMF, the World Bank, and the World Trade Organization (WTO).[10] LDCs have easy access to grants, so it is not surprising to see how reliant they have become on them. According to data in the EAC Statistical Portal, the percentages of government spending financed by grants in 2010 were 47 for Rwanda, 35 for Burundi, 16 for Tanzania, 10 for Uganda, and 4 for Kenya. Excluding grants, all EAC countries pierce the ceiling on budget deficits, as shown in Table 7.8. However, the fiscal deficit ceilings are "soft" ceilings that are easy to exceed. Article 10 (4) of the Protocol to Establish a Monetary Union states that a member country may be allowed to exceed the fiscal budget ceilings as long as the country is within the ceiling on the debt-to-GDP ratio.

(c) A ceiling on gross public debt equivalent to 50 percent of GDP in *net present value*

Turning now from government deficits in any one year, let us consider what happens over the course of many years. The national debt of any country is the accumulation of all past government deficits (and surpluses, if any).[11] It represents the total outstanding loans borrowed by the central government. Gross public debt is the total amount the government owes its creditors, that is, the face value of the debt. The net present value of debt reflects the real market value of the debt over its payment duration.

The net present value of debt is different from how debt is normally reported and how it is understood by the general public. The IMF/World Bank (2001) describes "net present value" as follows:

> The net present value (NPV) of debt measures the actual financial burden on a country of various kinds of debt and allows a more meaningful comparison of debt burdens across low-income countries than the face value of debt. This is because the face value of the external debt stock does not reflect the fact that low-income countries contract a significant part of the external debt on concessional terms (i.e., with an interest rate below the prevailing market rate and often long repayment periods). The NPV of debt is a measure that takes into account the degree of concessionality. It is defined as the sum of all future debt-service obligations (interest and principal) on existing debt, discounted at the market interest rate. Whenever the interest rate on a loan is lower than the market rate, the resulting NPV of debt is smaller than its face value, with the difference reflecting the grant element.

This description is particularly relevant for external debt. Because of inflation, the present value of a given debt stock decreases over time.

Table 7.8 *Budget Deficits, Including and Excluding Grants, as Percent of GDP*

	Burundi		Kenya		Rwanda		Tanzania		Uganda	
	Including Grants	Excluding Grants	Including Grants	Excluding Grants	Including Grants	Excluding Grants	Including Grants	Excluding Grants	Including Grants	Excluding Grants
2000	3.2	6.3	1.2	4.2	0.3	11.1	1.9	4.5	4.6	10.9
2001	0.9	8.7	2.2	2.8	1.3	9.7	0.3	3.8	2.3	10.2
2002	1.3	12.1	3.7	5.1	2.5	11.6	0.2	4.1	2.0	12.2
2003	6.4	16.6	7.3	8.6	2.2	9.8	0.0	6.5	1.6	9.8
2004	5.6	20.0	8.2	9.5	0.2	11.2	4.5	10.2	0.5	7.8
2005	2.2	14.2	5.3	6.3	0.3	11.0	5.3	11.2	2.2	7.1
2006	3.1	14.5	6.3	7.5	0.2	10.5	3.4	8.3	1.9	7.1
2007	2.9	28.9	5.0	5.8	1.0	13.1	3.6	8.6	1.9	4.9
2008	3.1	13.6	5.7	7.3	0.4	10.5	3.4	6.2	1.7	4.6
2009	3.1	12.4	7.4	8.9	0.8	12.4	5.2	11.3	4.7	7.2
2010	2.6	15.6	5.3	8.8	1.6	13.7	6.5	11.2	4.3	6.6
2011	1.7	3.9	13.5	13.9	0.1	11.6	5.6	8.9	3.7	7.2
2012	3.4	7.8	6.9	8.5	5.1	13.1	10.2	14.1	4.1	5.8
2013	2.6	9.1	5.7	10.1	5.1	14.4	4.3	8.2	5.9	7.5

Sources: Calculated using data from the East African Community Statistical Portal and various issues of *East African Community Facts and Figures.*[12]

Usually an interest rate is charged by the lender to offset inflation. However, developing countries, particularly LDCs, receive large proportions of their external loans with interest rates that are lower than the market interest rates. As such, the discounted value of the debt is lower than the face value of the debt.

Here is an illustration. A country takes a \$100 million loan to be paid annually (in equal amounts) for ten years. The concessional interest rate on the loan is 5 percent. Therefore, annual payments are \$12,950,457, calculated using the following formula, where "*A*" is the annual payment, "*P*" is the principal, "*i*" is the concessional interest rate, and "*n*" is the number of payment periods (years).

$$A = P\frac{i(1+1)^n}{(1+i)^n - 1}.$$

The total face value of the amount paid back (interest and principal) is \$129,504,570. The net present value (NPV) of the stream of loan repayments is calculated using the following formula:

$$NPV = \sum_{t=1}^{n} \frac{A_t}{(1+r)^t}$$

In this formula, "*t*" is time t (year 1–10), "A_t" is payment at time "*t*," "r" is the market interest rate, and "n" is the number of years. Suppose the market rate is 8 percent and constant. The net present value of the debt would be \$86,898,624, which is clearly less than the face value of the debt. Table 7.9 shows the face value of external debt and the NPV of external debt, both as percentages of Gross National Income (GNI).[13] Their relative difference reflects the magnitude of the concessional elements of loans, as shown in column 3 for each country in Table 7.9.

The NPV approach may explain, in part, why (except for Burundi) the size of debt in the EAC countries has not alarmed the World Bank and IMF surveillance teams. Recent joint IMF/World Bank sustainability analyses of the external debt stress of the EAC countries concluded that the stress was low for Kenya, Tanzania, and Uganda; moderate for Rwanda; and high for Burundi (IMF, 2012a; IMF, 2013a; IMF, 2013b; IMF, 2013c; IMF/World Bank, 2012; and, World Bank/IMF, 2012).

The NPV of debt expressed as a percent of GNI was way below 50 percent even for Burundi (since 2008) and, in fact, projected by the IMF to go down for Tanzania and Kenya. It is the NPV of the debt-to-exports ratio that put Burundi into the high risk category – it was above the IMF's threshold of

100 percent. Burundi's export revenues are also quite volatile because its export sector is highly concentrated. More than 75 percent of Burundi's export revenue comes from coffee and tea. What stands out in Table 7.9 are the sudden declines in the debt-to-GNI ratios for Burundi, Rwanda, Tanzania, and Uganda between 2005 and 2009. All LDCs in the EAC have benefited from the Heavily Indebted Poor Countries (HIPC) initiative and the Multilateral Debt Relief Initiative (MDRI).[14] Kenya has not benefited from either of these two initiatives.[15]

Up until 2004, *external* debt as a percent of gross national income in all four LDCs in the EAC was relatively high, as shown in Table 7.9. It was highest in Burundi, where it reached over 200 percent. The HIPC and MDRI initiatives sliced these countries' external debt as a percent of GNI by more than half. By 2009, Burundi's external debt as a percent of GNI was down to 39. Whether these countries will be able to sustain the current low levels of external debt is hard to say. The HIPC and MDRI initiatives brought Tanzania's external debt as a percent of GNI to 30 in 2008. However, within three years, it was over 40 percent.

The numbers in Table 7.9 do not include domestic debt, that is, loans borrowed by the government from within. Compared to the external debt, there is low reporting of the domestic debt. This is probably because internal borrowing is not monitored closely by the IMF and the World Bank. However, to get a better picture of the debt burden, it is important to have at least some idea of the size of the domestic debt. The domestic debt as a percent of GNI, with respective years in parentheses, were as follows: Burundi – 15 percent (2011); Kenya – 26 percent (2012); Rwanda – 9 percent (2010); Tanzania – 16 percent (2012); and Uganda – 13 percent (2011).[16] For Kenya and Tanzania, the total face value of the debt as a percent of GNI was above 50 percent for the year indicated in parentheses (IMF, 2012a; IMF, 2013a; IMF, 2013b; IMF, 2013c; IMF/World Bank, 2012; Ministry of Finance, Tanzania, 2013; National Treasury, Kenya, 2013; World Bank/IMF, 2012). However, note that even if domestic debt was included and taken at face value (instead of being discounted), as long as the NPV-approach is applied to external debt, the total debt as a percent of GNI for these countries, as of 2014, was below the ceiling.

Clearly the ceiling on public debt (equivalent to 50 percent of GDP in net present value) has left EAC countries with considerable policy space (which may be needed). Although this may sound like good news, countries should be cautious about borrowing and government spending, for several reasons.

Table 7.9 *Face Value and NPV of External Debt, Both as Percentages of GNI*

	Burundi			Kenya			Rwanda			Tanzania			Uganda		
	(a) Debt to GNI	(b) NPV of Debt to GNI	(a)–(b) (a)	(a) Debt to GNI	(b) NPV of Debt to GNI	(a)–(b) (a)	(a) Debt to GNI	(b) NPV of Debt to GNI	(a)–(b) (a)	(a) Debt to GNI	(b) NPV of Debt to GNI	(a)–(b) (a)	(a) Debt to GNI	(b) NPV of Debt to GNI	(a)–(b) (a)
2003	228	150	34	48	43	10	93	57	39	73	22	70	74	33	55
2004	216	15	93	43	34	21	91	15	84	72	22	69	72	33	54
2005	169	110	35	33	28	15	71	18	75	64	22	66	52	29	44
2006	162	105	35	29	26	10	17	8	53	34	16	53	14	6	57
2007	155	97	37	30	26	13	15	8	47	31	15	52	14	9	36
2008	125	80	36	22	19	14	15	8	47	30	14	53	16	10	38
2009	39	13	67	27	19	30	15	8	47	34	13	62	16	8	50
2010	34	14	59	27	20	26	14	12	14	38	23	39	18	7	61
2011	30	15	50	32	22	31	19	14	26	45	27	40	24	11	54
2012	27	13	52	31	21	32	18	n. a.	n. a.	41	10	76	23	9	61
2013	25	n. a.	n. a.	25	n. a.	n. a.	23	n. a.	n. a.	31	n. a.	n. a.	20	n. a.	n. a.
2014	22	9.4	57	27	13	51	26	17	35	30	16	47	20	11	45

n. a. – not available

Source: Various issues of World Bank's *Global Development Finance* and *International Debt Statistics.*

First, the NPV of debt is sensitive to the market interest rate used to discount the debt. Since the debt is paid over an extended period of time, what is used to discount the debt is actually an *expected* market interest rate. The NPV of debt can be inflated or deflated simply by using different interest rates.

Second, while the loan conditionality of the IMF and World Bank may seem strenuous and even suggest that they are not easy lenders, the fact remains that they are in the banking industry. They need borrowers. Their survival depends on it. Without being cynical, the collapse of the Greek economy in 2008/09 was a "shot in the arm" for the IMF.[17] Someone working with the World Bank confided in the author regarding a dilemma he once faced when he was giving advice to representatives of an African country. Based on what he knew, if he were to give his personal opinion, he would have advised them, explicitly, not to take the loan. However, his job did not allow for such a blunt suggestion. He tried to dissuade them by "beating around the bush," but they were so eager to take the loan, they did not get his hints. Back at his office, he was congratulated for helping the country decide to take the loan.

The respectable growth in real GDP in the last few years and discovery of oil and natural gas reserves in East Africa will bring about willing lenders. However, the EAC countries must be careful not to be too optimistic about the future and increase borrowing without careful examination. The debt crisis of the 1980s in Africa was caused, in part, by optimism about commodity prices which did not materialize (Humphreys and Underwood, 1989).

Third, there is the question as to what proportion of the loans is actually spent on public projects and how much is siphoned off by corrupt officials. Getting reliable data on economic activities in East Africa is a challenge even for official economic activities, let alone for illicit activities. However, a preponderance of evidence from international and domestic sources will convince even the most skeptical that corruption in the form of financial fraud in the public sector is rampant in East Africa.

The Corruption Perceptions Index (CPI) suggests that, except for Rwanda, East African countries are highly corrupt. In 2010, officials of the Kenyan Ministry of Finance told a parliamentary committee that the government could be losing close to one-third of the national budget to corruption as "individuals were taking huge sums meant for development projects" (BBC, 2010). Tanzania has suffered many scandals involving fraud and abuse – millions of dollars of public funds. They include: 1999 – the government buying an overpriced radar system for $40 million from a British company, BAE Systems, with one-third of the payment going to a middle person (Transparency International UK, 2011); 2005–2006 – the alleged theft of $131 million from the External Payment Arrears account (Issa, 2009); 2006 – a multimillion dollar contract awarded to a bogus company, Richmond Development Company, to supply electricity to Tanzania (BBC, 2008); 2013 – allegations that millions of dollars were lost from the import support account (Magolanga, 2013); and 2014 allegations that more than $120 million was illegally transferred from the Bank of Tanzania to government officials and individuals. Apparently, this money was moved from an escrow account created in 2006 following a dispute between the Tanzania Electricity Supply Company and Independent Power Tanzania Limited (Kabendera, 2014; The Guardian, 2014).

In 2012, the *New Vision*, a Ugandan newspaper, published a summary of nine major corruption scandals in Uganda, 2007–2012 (New Vision, 2012). Each scandal involved gross mismanagement and the siphoning of millions of dollars of public funds. Similar stories are common in Burundi which, according to the Corruption Perception Index, is the most corrupt country among the established members of the EAC.[18]

Burundi has consistently been one of the top ten corrupt countries out of about 180 countries surveyed by Transparency International every year. The EAC countries have made many declarations to fight corruption, but efforts have often been half-hearted and the problem has become chronic.[19] Only Rwanda seems to have succeeded in reducing corruption.

Fourth is a question which proceeds from the one raised above. How are the costs and benefits of borrowing being distributed? This question goes beyond corruption, the purpose of the loans, and the ability to pay back the loans. Even when loans are for development spending (as opposed to recurrent spending), such as improving technology and education infrastructure, and the economy is growing fast enough to pay back the loans, are the costs and benefits of borrowing being shared fairly?

Here is a hypothetical example, but not an unrealistic one in East Africa. Say a farmer has three children, two boys and one girl. The farmer goes to a local shopkeeper to borrow money to pay for his children's education. He and the shopkeeper agree the loan will be paid in three years. The farmer expects to be able to pay back the loan from the revenue he generates from selling his crops. The farmer uses the loan to send his two sons to school, but asks his daughter to stay home and help with farm work. In this example, the loan is used for a good purpose. Education is a good investment. However, the costs and benefits of the loan are not shared fairly.

In fact, they are shared on a prejudicial basis. The girl bears the burden of the loan while it is the boys who get the benefits.

On a national level, a loan used to increase the nation's ability to produce more goods and services can be considered a good investment. However, growth in the GDP, in itself, is not a sufficient criterion to determine the efficacy of a loan. To justify extensive borrowing, one must also consider how the burden of borrowing is shared and how the benefits are distributed. Otherwise, one group could be in the position of bearing the debt burden while another benefits from the economic growth that was induced by borrowing. (Of course, in the case of corruption, the nation could end up paying for the debt that was siphoned off by a few leaders.)

Loans that improve only roads in the cities, for example, would benefit urban residents, but the tax burden (to pay off the loans) would also fall on people in rural communities whose roads were not improved. Since rural people are generally low-income, bad loans are like a regressive tax, and they fail both the "benefits principle" and the "ability to pay" principle of a good tax. Loans that improve technology and education services, but only for those in major cities, would cause resentment, understandably, even when the economy as a whole was growing. If integration in the EAC continues to deepen, joint development projects and joint loans will be common and, thus, questions about the distribution of costs and benefits will not simply be a domestic matter. Borrowing should be for economic growth and development for all, that is, improvement in the standard of living for all, with special attention, in fact, given to those who have traditionally been left behind.

Fifth, concessional loans are unreliable and come with conditions. It is no wonder that grant flows are quite volatile (Gupta and McHugh, 2014). Notwithstanding what was noted above about the readiness of lenders, concessional loans (grants) are unreliable and often come with conditions that may conflict with a country's priorities or values. In February 2014, the World Bank postponed a $90 million loan to Uganda due to Uganda's strict anti-gay law. In March 2014, US Representative Ed Royce, Chair of the House Foreign Affairs Committee, asked the US Secretary of State, John Kerry, to re-evaluate "U.S. engagement with Rwanda, including future assistance" (Royce, 2014). Royce was concerned about the allegedly politically motivated assassinations of prominent Rwandan exiles who have spoken out against President Kagame and his regime. The point here is not that one can predict the trajectory of the US-Rwanda relationship, for example, but rather that there is always a delicate balance that a country dependent on grants must strike. There are no unconditional grants, not even from China.

Table 7.10 *Tax Revenue as a Percent of GDP*

	Burundi	Kenya	Rwanda	Tanzania	Uganda
2007	11.8	16.2	9.2	9.3	10.9
2008	11.1	16.8	8.9	9.9	10.4
2009	11.3	17.4	11.4	11.7	10.0
2010	11.2	17.3	11.0	10.7	10.5
2011	13.2	18.5	10.9	10.9	10.1
2012	15.0	15.7	12.3	10.1	9.8
2013	14.1	16.8	13.2	11.3	10.8
2014	12.6	16.3	n. a.	14.4	11.4

Source: Calculated using data from various issues of *East African Community Facts and Figures.*[20]

In 2013 when the President of China, Xi Jinping, was visiting Africa, he promised African leaders $20 billion in financial assistance with no strings attached. If you can believe that, you might as well believe that there are no labor violations in China and that China has never manipulated its currency. When President Xi said that China would not interfere with the internal affairs of African countries, he was implicitly placing the condition that African leaders must not interfere with China's internal affairs. And "internal affairs" can be interpreted broadly. If you complain that China has an unfair advantage in exports due to child labor or other labor rights violations, you are interfering with "internal affairs." Moreover, not unlike other donor countries, China expects its contractors to be given priority for, if not the exclusive right to, projects financed by China's loans (Gallagher et al., 2012). Nonetheless, it is important to mention that China has reduced the dependency of African countries on the West and the Bretton Woods institutions. Recently, Chinese contractors have been awarded contracts for the construction of major infrastructure projects in East Africa (BBC News, 2014, 2015; Rogers, 2015).

(d) Tax revenue equivalent to at least 25 percent of GDP

This criterion is linked to the criteria above on budget deficits and debt. It is meant to make governments less dependent on borrowing. The more revenue that governments are able to generate from taxes, the less they should have to borrow in the first place. Table 7.10 shows tax revenue as a percent of GDP for the EAC countries from 2007–2014, with Kenya being the only country whose numbers are less than 10 percentage points below the set floor of 25 percent. To reach and sustain such a floor, each country has a lot of work to do, which may include increasing the tax rates.

However, other solutions might be to find new sources of tax revenue, close tax loopholes, prevent tax evasion, and reduce tax incentives.

The tax revenue base in East Africa, as in other developing countries, is rather narrow because of the large size of the informal sector. The informal sector in East Africa is estimated to be about 40 to 60 percent of the total GDP (Institute of Economic Affairs, 2012; Verick, 2008). Administering tax collection in the informal sector poses challenges because of limited records, high volatility and unreliability of income, and high mobility of the participants in that sector. In addition, public services for the informal sector are often nonexistent or very limited, at best. As such, collecting taxes in the informal sector is considered unfair by those who make a living in that sector. Needless to say, the difficulty in collecting taxes and the lack of services are intertwined.[21] The lack of tax revenues limits the provision of services, and the lack of services makes collection of taxes seem exploitative.

Not only is the tax base in East Africa relatively narrow, tax avoidance and tax evasion, even in the formal sector, are additional challenges to reaching the tax revenue targets. Tax avoidance takes place as people take advantage of tax loopholes. An example would be the abuse of transfer pricing to reduce paying royalties and taxes on profits. Using multinational corporations (MNC) as an example, taxes are usually collected where profits have been made. However, buying and selling occur from one division of an MNC to another. Thus, an MNC can set internal prices so as to transfer profits from one country to another and avoid paying higher taxes. That is what is alleged to have been done by Resolute Goldmine in Nzega, Tanzania, in 2008. At that time, the price of gold was about $1,000 an ounce. According to the Chairperson of Tanzania's Parliamentary Committee on Public Accounts, Resolute Goldmine was selling gold mined in Tanzania to its sister company at $530 per ounce, thus denying Tanzania royalties and tax revenues (Kabwe, 2013). Kabwe also reported in 2013 that Tanzania was "losing about $1.25 billion a year in revenue, equivalent to five percent of its gross domestic product (GDP) – through corporate tax avoidance, evasion and corruption" (Makoye, 2013).

Closing tax loopholes in any country does not require an accounting genius. However, inertia on the part of the government and the propensity to safeguard special interest groups sustain the loopholes. Removing tax loopholes is not a simple matter politically because typically it is big companies and rich people, that is, those who are well connected to people in power, that are able to take advantage of the loopholes (International Tax Compact, 2010).

Tax evasion, by definition, is illegal. However, "creative accounting" can hide it. Kamau et al. (2012) show that creative accounting practices are widely used by private companies in Kenya to avoid and evade paying taxes. Illicit financial outflows are an indicator of tax evasion and, of course, corruption. Conservative estimates by Ndikumana and Boyce (2008) and Global Financial Integrity (2010) suggest that, over the years, billions of dollars have illicitly seeped out of African countries, including members of the EAC. According to Global Financial Integrity (2010, pp. 28 and 32), illicit financial flows from EAC countries, 1970–2008, amounted to $28.1 billion. It is interesting to note that the total external debt stock for the EAC countries in 2008 was $17.8 billion (World Bank, 2010a). Given that this is the overall picture in Africa, it is no wonder Ndikumana and Boyce (2008, 35) conclude that Africa is "a net creditor to the rest of the world." A more recent study by Global Financial Integrity (2014) paints the same picture of gross revenue losses. It estimates that trade misinvoicing alone cost Kenya, Tanzania, and Uganda almost $1 billion a year in lost tax revenue, as shown in Table 7.11. President Magufuli of Tanzania, who came to power in 2015, made it a priority of his administration to close tax loopholes and combat tax evasion.

In addition to losing tax revenue as a result of illicit financial outflows, governments' coffers may also be hurting due to excessive tax incentives. It is common, and not only in developing countries, to use tax incentives to attract investment. Small developing countries are under additional pressure to provide those incentives because of their weakness in infrastructure and skilled labor. They also lack large markets that would attract investors. The creation of Export Processing Zones (EPZs) has been one way that African countries have tried to attract investors. Products produced in these zones are primarily for export. EPZ incentives include tax holidays,

Table 7.11 *Summary of Estimated Average Annual Tax Revenue Loss Due to Trade Misinvoicing, 2002–2011*

	Annual Average Government Revenue ($ million)	Annual Average Tax Loss due to Trade Misinvoicing ($ million)	Tax Loss as a Percent of Government Revenue
Kenya	5,242	435	8.5
Tanzania	3,339	248	7.4
Uganda	1,916	243	12.7

Source: Global Financial Integrity (2014, vii).

accelerated depreciation of capital, exemption from customs duties, and exemption from a number of bureaucratic procedures and regulations. It has been observed that import-duty exemption "provides a perverse incentive to move capital out of the country illicitly through import over-invoicing" (Global Financial Integrity, 2014, 32).

A study by the Tax Justice Network-Africa (2012a) suggests that, combined, Kenya, Rwanda, Tanzania, and Uganda lose up to $2.8 billion a year from all tax incentives and exemptions. This loss is, on average, 3.4 percent of the total GDP of those countries in 2011. It should be noted that this estimate was given in gross terms. It does not take into account revenues generated because of the jobs being created and the overall economic growth due to technology and knowledge transfers. Nonetheless, the study by the Tax Justice Network cautions against a competition for investors by means of tax incentives which can lead to more and more tax incentives as each country tries to outdo the other.

(e) Enough foreign exchange reserves to cover at least 4.5 months of imports

It is especially important for developing countries to hold some of their "savings" in foreign currencies. This is because their own currencies are not acceptable for payments for imports. Table 7.12 shows the level of foreign reserves, measured in terms of the coverage of imports of goods and services, held in the EAC countries from 2004–2015. Not only do the levels of foreign reserves fluctuate from year to year, they are also quite volatile from month to month. Just as an example, in Kenya in April of 2014, the amount of official foreign reserves available was enough to cover 4.3 months of imports. The following month Kenya's foreign reserves were sufficient to cover 5.7 months of imports (Central Bank of Kenya, 2015). The volatility in the levels of foreign reserves reflects, in part, the volatility in export revenues and the prices of imports, especially the price of oil.

Central banks want to hold foreign reserves as a precaution, as self-insurance against shocks that may disrupt capital flows (Drummond et al., 2009). Foreign reserves are also held to allow a central bank to intervene in the foreign exchange market to reduce the volatility of exchange rates. In addition, foreign reserves give a country confidence (and even pride) and some leverage in negotiating for loans. The opportunity cost of holding foreign reserves is the interest income foregone, or, as some have expressed it, the foregone domestic physical investment on which reserves could have been spent (Neely, 2000; Gupta, 2008). The optimal level of foreign reserves differs widely between countries depending on, among other things, the

Table 7.12 *Foreign Reserves – Months of Imports*

	Burundi	Kenya	Rwanda	Tanzania	Uganda
2004	2.2	2.9	5.9	6.5	7.1
2005	2.1	2.5	6.2	4.7	6.0
2006	3.5	2.0	5.6	4.1	6.5
2007	3.6	2.1	4.7	4.5	6.1
2008	6.4	3.0	4.7	4.2	5.0
2009	4.4	4.2	5.4	4.5	5.7
2010	4.1	3.8	4.5	4.1	4.5
2011	3.8	4.0	5.1	3.3	4.0
2012	3.6	3.5	5.2	3.4	4.6
2013	4.3	4.1	5.0	4.6	4.6
2014	3.5	4.8	4.5	4.2	4.4
2015	3.5	4.6	4.6	3.8	4.2

Sources: IMF (2013d), p. 93 (for data for 2004–2012) and various reports by the IMF and respective central banks.

diversity of exports and export destinations, the reliance on aid, whether a country is landlocked or not, exchange rate regimes, and how risk averse policymakers are.

Nonetheless, the point must not be lost that the rationale for the macroeconomic convergence criteria is to create macroeconomic stability, which is fundamental to efforts to increase economic growth and development. The ultimate objective of establishing a monetary union is to increase the standard of living of the people within it. If successful, the monetary union will help reduce unemployment rates and make countries more capable of providing social services such as education and health care.

However, the macroeconomic convergence criteria, even if achieved, do not guarantee economic growth. Moreover, these criteria could easily be met by simply embracing contractionary fiscal and monetary policies. In fact, when one considers them purely in mechanical terms (with a standard "cookie-cutter" approach), it does not even require great expertise in economics or finance to achieve them. The criteria could easily be achieved through austerity measures – reducing the money supply and government spending and increasing taxes. Of course, this is not to suggest that that is how policies should be made in the EAC. Nonetheless, since the criteria do not, and maybe cannot, include real development variables such as the employment rate, real income per capita, access to social services, and income distribution, there is a danger in trying to meet the criteria when they may create avoidable economic hardship.

Once the monetary union is established, the legitimacy of, and the adherence to, the criteria set forth will greatly depend on how much progress a country is making, as determined by the measures of real development. At times countries will find the criteria to be too restrictive and politically unsustainable. Moreover, the uniformity of the criteria, while less complicated in structure, may not be practical, considering the wide economic disparity between countries. This may be the case unless the macroeconomic convergence criteria bring about real convergence – similar economic structures, subject to similar shocks (Ben Ltaifa et al., 2014).

It is not clear whether the criteria were established based on the conditions of the weakest member (Burundi) or on some "objective" economic standards. Whatever the case, it is not clear why, for example, Burundi, a landlocked country with a fragile economy and a very narrow export base, and Kenya, with a relatively robust and diverse economy, have the same foreign reserves floor. There is also an element of arbitrariness when the ceilings on the budget deficit and the public debt are the same for all member countries, irrespective of their economic differences. Surprisingly, in multilateral negotiations, African countries are emphatic in highlighting countries' economic differences, but when it comes to their own negotiations they seem to pretend to be equal. Coming up with country-specific criteria for a monetary union is probably politically unattainable, but economic differences cannot be ignored without consequences in the future. Perhaps this is just an unavoidable compromise on the road to a monetary union.

SOME ADDITIONAL CHALLENGES

The costs of a monetary union described at the beginning of this chapter represent some of the challenges in forming a monetary union. Other challenges include (a) the politics of integration; (b) uncertainty about the new currency; and (c) enforcement of fiscal discipline. Forming a monetary union is as much a political decision as it is an economic one. Needless to say, political factors must be considered in making such a monumental decision. Moreover, economic phenomena do not exist in a political vacuum. However, some leaders may want to speed up the process in order to gratify their political ambitions. A monetary union is seen as a step closer to forming a federation. Some in the EAC feel that the process to form a federation is not moving fast enough. As will be discussed in Chapter 8, President Museveni of Uganda, for example, wants the EAC to be an important part of his legacy. He was able to engage Presidents Kenyatta and Kagame of Kenya and Rwanda, respectively, to form the so-called "coalition of the willing."

According to Article 23 of the Protocol to establish the EAMU, "[t]he Summit shall, on the recommendation of the Council, establish an institution to be known as the East African Monetary Institute, which shall be responsible for the preparatory work for the Monetary Union." Notwithstanding the timetable for achieving a single currency, it is imperative that this institution be given the resources and political space needed to do its work appropriately, objectively, and transparently. It should not be constrained by a predetermined timetable which may not conform to the reality on the ground. For example, it would be prudent to have an explicit escape clause that gives countries the flexibility they need when they are confronted with large exogenous shocks.

Another important challenge in creating a monetary union involves the possibility that uncertainty about the new currency might unleash speculative behavior which could destabilize the value of national currencies and cause massive capital flight. How the conversion rates are set, between the national currencies and the new currency, must be completely transparent (Adam et al., 2014). Likewise, when the new currency is introduced, it must be made crystal clear to the public how soon the national currencies will become obsolete. When the EU introduced the euro in 1999, a transition period of three years was given before national currencies were eliminated.

Perhaps the greatest challenge has to do with enforcement of fiscal discipline. With a monetary union, when a country needs to stimulate its economy through expansionary policies, it can only apply fiscal policy, since monetary policy will have been surrendered to the regional monetary policy authority (in this case, the EACB). The ceiling on the budget deficit and public debt might require a country to implement austerity measures precisely when it would have liked to implement an aggressive expansionary policy. It is not clear what would happen to a country that met the criteria, became a member of the EAMU, but subsequently violated the fiscal deficit limit repeatedly. This is not an unlikely scenario, considering that external shocks would inevitably occur and affect these countries differently, akin to how the 2007–08 global financial crisis affected Euro zone countries and brought Greece very close to the exit gate. Enforcing fiscal policy ceilings is a difficult task when countries retain control over fiscal policies (Rusuhuzwa and Masson, 2012).

By losing control of monetary policy, countries will, in all likelihood, overutilize fiscal policy and disregard the fiscal policy ceilings. Okafor

(2013) saw this to be a potentially significant challenge for the West African Monetary Zone (WAMZ), if it were to become a monetary union. It is not clear what the penalties would be for not adhering to the criteria; it does not appear that not meeting the criteria would be enough to expel a partner state out of the EAC. Articles 145, 146, and 147 of the EAC Treaty allow, respectively, for withdrawal, suspension, and expulsion of a partner state from the EAC (East African Community, 2002, 116–117).[22] These provisions address the potential problem of partner states not meeting their financial obligations to the EAC Secretariat; however, they do not specifically address potential non-compliance with the macroeconomic convergence criteria.

Notwithstanding how committed the EAC members might be to forming a monetary union, it is only reasonable to assume that each country will be contemplating (quietly) various scenarios and have an exit strategy in place, just in case. It would be naïve not to do so. Moreover, Kenya, Tanzania, and Uganda already experienced the collapse of an East African monetary union in 1965. Each country will have to decide how it wishes to move forward, but all should be aware of both the benefits and challenges of establishing and maintaining a monetary union.

It is important to note that the single currency may not necessarily apply to the whole EAC region. The establishment of the EAMU requires a minimum of only three countries. This is in line with the principle of variable geometry stated in Article 7(1)(e) of the EAC Treaty. The principle of variable geometry "allows for the progression in co-operation among groups within the Community for wider integration schemes in various fields and different speeds" (East African Community, 2002, 15). The principle of variable geometry is an acknowledgment that countries have different economic structures and are at different economic levels and, thus, should have the flexibility to move towards deeper integration at different speeds. Nonetheless, if the EAMU were to be formed with only three or four partner states, the ones not included may feel isolated, depending on the circumstances under which they were left behind. If a country felt it had been sidelined, that could cause tension between partner states. For example, if Tanzania was left behind, it could react by focusing its efforts on integration in SADC and put the EAC matters on the back burner. It is important, therefore, that a consensus be reached as to how the EAC should move forward.

Incidentally, in 2008, the Council of Ministers of the EAC requested from the East African Court of Justice (EACJ) an advisory opinion regarding the compatibility of the principle of variable geometry and the principle of consensus, which states that "the decisions of the Summit shall be by consensus" (East African Community, 2002, 20).[23] Specifically, the Council of Ministers sought opinions on

(i) whether the principle of variable geometry is in harmony with the requirement for consensus in decision making;
(ii) whether the principle of variable geometry is applicable to guide the integration process, the requirement on consensus in decision-making notwithstanding;
(iii) whether the requirement on consensus in decision-making implies unanimity of the Partner States (EAC Secretariat, 2009, 5–6).

The EACJ found:

> that the principle of variable geometry, as its definition suggests, is a strategy of implementation of Community decisions and not a decision making tool in itself . . . that the principle of variable geometry can comfortably apply, and was intended, to guide the integration process and we find no reason or possibility for it to conflict with the requirement for consensus in decision-making . . . In conclusion, we answer issues (i) and (ii) in the affirmative and issue (iii) in the negative. (EAC Secretariat, 2009, 34 and 41)

While the EACJ found the two principles to be in harmony with each other, the judges cautioned:

> that variable geometry should be resorted to as an exception, not as the rule, as indeed institutionalized flexibility might lead to break-up of the Community or its transformation into "a mere free trade area." (EAC Secretariat, 2009, 34)

The clarification provided by the EACJ should be of great relevance at the political federation stage. If the EAC reaches that stage, it is highly unlikely that the current six partner states would form a federation all together at the same time.

For a regional economic bloc on the move, the next natural level of integration after achieving a customs union and a common market is a monetary union. However, in practice, the EAC is not yet a full-fledged customs union and has only made baby steps towards becoming a common market. The ten-year transition period towards a monetary union may seem like a long time, but if the implementation of the protocol to establish the East African Customs Union is any indication, ten years may not be nearly long enough.

With a customs union or a common market, a country can be halfway in and halfway out. That has been the case so far in the EAC, notwithstanding the progress that has been made since the 1990s. Countries might agree on common external tariffs but in fact maintain and even increase non-tariff barriers. Countries sign on for the establishment of a common market, but in reality they might make the application for work permits by workers from other member states cumbersome and more expensive. With a monetary union, however, that kind of half-heartedness cannot be accommodated. A single currency will actually mean a single currency. There will not be, for example, a common currency for some transactions and a national currency for other transactions. Maintaining a monetary union has little "wiggle" room. Countries must establish it or join it only when they are adequately prepared and fully committed.

The EAC has a lot to teach other regional blocs, but it also has a lot to ponder. The Euro zone has not been a source of confidence in monetary unions, even though its membership includes some of the most developed countries in the world. Of course, while the Euro zone's experience of nearly unraveling in the years around 2010 should not make the EAC extremely nervous, it should give the EAC real pause to think. Referring to the European experience, the IMF Managing Director Christine Lagarde has urged the EAC not to rush into a monetary union. Speaking in Kenya in January 2014, Lagarde cautioned the EAC that "[t]he recently signed road map to East African monetary union is very ambitious. Don't rush, take all the steps and learn from the mistakes of Europe and other monetary unions" (Omondi, 2014).

Deepening the level of integration in a regional economic bloc is a step-by-step process. However, when a regional bloc fails, it does not simply take a step backward; it crumbles. It is, therefore, important to be cautious about each additional level of integration. If it is achieved prematurely, it can undo what has already been achieved, and that would be a major setback.

Notes

1. Moreover, Nigeria has been severely hurt by low oil prices. The price of oil fell from an average of $100 a barrel, between 2010 and 2014, to an average of $40 a barrel in the first half of 2016. Between June and August 2016, the Nigerian naira depreciated by 60 percent, relative to the US dollar. It was projected by the IMF that Nigeria's economy would contract by 1.8 percent in 2016 (IMF, 2016).
2. Beetsma and Giuliodori (2010) provide an excellent overview of studies on the benefits and costs of monetary unification, starting with a seminal article by Mundell (1961) on optimum currency areas.
3. Two main tools are used to steer an economy in the right direction – fiscal policy and monetary policy. Fiscal policy involves changing government spending and/or taxes.

It is controlled by lawmakers. Fiscal policy can be used to stimulate the economy or reduce inflation. Monetary policy involves changing the supply of money to influence interest rates and spending in the economy. It is controlled by the central bank. The primary objective of monetary policy is to stabilize prices, with the ultimate goal of increasing employment and economic growth.

4. The percentages are calculated by simply comparing the exchange rate index in 2016 with that in 2001 (the base year).
5. A positive number indicates a depreciation of the local currency; more local currency was needed to buy a dollar. A negative number indicates an appreciation of the local currency; less local currency was needed to buy a dollar.
6. Table 2.4 shows the structure of exports.
7. For the finer details of the macroeconomic convergence criteria for the EAMU, see the collection of articles in Drummond et al. (2014).
8. Merchandise (service) trade is the sum of merchandise (service) exports and imports.
9. An extreme example occurred in 2007/08 in Zimbabwe, where hyperinflation reached the inconceivable level of 230 million percent. That is, on average, prices were increasing at a rate of 7 percent per second. Needless to say, Zimbabwe's currency became completely worthless. Zimbabwe adopted the US dollar and the South African rand as official currencies.
10. As an example, LDCs have been exempted from implementing the WTO's Agreement on Trade-Related Aspects of Intellectual Property Rights (TRIPS) until 2021. TRIPS and many other agreements were reached in 1995 when the WTO replaced the General Agreement on Tariffs and Trade (GATT). Implementation of the TRIPS agreement has been reviewed every few years and each time, so far, the exemption for LDCs has been extended. The last extension was given in 2013 for a period of eight years, with a further extension possible when this grace period is over (WTO, 2013).
11. None of the EAC countries has had a surplus in recent years.
12. Occasionally, the data from these sources did not agree with each other and the author had to verify with other sources.
13. The World Bank reports debt as a percent of GNI instead of as a percent of GDP. However, the difference in numerical values between GNI and GDP in these countries is marginal. The growth of GNI and GDP follow the same trend.
14. The HIPC initiative was launched in 1966 by the IMF and World Bank to provide debt relief to poor countries. The MDRI was an extension of the HIPC initiative. Most of the countries that were eligible for the HIPC initiative and the MDRI were in Sub-Saharan Africa.
15. All EAC countries, including Kenya, have benefited from the rescheduling of debts by the Paris Club, an informal group of developed countries which are big lenders. However, the rescheduling of debts only provides temporary relief – it amounts to "kicking the can down the road," so to speak.
16. There is some discrepancy between the external debt-to-GDP ratios in the World Bank's *International Debt Statistics* and those in other publications. This is more noticeable regarding Kenya. In Kenya, the domestic debt-to-GDP ratio has exceeded the external debt-to-GDP ratio since 2010; according to the Republic of

Kenya's *Quarterly Economic and Budgetary Review* (Second Quarter 2013/2014), the total debt-to-GDP ratio in 2012 was 51 percent, 46 external and 54 internal.

17. Just before the collapse of the Greek economy, there were some serious discussions about the relevance of the IMF (The International Economy, 2007).
18. It should be noted that in 2015, South Sudan, which joined the EAC in 2016, had a lower CPI than Burundi. (The lower the CPI, the more corrupt the country is considered to be.)
19. President Magufuli of Tanzania, who came to power in October 2015, has placed fighting corruption in all forms and at all levels among his top priorities.
20. The data source records GDP in calendar years. Except for Burundi, which reports its tax revenue in calendar years, the other countries report it in fiscal years (July–June). In calculating tax revenue as a percent of GDP for 2007, for example, the tax revenue for 2006/2007 was divided by the GDP for 2007, and so forth.
21. For discussions on the challenges and possibilities of taxation in the informal sector, see Auriol and Warlters (2012) and Tax Justice Network-Africa (2012).
22. "A Partner State may withdraw from the Community provided [that] the National Assembly of the Partner State so resolves by resolution supported by not less than two-thirds majority of all the members entitled to vote" (Article 145, 1 (a)).

    "The Summit may suspend a Partner State from taking part in the activities of the Community if that State fails to observe and fulfill the fundamental principles and objectives of the Treaty including failure to meet financial commitments to the Community within a period of eighteen (18) months" (Article 146, 1).

    "The Summit may expel a Partner State from the Community for gross and persistent violation of the principles and objectives of this Treaty after giving such Partner State twelve months' written notice" (Article 147, 1).
23. For more details, see Chapter 10 in Mwapachu (2012).

8

Aspirations for an East African Political Federation

The first political union of independent states in Africa was that between Tanganyika and Zanzibar in 1964, to form Tanzania. An East African political federation would be the second. Given the current membership of the East African Community (EAC), an all-inclusive EAC political federation would be a system of government that has a single national authority and six state authorities – Burundi, Kenya, Rwanda, South Sudan, Tanzania, and Uganda.[1]

EARLY EFFORTS FOR AFRICAN UNITY

Though an EAC federation would be just the second political union in Africa, there certainly has been no shortage of calls from African leaders for African unity. Writing about the momentum the pan-African movement had gained by the end of WWII, Kwame Nkrumah (1963, 135) remarked that the fundamental purpose of the movement was "national independence leading to unity." Nkrumah was the first president of Ghana from independence in 1957 until 1966, when he was overthrown by a military and police coup d'état. Nkrumah worked tirelessly for independence and unity in Africa. When Guinea attained its independence in 1958 (a year-and-a-half after Ghana), Ghana and Guinea established a special bilateral relationship which, according to Nkrumah (1963, 141), was "a nucleus for a Union of African States." That nucleus was joined by Mali in 1960 and was officially named the Union of African States. Other independent African countries were welcome to join. However, the union collapsed before it could even be described as a genuine economic bloc, let alone a political union.

In the early 1960s, the political situation in Africa was too unstable for a loosely formed union to survive. The African leaders who had just come to power were overwhelmed by the struggle to hold their own countries together, while at the same time trying to gain influence on a continent-wide level. Although these leaders may have had similar goals – independence and unity – their interpretation of unity and their ways of pursuing it were not aligned. Commenting on the division among African leaders in his analysis of Nkrumah's efforts to push for African unity, Gebe (2008, 169) notes:

> Within the larger African political landscape, the front of the African leaders became divided over the form and best strategy towards continental unity. Three groups finally emerged, the radical Casablanca Group that desired an immediate and total union of Africa, the moderate Monrovia Group that wanted a gradualist approach to the issue of unity and lastly, the Brazzaville Group whose political aspirations were somewhat linked to a continuing association with metropolitan France. These divisions and the dynamics of the independence struggle on the continent, including different colonial experiences and socio-economic conditions, made it impossible for the realization of the vision of a truly united Africa as envisaged by the radical group. The Organization of African Unity which was eventually established on May 25, 1963 was, strictly speaking, a compromise arrangement but with the expectation that the continent could move towards the development of the necessary structures and institutions.[2]

A number of factors contributed to the disagreement regarding the form of, and the pace towards, African unity. They included the newness of these countries, dependence on the colonial masters, the Cold War, and the autocratic and brutal leadership of some post-colonial African leaders. In a political sense, immediately following independence, African countries were new to their own people. Many challenges had to be addressed: how to hold a country together when the main political bond had come from having a common enemy who was no longer there; how to develop a country that had been used and abused by the colonial powers; and how to forge relationships with neighboring countries which were not necessarily neighborly. When one was dealing with these types of challenges and many more, earnest efforts towards unity were a luxury many leaders could not afford, even though unity might have been part of the long-term solution for them.

Political independence did not and could not have meant economic independence immediately. African economies were inextricably linked to the European market, and the newly independent countries were unavoidably dependent on financial aid. African countries signed agreements with the European countries, including the Yaoundé Convention signed in 1963. The Yaoundé Convention applied to 18 African countries that were independent at that time. Under this convention, the European Economic Community promised support to African countries and allowed most dutiable imports from African countries to enter the European market duty-free. When the economic survival of African countries and the survival, in power, of some leaders were in the hands of external powers (whether by choice or due to circumstances), the ability of African countries to plan their own future, and decide with whom it would be forged, was very limited.

Moreover, the Cold War made African unification nearly impossible. Choosing a side, West (capitalism) or East (socialism), was sufficient for a country or, in many cases, a country's leader to receive aid and protection, no matter how corrupt or brutal that leader might have been. Neighboring countries were at odds with each other simply by choosing different sides and adopting different economic systems.

While this may not have been unique to Africa, political independence in some African countries was, in effect, simply a change in oppressors – from a foreign oppressor to a domestic one. Even worse, some of those domestic oppressors colluded with former foreign oppressors. While Africa had prominent and visionary leaders like President Nyerere of Tanzania and President Nkrumah of Ghana, post-independent Africa was also cursed with many dictators – leaders preoccupied with holding and expanding their power.

If African leaders have been united, it has been in *not* holding each other accountable. One distinctive feature of the Organization of African Unity (OAU) was its willingness to tolerate African dictators. For example, when the dictator Idi Amin of Uganda came to power in 1971 and killed thousands of innocent people, the OAU was, for all practical purposes, silent. In fact, Idi Amin was honored with the chairmanship of the OAU in 1975![3] As another example, one would have thought that the declarations on accountability by the African Union (AU) and regional blocs such as the Southern African Development Community (SADC) would have produced effective measures to bring an end at last to the autocracy of Robert Mugabe who has been in power in Zimbabwe since 1980.[4] Instead, in 2007, Mugabe was on stage with another dictator – Muammar Gaddafi of Libya – and other African presidents in Accra speaking about pan-Africanism and, as usual, blaming the West for all the problems in Zimbabwe. He has even been able to convince some people that anyone critical of him and his regime, regardless of the specifics of the criticism, is a puppet of the West. Since Gaddafi's death in 2011, Mugabe has increasingly become the loudest voice for an African political union (Smith, 2013). Mugabe was chosen the 2015 chairperson of the AU.[5]

Holding each other accountable has been avoided by African leaders with the excuse that they do not want to interfere with other countries' internal affairs. However, a leader who abuses human rights in his or her own country or who does not respect democracy cannot and should not be taken seriously in suggesting a politically unified Africa. Political unity must come through a genuinely democratic process.

The main agenda item for the 2007 summit of the African Union (AU) was a debate over an AU study conducted a year earlier titled, "An AU Government: Towards the United States of Africa" (African Union, 2006). The study suggested establishing a "Union Government" that "will be a political transitory arrangement towards the United States of Africa." In his analysis of the study, Sturman (2007, 7) writes:

> . . . the document lacks substance. It is deliberately vague on both the rationale for and the content of a United States of Africa. It does not use the word 'state' to describe this entity, nor does it mention whether or how the national sovereignty of the 54 existing African states would be superseded.

Moreover, the study proposed a clearly unrealistic "road map." According to the road map, the United States of Africa would be formed by 2015. This far-fetched proposal had the support of Muammar Gaddafi (Sturman, 2007; African Network on Debt and Development, et al., 2007). Presumably, if you are a dictator you can make things happen fast!

It should be noted that the AU has a Pan-African Parliament (PAP) based in Midrand, South Africa. Each AU member sends five representatives elected by its legislature. The role of the PAP is an advisory one, not one with governing authority. Should an AU government be established, the representatives will be directly elected by the people, making it a sovereign authority over African states.

Turning now to East Africa, it should be noted that aspirations for an East African federation are neither new nor unrealistic. The idea for it is almost a century old. As discussed in Chapter 3, the first study on the potential for a federation of Britain's five territories in Eastern Africa (Kenya, Northern Rhodesia [Zambia], Nyasaland [Malawi], Tanganyika and Uganda) was conducted in 1924. The British were not trying to promote African unity per se; they were looking for ways to rule and dominate those countries more efficiently and, thus, more profitably, for the British. However, in the late 1950s and early 1960s, prominent African leaders like Kwame Nkrumah of Ghana and Mwalimu Julius Kambarage Nyerere of Tanganyika advocated passionately for African unity for the empowerment of Africans (Nyerere, 1960 and 1961; Nkrumah, 1963).

Perhaps no one, certainly no leader, in East Africa was as strongly committed to an East African federation as Nyerere. He saw the struggles for freedom and unity as one struggle, to be won simultaneously. He was willing to postpone the independence of Tanganyika to wait for Kenya and Uganda, if that meant East Africa (Kenya, Tanganyika, and Uganda) would attain freedom as a federation. He saw the likelihood of a federation after each country had gained its independence separately to be slim, at best. The lengthy quote which follows captures some of the richness of his appeal for an East African federation at the time of independence.

> In the struggle against Colonialism the fundamental unity of the people of Africa is evident and is deeply felt. It is, however, a unity forged in adversity in a battle against an outside Government. . . . The feeling of unity which now exists could, however, be whittled away if each country gets its independence separately and becomes open to the temptations of nationhood and the intrigues of those who find their strength in the weakness of small nations.
>
> There is one way to ensure in East Africa that the present unity of opposition should become a unity of construction. The unity and freedom movements should be combined, and the East African territories achieve independence as one unit at the earliest possible moment. That means a Federation of Territories now administered separately . . . The argument of "bado kidogo," "you are not ready," is the same argument the imperialists have always used to delay our independence . . . Furthermore, Federation after independence means the surrender of sovereignty and all the prestige and symbols of such sovereignty. Surely, if it is difficult now to convince some of our friends that Federation is desirable, when it does not involve surrendering any sovereignty, it is going to be a million times more difficult to convince them later. (Nyerere, 1960, pp. 1, 3, and 4)

In his eloquent appeal for an East African federation at independence, Nyerere provided examples of countries that achieved unity and independence simultaneously. They included the United States and Nigeria. Whether these served as good examples from which the East African countries could have learned is beyond the scope of this study. However, there are some important differences. For the United States, the colonies literally joined forces to fight for independence. Kenya, Tanzania, and Uganda had a common enemy, but they did not actually join forces to fight for independence. Tanganyikans and Ugandans, for example, did not fight for the independence of Kenya. As for Nigeria, the North and the South were amalgamated by the British in 1914, so "unity" was not something that started when Nigeria attained its independence in 1960. Moreover, the ongoing instability in Nigeria can be linked, in part, to that action by the British.

An East African federation did not materialize at independence. At that time, Uganda was reluctant to surrender its sovereignty, particularly in matters of citizenship and foreign affairs. One might say history has proven Nyerere correct. Some may even consider his statements about the difficulty of forming a federation after independence separately to be prophetic.

Would a federation of the "newly born" countries have survived? It seems hard to imagine, given that a less ambitious integration, the former EAC, collapsed after just ten years. As discussed in Chapter 4, the former EAC died in part due to ideological differences, particularly between Kenya and Tanzania. Kenya nurtured a capitalist economy, while Tanzania embarked on building a socialist economy.

It is not possible to know what kind of economic system would have been adopted in East Africa, had an East African federation been established at independence. However, it can be said, unequivocally, that Nyerere was a leader of high moral principles centered on freedom and equality for all human beings. Nyerere saw the capitalist system as exploitative. As much as he cared for unity and as pragmatic as he was, it is hard to imagine him staying in a union that did not abide by his principles. In fact, Mkali (2012, 92–99) is correct in suggesting that had Nyerere known some of the secret deals made in Kenya and Uganda, he would not have proposed establishing a federation. Among them was a secret deal between the British government and Jomo Kenyatta (the first president of Kenya) not to carry out land reforms at independence that would have redistributed land from the hands of white settlers. Another was a deal that would preserve the 1900 Buganda Agreement under which land was confiscated from ordinary people and given to the British colonialists and local chiefs (Mkali, 2012).

Nyerere was the first leader in the world to recognize Biafra (the southeastern region of Nigeria) when it seceded from Nigeria in 1967.[6] He saw that the people of Biafra were being oppressed by the northern Nigerians. Nyerere was a staunch supporter of African unity, but also an atypical politician of high moral standards (Mwakikagile, 2002).

THE UNION OF TANGANYIKA AND ZANZIBAR

As fate would have it, the Zanzibar Revolution in January 1964 provided Nyerere a new opportunity for building unity. He and Sheikh Abeid Amani Karume, the first president of Zanzibar, arranged to form a union between Tanganyika and Zanzibar. Nyerere, of course, was an ardent advocate for pan-Africanism. Karume was an enthusiastic counterpart, not so much because he was a pan-Africanist, but because he felt that his leadership and the survival of the new Zanzibar needed a strong, geographically close partner. For Karume, the union was a "marriage" of convenience, not necessarily of ideology, although there is nothing to suggest that he was opposed to it. Tanganyika and Zanzibar united in 1964 to form Tanzania.

On April 26, 2014, Tanzania celebrated 50 years as a union. Addressing the people of Tanzania and African leaders, President Kikwete of Tanzania praised the union and offered it as a model for Africa. Aware of the ambition for an East African federation, he remarked that,

> [w]e could not achieve political federation during the reign of Jomo Kenyatta and Mwalimu Julius Nyerere but I am very confident that this time around Uhuru Kenyatta and I and other leaders in the region will achieve that dream . . . If we have succeeded in keeping the union of our two countries intact for 50 years, it is testimony that political federation is achievable. (Mbashiru, 2014)

Holding a union together for 50 years is impressive, but Tanzania does not necessarily provide a good model to be emulated in forming a federation. It is no secret that the union of Tanganyika and Zanzibar was an arranged "marriage" between the leaders of Tanganyika and Zanzibar, Mwalimu Nyerere and Sheikh Karume. Some of the details of their maneuvers were revealed in 2014 by Pius Msekwa and Salum Rashid who were, at the time, Tanganyika's Secretary of Parliament and Zanzibar's Secretary of the Revolutionary Council, respectively.

A deal for a union was negotiated and finalized secretly by Nyerere and Karume. Subsequently, Nyerere asked Msekwa to convene the Parliament hastily to ratify the deal (Nuzulack, 2014). Salum Rashid never saw or signed a Zanzibar Presidential Decree declaring the establishment of the union, even though, apparently, he and Karume were supposed to sign it (Juma, 2014). Of course, Nyerere and Karume had good and noble intentions in forming the union. More importantly, their leadership left a country capable of maturing to the point where people could freely (more or less) debate and decide, as they saw fit, the way to move forward.

Nonetheless, the way Tanzania was formed and the two-government structure put into place are not examples to be followed. The union of Tanganyika and Zanzibar came about the way it did because the two nations did not have nearly the level and type of democracy that is enjoyed today. Tanganyika was a one-party state at the time. Can anyone imagine in a truly democratic society that two leaders, for example, the presidents of Kenya and Tanzania, would meet secretly and reach a binding deal to unite Kenya and Tanzania and simply ask their Parliaments to rubber stamp the deal? It is unthinkable. But that was what happened regarding Tanganyika and Zanzibar. There was no public debate or referendum whatsoever. After the 2009–2010 fact-finding missions examining areas of tension between the Tanzanian mainland and Zanzibar, the Kituo cha Katiba (2010, 5) warned the EAC that "[s]ecrecy and ignoring the people as the formation of the Tanzanian Union shows can lead to subsequent problems." The Tanzanian Union agreement was reached in the "blink of an eye," making the pace suggested for fast-tracking the EAC political federation look like a snail's pace. (Fast-tracking an East African political federation is discussed later in this chapter.)

Tanzania has a two-government structure – the government of Zanzibar and the Union government. This two-government structure of the Tanzanian Union should not serve as a model for a potential East African federation. Tanganyika does not have its own government. In a political sense, Tanganyika ceased to exist in 1964. Perhaps this reflects Tanganyika's confidence in its stature that whether it had its own government or not, it would still be the main guardian of the union. Tanganyika (that is, the Tanzanian mainland) has a population 33 times larger than Zanzibar, and geographically it is 360 times larger than Zanzibar. One must wonder whether a two-government structure set the other way around, where Zanzibar lost its political identity, was ever considered and also whether such a union would have lasted 50 years.

A potential East African federation must be a union of equals, from a political point of view. If, for example, three countries form a federation, there should be a federal government and each state should have its own government. However, it is not clear how Tanzania's current structure would fit into an East African federation.

THE BENEFITS AND CHALLENGES OF A POLITICAL FEDERATION

Given the current membership of the East African Community, an East African federation would be a system of government with a single regional authority and six state authorities – Burundi, Kenya, Rwanda, South Sudan, Tanzania, and Uganda. The advantages of a federation would be the same as those associated with regional economic integration in general – increased competition, increased investment, economies of scale, increased political and economic leverage, learning good practices from each other, and political stability, all of which would tend to lead to increased economic growth.

Of course, these countries would not be jumping from an autarky position (self-sufficient, closed economies) or isolationism to a federation. If the level of a federation is achieved, it would most likely be a step up from a monetary union. The benefits of having a federation must, therefore, be considered in marginal terms. If the protocols to establish a customs union and a common market are fully implemented and a monetary union is established, the additional economic benefit of having a federation will be moderate. Moreover, land would most likely continue to be kept out of the EAC agreements. (See discussion below.)

The political stability argument for having a federation may not be as strong as it sounds. The EAC countries are not a real threat to each other. With the exception of the Tanzania-Uganda war which was initiated by the dictator Idi Amin of Uganda in 1978, conflicts in East Africa, specifically in Burundi, Rwanda, and Uganda, have been civil wars, even when a rebel or liberation group was fighting from a neighboring country. Some might argue that in a political federation, the peaceful culture of a large, diverse country like Tanzania, for example, might spill over to a turbulent country like Burundi and defuse tensions there. That may be the case, but the net spillover could be the other way round, where conflict in Burundi spills over into Tanzania.

An EAC political federation in itself would not end civil wars, and whatever needs to be done to end them does not require a political federation. Incidentally, even if there was a military threat from the outside to one of the member countries, a joint military response does not require a political union. The EAC could establish an agreement similar to the North Atlantic Treaty Organization (NATO) to deal with military aggression against any of its members.

There have been instances of terrorist attacks in East Africa, but again intelligence-sharing and joint counter-terrorism do not require a political union. In fact, a political union may spread terrorism to areas that were initially relatively safe, as borders become more porous. It is partly for that reason that Tanzania has, so far, not joined Kenya, Rwanda, and Uganda in issuing the single East African tourist visa launched in 2014.

When a group of countries form a political union, each partner state loses some of its identity and gains some of the common identity. A country may have a net gain or net loss, depending on the kind of reputation it is bringing to the union, relative to the reputation of its partners. The rest of the world will generalize from what is happening in one country, particularly negative events, to the whole region. A terrorist attack in one city or a civil war in one country might generate a travel warning for the whole region, not just to the specific country where violence took place.

IS EAST AFRICA READY TO BE A FEDERATION?

When one considers the history of each of the EAC countries, especially from the 1960s to the 1980s, significant progress can be seen, as each country now has a multiparty system. But genuine democracy takes time to build. The East African countries are at different stages of democracy; each of them needs to strengthen its democracy first, before it takes on the complexities of a federation.

Burundi: It gained independence in 1962, but has been engulfed in civil strife for most of its history (Bertelsmann Stiftung, 2012). There were, however, some signs of normalcy between 2005 and 2015.

The constitution that was reached through a referendum in 2005 set a two-term presidential limit (with five years per term). In addition, it tried to balance power by having two vice president positions, one each for the majority Hutu and minority Tutsi ethnic groups. However, President Nkurunziza and his close loyalists wanted the constitution to be interpreted in a way that would allow him to run for a third term. For the first term (2005–2010), Nkurunziza was elected through a parliamentary vote, and for the second term (2010–2015) he was elected through a popular vote. Arguing that the first term did not count since he was not elected through a popular vote, in April of 2015, Nkurunziza (endorsed by his party, the National Council for the Defense of Democracy-Forces for the Defense of Democracy [CNDD-FDD]) decided to run for a third term and won. So much for defending democracy! Nkurunziza's argument would make one think that the job description for president was different the first five years he served.

The United States had warned Nkurunziza not to interpret the constitution so as to give him a chance for a third term, and the leadership of Burundi's Roman Catholic Church had argued Nkurunziza should not stand for a third term. Even though Burundi is very dependent on foreign aid and Catholics represent 70 percent of its population, Nkurunziza did not bow to pressure. His decision led to protests, an attempted coup to overthrow him, and deaths. Thousands of refugees crossed into Tanzania to seek shelter. When Nkurunziza was reelected as president in July 2015, the election lacked credibility in the eyes of international observers, including EAC observers, and, of course, opposition parties in Burundi. The election was described as being "tainted by government intimidation and violence" (Buchanan, 2015; Analo, 2015). Following the disputed election, Burundi returned to a state of political instability that has characterized most of its recent history. On top of that, tensions have been high between Burundi and its neighbor and partner country in the

EAC, Rwanda. Burundi has accused Rwanda of training rebels to overthrow Nkurunzinza. Apparently, a UN report also makes the same accusation, but Rwanda has vehemently denied any involvement with Burundi's internal affairs (Gettleman, 2016).

What was conspicuously missing in the months leading to the decision by Nkurunziza and his party was a public warning to Nkurunziza from the EAC leaders. In fact, it is not even clear why the EAC sent an observer team to an election that violated the constitution. In general, the diplomatic gesture of the EAC, sending poll observer teams to its member countries' elections, should be supported and commended. However, such gestures should be made together with explicit calls from the EAC for its members to respect their constitutions. Otherwise, poll observer teams may appear to be condoning undemocratic elections.

This underscores the point that African leaders are not known for holding each other accountable. Moreover, which leader in East Africa had the moral authority to counsel Nkurunziza? President Museveni of Uganda clearly did not. It is alleged that he bribed the Members of Parliament to have the constitution changed to remove presidential term limits in Uganda (The Observer, 2012). Museveni has been in power since 1986. President Kenyatta of Kenya was indicted by the International Criminal Court (ICC) for crimes against humanity in connection with the 2007 post-election violence in Kenya in which more than 1,000 people died (Gayathri, 2013). While those charges were later dropped, they still left Kenyatta weak in terms of his moral authority. President Kagame of Rwanda has done wonders for the economy of Rwanda, but at the same time his regime has become increasingly repressive. He too was contemplating changing the constitution – and subsequently did so – so he could stay in power beyond 2017 (Smith, 2014; Aglietti, 2014).

That only left President Kikwete of Tanzania, who, incidentally, was Chair of the EAC when the situation was boiling in Burundi. But Tanzania has been ruled by the same political apparatus since its independence in 1961. Even if President Kikwete had wanted to counsel President Nkurunziza, he would have had to think twice about it. When Kikwete offered well-intentioned advice to Kagame in 2013 on how to deal with the rebels of the Congo-based Democratic Forces for the Liberation of Rwanda (FDLR), Rwanda was offended. The relationship between Kikwete and Kagame was never the same. That is why when they exchanged warm gestures at an EAC summit in February of 2015, *The Citizen*, a major newspaper in Tanzania, used the headline, "JK, Kagame break the ice at EAC summit" (Ubwani, 2015).

In many ways, Burundi is on its own, and there is no real indication that a federation would help bring political stability to Burundi. If anything, Burundi may be a threat to a federation, as countries may take different sides in its political landscape. Burundi must find a way to clean up its political mess and build strong institutions before it moves into a federation.

Incidentally, it was only after the elections and subsequent insecurity that other EAC leaders showed some unity against Nkurunziza. The position of chair of the EAC was to rotate from the President of Tanzania to the President of Burundi in 2016, but Burundi was denied that leadership role. Instead, the President of Tanzania was given a one-year extension to chair the EAC. To make clear that this stance was directed at Nkurunziza himself, the EAC leaders accepted the appointment of Libérat Mfumukeko, a Burundian, as the new Secretary General of the EAC. It was Burundi's turn to nominate its citizen to assume that position when Richard Sezibera's five-year term ended in April 2016.

Kenya: It was ruled by the Kenya African National Union (KANU) from 1963 until 2002. In 1992, the constitution was changed to allow a multiparty system. Presidential elections have in fact been competitive since 2002. The disputed 2007 elections were followed in early 2008 by country-wide violence. The riots left more than 1,000 people dead, including about 100 people who were killed in a church where they had taken shelter. At least 600,000 people were left homeless.

The violence was triggered by the rigging of elections, and the killings were along ethnic lines. Still, the root causes had to do with a number of longstanding issues, the top one being land disputes (Oucho, 2010; Mkali, 2012). On the surface, the violence showed a people who had an identity crisis. Clearly many put their ethnic identity first and national identity second. The violence was a painful reminder of the severe deficiencies in the political system, as well as a bold demonstration of the quest for free and fair elections. It was also a wake-up call that land disputes, which date back to the colonial era, will not simply fade away.

The formation of a coalition government could be credited with ending the violence, although by and large it was a dysfunctional coalition. There was a comedy-like, tug of war between President Kibaki and Prime Minister Odinga. Nonetheless, under their leadership, a new constitution was signed into law in August 2010 which reduced the power of the executive branch and put more effective checks and balances in place for the governance of the country. If the spirit and the letter of the new constitution are fully implemented, one can argue that Kenya is on a positive trajectory in its governance. That is a big "if." Kenya needs to gain experience with its new constitution before it propels itself into a federation. It also needs to find a real solution to the land question. Otherwise, it will bring a "ticking time bomb" into the federation.

Rwanda: If economic indicators and the reduction of corruption were the only important factors in determining a country's readiness for a federation, Rwanda would be the EAC country most ready for a federation. According to World Bank data, between 2001 and 2015, Rwanda's real GDP increased by an annual average of 8 percent. The poverty rate dropped from 58 percent in 2001 to 39 percent in 2014. According to Transparency International, Rwanda is the least corrupt country in the EAC. In just a few years, it has gone from being among the most corrupt countries in the world (together with its EAC partner states) to being one of the top two least corrupt countries in mainland Africa. (The other one is Botswana.) Its Corruption Perception Index (CPI) improved from 28 in 2007 to 54 in 2015. As such, President Kagame deserves to be commended, especially given the dark history of civil wars and the country's genocide (Clark and Kaufman, 2003).

However, regarding human rights and the freedom of speech, Rwanda is not impressive. Kagame's administration has become increasingly repressive (Human Rights Watch, 2014). Rwanda has also been accused of fueling conflict in the Democratic Republic of Congo. Whether the repression or involvement in the DRC are necessary evils to guarantee Rwanda's security is irrelevant to the question about forming an East African federation.[7] Countries that blatantly repress freedom of speech should not be part of a federation built on respect for human rights.

President Kagame and his supporters pushed for a referendum vote in 2015 that amended the 2003 constitution. Article 101 of the 2003 constitution stated that, "The President of the Republic is elected for a term of seven years renewable only once. Under no circumstances shall a person hold the office of President of Republic for more than two terms" (Republic of Rwanda, 2003). Taken at face value, the 2015 amended constitution actually reduces the maximum number of years one could be president from 14 to 10 – that is, two five-year terms (Republic of Rwanda, 2015). However, the new constitution allows Kagame to run for a third seven-year term before the five-year terms take effect, for which he will be also be eligible to run. In other words, the clock starts anew in 2024, meaning Kagame could potentially be in power until 2034 (McVeigh, 2015). He has already announced that he will run for office in 2017.

Of course, every country has the right to change its constitution as it wishes. However, changing the constitution for the sole purpose of increasing the number of years someone remains in power is contrary to the spirit necessary for a federation based on democratic principles. Rwanda needs time to establish genuine democratic institutions before it moves into a federation.

Tanzania: It has been ruled by the same political apparatus since its independence in 1961. The Tanganyika African National Union (TANU) ruled from 1961 to 1977. TANU and Zanzibar's Afro-Shirazi Party united in 1977 to form the Chama Cha Mapinduzi (CCM), which continues to rule in Tanzania. Although a change in the constitution in 1992 established a multiparty system, the CCM has won all five elections since then. Part of the reason for such political dominance by the CCM is the lack of real separation between the state and the party. So far, the Presidency has always been won by the CCM. To consolidate power, the CCM has always chosen the chair of its party to be whoever was president. This tradition or strategy is a remnant from the one-party political system and has worked to the CCM's great advantage. As he took over the chairmanship of the CCM party in 2016, President Magufuli publicly asked civil servants to abide by the CCM manifesto (Mtulya, 2016).

On top of all this, power is concentrated in the executive branch of the government. For example, the president appoints all Regional and District Commissioners – naturally people loyal to his party. The Tanzanian mainland has 26 regions and 166 districts; the president can also increase the number of regions and districts. In addition, cabinet members (ministers and deputy ministers) appointed by the president, loyal to his party of course, also hold positions as members of parliament (MPs). The weakness of this system becomes conspicuous during annual parliamentary budget debates. The cabinet members, the people that present the respective budgets of their ministries, are also MPs. In other words, the people who are accountable to the parliament are also MPs, and very influential MPs, one must add. The situation is analogous to having senior administrators of a company serve as board members of the same company. The president also appoints Permanent Secretaries for various ministries, executive directors for local governments, and many other officials.

Given that Tanzania itself is a union, it must consider many questions. Would Tanzania enter the EAC federation as a single state or as two states? If it did not enter as a single state, it would mean Zanzibar and the Tanzanian mainland could decide separately whether to join the EAC. What would be the implications if one votes to join and the other votes not to join? Even if they were both to join, what would be the structure of the EAC federation when some of its members are already a union? Clearly Tanzania has a lot to ponder before it commits to a federation.

Moreover, while Tanzania has been blessed with peace and harmony (which must never be taken for granted), it cannot be considered a shining example of a country adhering to democratic principles. A number of commentators and analysts have expressed that the 2015 Tanzanian Cybercrimes Bill has a high propensity to limit freedom of opinion and expression (Ndumbaro, 2015; Marari, 2015; Marere, 2015).[8] In addition, in 2016 police banned political rallies that were planned by opposition parties (Kabendera, 2016; Mhagama, 2016).[9]

Likewise the October 2015 general elections in Zanzibar left a lot to be desired. Zanzibar's elections were nullified by the Chair of the Zanzibar Electoral Commission (ZEC) without clear and convincing reasons. The main opposition party in Zanzibar, Civic United Front (CUF), strongly condemned the decision as they saw elections to have been free and fair and believed that they won in Zanzibar. Both the Zanzibar Law Society and Tanganyika Law Society thought the decision to nullify the Zanzibar elections was illegal (Mtulya, 2015). A number of external observers, including the EAC observers, denounced the nullification. The United States went so far as suspending $473 million in aid to Tanzania. Nonetheless, the Chair of the ZEC ordered a re-run of elections. CUF boycotted the re-run, so it came as no surprise that the CCM won overwhelmingly. What happened in Zanzibar adds to doubts about Tanzania's adherence to the principles of democracy and points to the need for Tanzania to grow its democracy before moving into a federation.

Uganda: It went through a tumultuous period under Idi Amin, 1971–1979, and Milton Obote's second presidency, 1981–1985. Obote was overthrown in 1985 and President Museveni took power in 1986. Museveni has been in power for 30 consecutive years and was just elected in 2016 for another five-year term. Given that the country has a very young population, 75 percent of Ugandans have only had one president all their life.

Uganda had a two-term presidential limit (five years per term) which would have ended Museveni's presidency in 2005.[10] However, in his second term, he pushed for and succeeded in having the constitution changed, removing the term limits. When he was asked in 2011 if he would run again in 2016, Museveni's response was, "[o]ne of the real points for me politically is the East African federation. I cannot leave this issue if I think there is a possibility of advancing it. This is something [for which] I have been working all my time in politics and is one of the reasons why I continue to be in power" (The Observer, 2011). This is the classic case of a leader thinking that he is indispensable, a very dangerous mindset for a democracy. At some point in 2011, when President Museveni was asked how he would react if Ugandans contested election results with demonstrations, Museveni responded that "[w]e just lock them up . . . bundle them into jail and [bring them] to the courts" (The Herald, 2011). There you have it – one theoretical model for democracy! But certainly not one fit for an EAC political federation.

Some MPs in Uganda have been pushing for the restoration of two five-year term limits for the presidency, but so far they have not succeeded. Some, perhaps avoiding conflict with Museveni, have proposed a restoration of term limits that would not be enforced retroactively, that is, that would not apply to Museveni (Gatsiounis, 2012). That proposal has not gained traction. Museveni ran in and won the 2016 elections.

Uganda also has a challenge akin to that of Tanzania, as there are people specifically in Buganda and Bunyoro demanding that Uganda "become a federal state with different regions becoming semi-autonomous entities" (EAC Secretariat, 2011, 10). Uganda should resolve its persistent friction regarding statehood before it joins an EAC federation. An EAC federation must not, and cannot, be used to mask internal conflicts.

FAST-TRACKING AN EAST AFRICAN POLITICAL FEDERATION

The stated ultimate goal of the EAC is to form a political federation. Despite the concerns discussed above about the readiness of the EAC countries to become a federation, some seem to want to "sprint" to do so. In 2004, the heads of the EAC (only Kenya, Tanzania and Uganda at the time) established what came to be known as the Wako Committee "to examine the possibility of expediting and compressing the process of integration so that the ultimate goal of a Political Federation is achieved through a fast track mechanism" (EAC Secretariat, 2007). The Wako Committee submitted its report in just three months. It outlined a road map of action that took fast-tracking quite literally. Under its action plan, the EAC would have achieved a political federation in 2013.

The study by the Wako committee was followed by individual country surveys to determine the level of awareness of the EAC, attitudes about a political federation, and opinions about fast-tracking the political federation (EAC Secretariat, 2007a). Taking the results of the studies at

Table 8.1 *Levels of Support for Integration and a Political Federation, According to the Wako Committee (percentage)*

	Kenya			Tanzania			Uganda		
Support for:	Yes	No	Other	Yes	No	Other	Yes	No	Other
integration	85.8	11.0	3.2	66.5	21.2	12.5	88.2	7.3	4.6
political federation	69.9	27.0	3.1	74.4	21.5	4.2	77.2	14.4	7.9
fast-tracking	64.9	35.1	0.0	25.4	74.6	0.0	56.3	28.4	15.4

Source: EAC Secretariat (2007a).

Table 8.2 *Awareness of the Proposed Political Federation of East Africa (percentage)*[11]

	A Great Deal	Some	A Small Amount	Nothing	Don't Know/ Have Not Heard Enough
Kenya	10	15	33	25	17
Tanzania	21	17	30	29	3
Uganda	13	14	35	28	10

Source: Afrobarometer (2008, 2008a, 2008b).

face value, in all three original EAC countries there was strong support for a political federation, as shown in Table 8.1. However, according to the results, Tanzanians were opposed to fast-tracking into a federation; still, support for a political federation in Tanzania was high and, surprisingly, higher than the support in Tanzania for integration in general.

Overall, one must not read too much into the results of those studies. From a statistical point of view, it is not clear how much those results really reflected the views of the general population. It does not seem the participants of the surveys were chosen at random. For example, in Tanzania where females constitute 51 percent of the population, only 24.6 percent of the 9,519 people who received questionnaires were female.

Using random samples, more careful studies conducted by Afrobarometer (2008, 2008a, 2008b) three years later suggested little awareness of the proposed political federation of East Africa and little support for it, as shown in Tables 8.2 and 8.3. However, the survey questions by

Table 8.3 *Approval of the Proposed Political Federation of East Africa (percentage)*[12]

	Strongly Approve	Approve	Disapprove	Strongly Disapprove	Don't Know/ Have Not Heard Enough/Neither Approve Nor Disapprove
Kenya	8	11	22	25	34
Tanzania	7	14	18	43	17
Uganda	15	22	13	17	32

Source: Afrobarometer (2008, 2008a, 2008b).

Afrobarometer did not mention that a federal (unitary) government would not eliminate state governments. Those who were not aware of the proposal for a political federation may have disapproved of it, thinking their state government would be eliminated altogether.

Many people in government, business, academics, media, and civil society are knowledgeable about the EAC and can articulate their reasons for or against forming a federation. However, the question about support for a political federation, let alone fast-tracking it, is presumptuous until the majority of people are clear about the benefits and challenges of a political federation. Awareness of the proposal to form a federation is not enough for people to make an informed decision as to whether to support it or not. While it can be assumed that the level of awareness has been growing over time, discussions about a federation have not yet percolated down to the grassroots level. Parliamentary candidates have not yet had to debate or state their positions on the issue of a political federation during campaigns, even when there were opportunities to do so.

In 2014, Tanzania went through some deep "soul searching" about its union as it debated a proposed new constitution. The structure of the Tanzanian Union was front and center in that debate. Remember that Tanzania has had a two-government structure since 1964 – the government of Zanzibar and the Union government. Initially, the proposed new constitution recommended a three-government structure, with the addition of a government for Tanganyika (the Tanzanian mainland). President Kikwete and his ruling party opposed the recommendation and were able to have it removed. One would have thought that the debate about the

Tanzanian Union would have included a discussion on how the Union structure would fit into a potential EAC political federation. However, that discussion was conspicuously absent and, as of 2017, the whole initiative about a new constitution was put on hold.

THE NEED FOR DISCUSSION ABOUT A POTENTIAL EAC POLITICAL FEDERATION

Since there have not been real public discussions about a potential EAC political federation, it is not clear which groups are for it, which are against, and what the motives and fears are. Surveys conducted by various groups over the years do not amount to full public discussions. Making people aware of the proposed political integration, identifying fears and concerns, and suggesting ways to address them, as the EAC Secretariat (2011) does, is extremely important. However, the full value of awareness is derived from having open, completely free, non-paternalistic discussions. It would not be an honest debate if all that was done was to try to persuade people that a federation is good for them or that it is bad for them. Discussions and debates about a political federation must happen at all levels, so that when eventually a referendum is held, people will be well informed as to what is at stake. In those discussions, the land issue will no doubt receive special attention, especially in Tanzania.

It is apparent that all EAC leaders are in favor of a political federation, with President Museveni of Uganda seemingly at the forefront. It is also apparent that the push for a federation is coming from within and not from external forces. However, the discussion cannot only be among leaders. Moreover, Museveni has maintained power since 1986. His calls for a federation would have had strong moral authority if he had left power after his successful leadership in his first two terms. Whether it is fair or not, the more he clings to power, the more he is seen as someone who just wants more power, which further calls into question his intentions for the EAC federation.

It is worth noting that in the last 20 years, it has been the autocratic leaders who have been major lobbyists for the political unification of Africa. In the lead was President Gaddafi of Libya. In fact, the precursor to the establishment of the AU was a special OAU summit of African heads of state initiated and hosted by Gaddafi in Sirte, Libya, in 1999, at which point it was declared (in the Sirte Declaration) that steps towards integration must be accelerated. Often times, dictators and autocratic leaders seek to divert attention away from discontent at home by engaging in grandiose international initiatives. Some element of that phenomenon might be taking place currently in East Africa.

THE LAND ISSUE

Land is a contentious issue in negotiations about a political federation. The position of Tanzania is that land must remain under national jurisdiction, even if the EAC were to become a federation. At the EAC meeting of the Council of Ministers in 2011, Tanzania's Deputy Minister of Industry and Trade, Lazaro Nyalandu, stated unequivocally that land will not be part of the EAC.[13]

> We'll never allow that, because to do so is to betray our own people. There are member countries that are struggling to bounce-back with the issue of land in the regional bloc's set-up . . . The [Tanzanian] government is committed to ensure that all resources of its people are well protected for their own benefit . . . As leaders, we'll never surrender the land of Tanzanians for the interest of the East African Community. (Kabeera, 2011)

This position has been reiterated by Tanzanian leaders on many occasions. "Land is out of the EAC 'empire'" is the message Tanzania's Minister for East African Cooperation, Samwel Sitta, gave to the newly elected Tanzanian members of the East African Legislative Assembly in 2012 (Tambwe, 2012). Tanzania has not ratified the EAC Protocol on Environment and Natural Resources in light of concerns that the protocol contradicts "the one on the EAC Common Market, particularly access to the use of land and premises, which should be governed by national policies and laws" (*The Citizen*, 2015).

If Tanzania's position is at one end of the spectrum, Rwanda's is at the other end. According to Rwanda's Director of Land Administration, Francois Ntaganda, everyone regardless of his or her nationality is allowed to own land in Rwanda: "We don't have any problem with land; anybody in the world is free to own a [sic] land in [Rwanda] as long as you negotiate properly and buy it; we don't discriminate" (Kabeera, 2011).

In reality, Rwanda has a big "problem with land." It has very little of it. The difference between Tanzania's position about land and that of its partner states may reflect differences in economic philosophies, but more importantly, it reflects the vast difference in land availability. Here is a rhetorical question. If land in the EAC was available for ownership by all EAC citizens on an equal basis, where would Kenyans, for example, go

Table 8.4 *Land and Population Density in the EAC (2012)*

	Total Land Area (sq. km. in thousands)	Forest Area (sq. km. in thousands)	Arable Land (sq. km. in thousands)	Arable Land per Capita (sq. km.)	Population Density per sq. km.
Burundi	26	2	9	0.10	384
Kenya	569	35	51	0.13	76
Rwanda	25	5	12	0.11	465
Tanzania	886	331	116	0.25	54
Uganda	200	29	68	0.19	182

Source: World Bank (2013a).

to buy land – Tanzania, where the population density is 54 per square kilometer, or Rwanda where the population density is 465 per square kilometer? Land is relatively abundant in Tanzania and relatively scarce in other EAC countries (not including South Sudan which joined the EAC in 2016), to various degrees, as shown in Table 8.4.

Theory tells us that economic openness increases the real income of the owners of whatever factor of production is relatively abundant, and thus they would be in favor of openness. Removing controls on land ownership would result in an influx of foreign buyers of land in Tanzania and increase the real value of land just as an increase in the demand for coffee produced in Tanzania would increase its price. But land and coffee are very different – the latter is just a consumer commodity. Land is a stationary, finite (supply is perfectly inelastic) natural resource, the "physical address" of a nation. Most countries have restrictions on land ownership by foreigners; Tanzania is not unique in that regard. Those restrictions are due to security concerns. They are also in place to protect small native holders of land who may be taken advantage of by their not knowing the full value of their land. The bureaucrats who process land transactions may also be in favor of restrictions that create more opportunities for bribes.

In Tanzania, land is in the hands of the president. The Land Acts of 1999 maintains that, "[a]ll land in Tanzania shall continue to be public land and remain vested in the President as trustee for and on behalf of all the citizens of Tanzania" [The United Republic of Tanzania, 1999, Part III (4)(1), 1999a, Part II (3)(1)(b)]. It is an understatement to say that this land "trusteeship" arrangement gives too much power to the executive branch and has a great deal of potential for abuse.[14] That aside, Tanzania is against any arrangement that would make its land available to other East Africans for ownership on equal terms.

Tanzania does not have entrenched land problems similar to those experienced, for example, in Kenya or Uganda. However, that does not mean that it has escaped land conflicts. Tanzanian newspapers carry stories on land disputes almost daily, many of them involving foreign investors (Kiishweko, 2012).

Each EAC country has its share of major land issues which need to be addressed adequately before making any attempt to bring land into the EAC jurisdiction. Tanzania is doing itself and everyone else a favor by asking that land not be brought under the EAC. Land disputes are protracted, sometimes over decades and even centuries. Those disputes will not melt away by placing them in one pot or simply unleashing market forces. In fact, blending EAC countries' land issues together may escalate existing disputes and create a hybrid of new problems if those who have been deprived of land feel that their complaints are being swept under the rug.

This does not mean that land must stay out of the EAC forever. When the structure of the EAC economies has changed to be less dependent on subsistence farming and each country has adequately dealt with its major land disputes, the EAC can revisit the land issue. Meanwhile, a lesson can be learned from Rwanda's efforts to implement and enforce its 2004 National Land Policy and subsequent land laws. The laws protect the rights of all land holders and, notably, give women equal rights to inherit land. While it may take years before women's inheritance rights are fully realized given the deeply rooted patriarchal system in Africa, especially with regard to land, Rwanda's efforts are exemplary (Crabtree-Condor and Casey, 2012).[15]

THE POLITICS OF OIL AND GAS RESERVES

There are indications that the economies of Kenya, Tanzania, and Uganda will look quite different in 10–15 years as a result of the discovery of large reserves of natural gas and oil in these countries. These three countries could potentially become big producers and exporters of natural gas and oil, a development that could transform their economies. With an increased inflow of foreign direct investment and increased export revenue, these countries could become less dependent on financial aid and, at the same time, improve their infrastructure and the provision of social services. However, natural resources have often been a curse in many African countries. Of course, nothing about natural resources intrinsically makes them a curse. Likewise, nothing about natural resources intrinsically makes them automatically a blessing.

With good governance and low corruption levels, diamonds in Botswana have been a blessing (Lewin, 2011). In Angola, the Democratic Republic of Congo, Liberia, and Sierra Leone, diamonds and other minerals have been used to finance brutal wars – hence, the brand name "blood diamonds," or the label "conflict minerals." The four countries in Sub-Saharan Africa that produce the most oil are Angola, Chad, Equatorial Guinea, and Nigeria. For each of these countries, over 90 percent of their export revenues is generated from oil exports. But these countries have something else in common. They are among the most corrupt countries in the world according to Transparency International, which publishes the annual Corruption Perception Index. Oil rents are the epicenter of corruption in those countries and have failed to transform the lives of ordinary people.[16]

Take Equatorial Guinea as an example.[17] While Equatorial Guinea may be an extreme case, it illustrates an important point. According to World Bank data, Equatorial Guinea was among the top 25 countries in the world in 2012, in terms of GDP per capita, derived using purchasing power parity (PPP).[18] Its annual average GDP per capita (PPP) from 2009 to 2012 was over $37,000, a level comparable to that in Western Europe. (Of course, Equatorial Guinea's GDP per capita fluctuates wildly with the price of oil.) The rapid economic growth in Equatorial Guinea since the late 1990s is almost solely due to exports of oil. Yet that growth in trade and GDP has not translated into comparable development. In 2012, Equatorial Guinea was 136th in the Human Development Index (HDI) ranking. Many countries with lower GDP per capita than Equatorial Guinea are ranked high in the HDI. Equatorial Guinea was still categorized as a least developed country as of 2016, although according to a 2013 resolution of the United Nations Economic and Social Council, Equatorial Guinea will graduate from the least developed country category by 2017 (United Nations, 2013). Of course, even with good policies, economic growth does not translate into a higher standard of living across the board overnight. However, the disparity between economic growth or wealth and economic development in a number of mineral-rich African countries cannot be easily explained by the time lag that exists between economic growth and real development.

Equatorial Guinea is among the top ten countries perceived to be most corrupt. In fact, if one considers the last 15 years, there seems to be a correlation between economic growth and the level of corruption in Equatorial Guinea. Of course, correlation does not imply causation. Nonetheless, it is tempting to hypothesize that when greed begets more greed, natural resources may not only fail to bring about real human development – they may actually give those in power the arrogance and means to exploit the population. Yet even with this possible conclusion, we cannot say that oil or natural gas reserves are necessarily bad any more than we can say fertile land is bad because a few people may grab it and use it to oppress and exploit others.

In the EAC, where imports of fuel siphon off 20 percent of total import spending, oil and natural gas rents can reduce trade deficits, increase employment, and improve the economies of the whole region. But that will not happen automatically. It requires that these countries find a cure for corruption which, except for Rwanda, looks like a cancer that has metastasized.[19] Short of that, oil rents will simply be a windfall for clever oil and gas companies and corrupt officials. Moreover, a lack of transparency in awarding drilling and construction contracts, disagreement over the ownership of the natural resources, concerns over environmental damage associated with drilling, and safety in the transportation of natural resources can lead to increased internal and cross-border conflict.

For the positive effects of natural gas and oil to be realized, the EAC countries must also have effective policies and regulations that take into account broader development goals, environmental issues, and revenue-sharing concerns. In preparation for a political federation, the EAC countries must determine how the federal government would be financed. It is not yet clear if and how the EAC countries would share oil and natural gas earnings. Creating a transparent, agreeable, and enforceable revenue-sharing formula and mechanism is a daunting task for a single country, let alone for a federation.

Tanzania, traditionally a peaceful country, was challenged by violent riots in Mtwara (southern Tanzania) in 2013 over a gas pipeline under construction to transport gas from Mtwara to Dar-es-Salaam (Bariyo, 2013). Mtwara residents felt they were being marginalized when it came to the benefits of the natural resources extracted in their own backyard. The military had to be deployed to restore peace. Subsequently, Prime Minister Pinda calmed the tension by announcing that gas will be processed in Mtwara before it is transported to Dar-es-Salaam, thus creating jobs in Mtwara (Mwananchi, 2013).

In 1999, before starting to produce and export oil, Chad teamed up with the World Bank to draw up an elaborate plan that would supposedly ensure profitable production, adequate distribution of the profits to the population and between generations, a higher standard of living, and protection of the environment. As one commentator cynically remarked, they might as well have also agreed that "pigs would fly" (Save Virunga, 2013). Chad's leaders were quickly intoxicated with the aroma of oil revenue and found excuses to abandon the plan. Instead of alleviating poverty, oil production has reinforced corruption and inequality in Chad.

More discoveries of natural resources in the EAC and the prospects of having to share the proceeds may bring protective attitudes similar to Tanzania's attitude about land. However, these discoveries could also bring more unity. The development of the energy sector can provide unique opportunities for joint infrastructure projects, especially since some of the partner countries are landlocked. It is no secret that landlocked countries have a greater need for joint transportation projects than transit countries. In 2014, at a time when Kenya, Rwanda, and Uganda seemed to have been enjoying a special bond, they agreed to collaborate on two oil pipeline projects: an 870-kilometer extension to Uganda and Rwanda of an existing pipeline that runs from Mombasa, Kenya, at the Indian Ocean to Eldoret in western Kenya; and a new 1,500-kilometer pipeline that would connect oil fields in western Uganda with Kenya's Lamu port, also on the Indian Ocean. It was envisioned that the new pipeline would also be used to export oil from South Sudan (Mumo, 2014). Currently, there are only three cross-border, international oil pipelines in Africa – the Chad-Cameroon pipeline, the Tanzania-Zambia Mafuta pipeline (TAZAMA), and the South Sudan-Sudan pipeline.

Successful joint infrastructure projects can glue neighboring countries together and make it easier for them to form a political federation. At the same time, they are a risk because their full benefits depend on the continual cooperation of all the partners. As it happened, it did not even take Kenya and Uganda being on bad terms for Uganda to change its mind. The dynamics of EAC politics among the leaders changed when Tanzania got a new president in 2015. President Magufuli's authoritarian leadership style aligned better with that of Presidents Kagame and Museveni of Rwanda and Uganda, respectively. Within a short period of time in office, he was able to establish a close working relationship with them. He was even able to work out a deal that led Museveni to agree to change his initial, apparently non-binding agreement with Kenya. The new oil pipeline that would have connected Ugandan oil fields with a Kenyan port will now take an alternative route through Tanzania to the port of Tanga in Tanzania (Mail and Guardian Africa, 2016).

Landlocked countries like Burundi, Rwanda, South Sudan and Uganda face special risks since they rely on transit neighboring countries for trade (Faye et al., 2004). Other things being equal, these countries need the EAC more than

Kenya and Tanzania do. The new planned oil pipeline that would have linked the oil fields in western Uganda with the Lamu port in Kenya was of greater significance to Uganda than it was to Kenya. This is not to suggest that Kenya would not have benefited from the investment. However, Uganda would have been more vulnerable to any occurrences that would interfere with the use of the pipeline. South Sudan exemplifies that type of vulnerability with its reliance (so far) on Sudan to export its oil. The relations between South Sudan and Sudan cannot be compared with those between Kenya and Uganda, of course, but even neighborly countries can go through challenging times in their relationship.

An EAC political federation would put the proposed joint oil pipeline projects in a more stable and predictable political environment. Nonetheless, federations can collapse, as has happened with the Soviet Union (1922–1991), Yugoslavia (1922–1991), the Arab Federation of Iraq and Jordan (February–July 1958), the United Arab Republic political union of Egypt and Syria (1958–1961), and the West Indies Federation (1958–1962).[20] Countries alone can even break apart, as Ethiopia and Sudan have done.[21] Had the 2014 Scotland independence referendum gotten a majority "yes" vote, it would have ended Scotland's union with Wales and England as Great Britain. The European Union is not a political federation, yet very few could have predicted that the United Kingdom would have voted, in 2016, to leave the EU. Soon after the British exit (Brexit) result, Scotland, which voted against the United Kingdom leaving the EU, was talking about a new referendum to leave the United Kingdom (Hope, 2017). At the same time, Shetland islanders were talking about breaking away from Scotland, if Scotland left the United Kingdom (Mortimer, 2017).

No matter how promising the political situation looks at this point in EAC history, joint oil pipeline projects and other large interdependent projects must be safeguarded by sound, binding legal contracts that spell out the costs for any breach of contract. A friendly relationship between two presidents or even between the peoples of two countries is not sufficient to safeguard a long-term agreement. Political oral agreements are not sufficient in a court of law.

At the same time, while the economic benefits of harvesting natural resources may seem obvious, the EAC countries must conduct careful and transparent studies of the environmental impact of drilling and pipeline construction. The additional benefits must be weighed against additional costs to determine the most optimal pipeline route and adequate protections against leakage. In conducting environmental impact assessment, it is imperative to engage local communities, environmental groups, and other stakeholders. Winning the support of local communities and consultation with environmental groups would reduce the likelihood of sabotage of the project and may also preempt lawsuits that may hold the project back. In 2014, the East African Court of Justice (EACJ) ruled against Tanzania on its proposed highway across the Serengeti National Park. The case against that project was filed in 2010 by the African Network for Animal Welfare (ANAW), a non-profit organization based in Kenya (Ubwani, 2014).

It is well understood that the Europeans used the "divide and conquer" strategy in colonizing Africa. Therefore, it may seem obvious that the logical thing for African countries to do is to reverse what the colonialists did and unite. Moreover, "unity is strength." Yet what is often less appreciated is that African "nations" were not necessarily in harmony with each other before colonialism. In fact, in some areas it was the existing conflicts between tribes or ethnic groups that were used by the Europeans to take advantage of Africans. Efforts to establish a federation must, therefore, be carried out not with a false sense of nostalgia or as if African nations have an intrinsic propensity for unity. A federation should only be pursued if the value of unity – assuming the federation is done right – would be worth sacrificing some national sovereignty to the federal government. It would be naïve to assume that just because countries have good relations, they will make a viable federation. Two people can be good neighbors and good friends with each other for a long time, but rooming together may ruin their friendship.

A federation cannot be pursued as an experiment or something based on a desire to "undo" colonialism. One key question the EAC countries need to ask themselves is how committed they are to a federation. In other words, how binding should an agreement to establish a federation be? According to Article 145, 1 (a) of the EAC Treaty, a country "may withdraw from the Community provided [that] the National Assembly of the Partner State so resolves by resolution supported by not less than two-thirds majority of all the members entitled to vote" (East African Community, 2002, 116). Would this also apply to a country wanting to pull out of a federation? Notwithstanding what might be allowed by Article 145 of the EAC Treaty, could a country pull out of the federation following a referendum in that country when, for example, at least 51 percent of the voters wanted to secede? Would the federation go to war to try to prevent a state from seceding? These questions should be open for honest discussion; they must not be simply assumed away.

The EAC countries have made significant progress towards integration, but not enough to predict that a political federation at this point would be viable. The EAC countries must not move to become a political federation simply because the idea has been floating around for decades. Talking about it and even wanting it for a long time does not necessarily mean the prerequisites are in place for a viable federation. Maturity of democracy in each country is a prerequisite for the formation of a viable and sustainable East African federation. It provides a vitally important environment for an honest and open debate and a meaningful referendum on federalism. Moreover, the experience of some countries splitting up even after decades of being a country or federation is a sobering reminder that a political federation cannot be approached simply as "the next logical step" after a monetary union.

An East African federation cannot be an "arranged marriage" brought about by overzealous politicians. Such a union is likely, sooner or later, to break up. Yet that can be avoided if countries do not rush into it. What is needed at this point is for East African countries to continue to solidify their current level of economic integration, implement policies that increase the standard of living for all people, improve domestic governance with checks and balances, and develop genuine democracies at home. A federation might come later; there is no need to rush into it. Speed is not always a virtue. As the Swahili proverb states, "haraka, haraka haina baraka" – literally, "haste, haste has no blessing."

Notes

1. South Sudan joined the EAC in 2016. Given its newness as a country and its level of instability, it is on the periphery with regard to this much deeper level of integration. If and when an EAC political federation is formed, South Sudan will either be left behind or will simply be invited to tag along if it wants.
2. The Casablanca Group was comprised of the Algerian Provisional Government, Ghana, Guinea, Libya, Mali, Morocco, and the United Arab Republic (Egypt). The Monrovia Group was comprised of Cameroon, Central African Republic, Chad, Dahomey (Benin), Ethiopia, Gabon, Ivory Coast (Côte d'Ivoire), Liberia, Malagasy Republic, Niger, Nigeria, People's Republic of Congo, Senegal, Sierra Leone, Somalia, Togo, Tunisia, and Upper Volta (Burkina Faso). The Brazzaville Group, which was mainly comprised of former French colonies, consisted of Cameroon, Central African Republic, Chad, Dahomey (Benin), Gabon, Ivory Coast (Côte d'Ivoire), Madagascar, Mauritania, Niger, People's Republic of Congo, Senegal, and Upper Volta (Burkina Faso) (Nkrumah, 1963; Genge, Kornegay, and Rule, 2000). Note that many countries belonged to more than one group.

3. The OAU was established in 1963. It was succeeded by the African Union in 2002.
4. To its credit, however, in 2007, the AU denied President Omar Al-Bashir of Sudan the chairmanship of the AU because of the horrific atrocities that were taking place in Darfur. Also, in 2009, the AU suspended Madagascar's membership over a coup that forced an elected president out of office. The suspension was lifted in 2014 after a democratically elected leader took office. Likewise, the AU suspended Egypt in 2013 when the military ousted President Morsi. However, Egypt was allowed back into the AU in 2014 following Egypt's extensive diplomatic appeals.
5. Incidentally and sadly, as Schneider (2015) alludes to, Mugabe was chosen by default. He writes: "Mugabe was nearly the only viable candidate, elected almost by default. The chair rotates between the continent's five regions. This year it is the turn of Southern Africa. The majority of the region's leaders would be unable to serve as chair as they were so recently elected . . . Other candidates would have been unviable. For example, South Africa's Jacob Zuma is the ex-husband of Dlamini-Zuma [Chairperson of the African Union Commission], which rules him out, Botswana's Ian Khama's foreign policy – he is a supporter of the International Criminal Court (ICC) and rejected Zimbabwe's 2013 elections – is too maverick for the majority of AU member states, and King Mswati III of Swaziland has no electoral legitimacy as an absolute monarch."
6. Nigeria won Biafra back in 1970 after a brutal civil war.
7. On the question of whether President Kagame's authoritarian development model can be reconciled with democracy and human rights, see Friedman (2012).
8. In 2016, one individual was sentenced to three years in prison or a fine of 7 million shillings (equivalent to $3,200 at the time) for insulting the president (Gaffey, 2016). The government has also used The 1976 Newspapers Act, section 25 (1), to ban two radio stations and a few newspapers in a process that the Tanzania Editors Forum has described as the government being the complainant, the prosecutor, and the judge (Rwebangira, 2016; Mwananchi, 2016).
9. See an in-depth reflection by Zitto Kabwe, a Member of Parliament and the leader of one of the opposition parties in Tanzania, ACT-Wazalendo (Kabwe, 2016).
10. Even though Museveni had been in power since 1986, the first elections during his time in office were held in 1996.
11. The question that was asked was: "How much have you heard about the proposed federation of the East African States, that is, the formation of a unitary government for Kenya, Tanzania, Uganda, Rwanda and Burundi, with a joint army, parliament, presidency and economy?"
12. Here was the inquiry: "People have different ideas about how much integration of the economies and political systems of the East African States is the right amount. Some don't want any integration. Others support complete unification of the governments. Please tell me if you approve or disapprove of [the] formation of a unitary government, including having one East African President."
13. For an extended discussion about the land issue and for a strong appeal to Tanzania not to be part of an EAC political federation, see Mkali (2012). Mkali feels so fervent about this issue that he sent copies of his book to all Tanzanian members of parliament, including those who serve in the EAC Legislative Assembly.
14. For a critical discussion of this archaic system, see Shivji (1999).

15. In 2015, women leaders from 16 African countries met in Tanzania to strategize on ways to ensure women's right to own land. They decided to mobilize women from all over Africa to climb Mt. Kilimanjaro, the highest mountain in Africa, to raise awareness about land rights (Tanzania Gender Networking Program, 2015).
16. Oil rents are the difference between the value of crude oil and the cost of producing it. See Arezki and Brückner (2009) for the link between oil rents and corruption.
17. This example is taken from Mshomba (2010).
18. Purchasing power parity (PPP) takes into account countries' different relative costs of living.
19. President Magufuli of Tanzania, who came to power in October 2015, has declared war on corruption. Given his tenacity, Tanzania is on a positive trajectory with regard to corruption.
20. For the history of the Arab Federation of Iraq and Jordan and the United Arab Republic political union of Egypt and Syria, see Chaurasia (2005).
21. Eritrea split from Ethiopia in 1991, and South Sudan broke away from Sudan in 2011.

9

Aspirations for Continent-wide Integration

While regional economic blocs can be achievements in their own right, the African Union's aspiration is for continent-wide integration. The Abuja Treaty envisioned regional economic blocs as the building blocks of the African Economic Community, creating a continental economic and monetary union by 2028 (Organization of African Unity, 1991). Of the 17 regional economic blocs in Africa, the African Union (AU) considers eight of them to be pillars or official "building blocks" of the African Economic Community (UNCTAD, 2012b). They are:

CEN-SAD	Community of Sahel-Saharan States
COMESA	Common Market for Eastern and Southern Africa
EAC	East African Community
ECCAS	Economic Community of Central African States
ECOWAS	Economic Community of West African States
IGAD	Intergovernmental Authority on Development
SADC	Southern African Development Community
UMA	Arab Maghreb Union

All African countries belong to at least one of these regional groupings, with most belonging to two, as shown in Figure 9.1. Algeria, Botswana, Lesotho, Mozambique, Namibia, and South Africa belong to just one of the eight building blocks. Kenya and Rwanda belong to three. The rest of the countries belong to two.

Given the enormity of the African continent, the sheer number of countries, and the diversity among them, it is only logical that the path to a continental African Economic Community would be a step-by-step process of uniting the established blocs. The discussion in the preceding chapters shows the progress that has been made in establishing regional

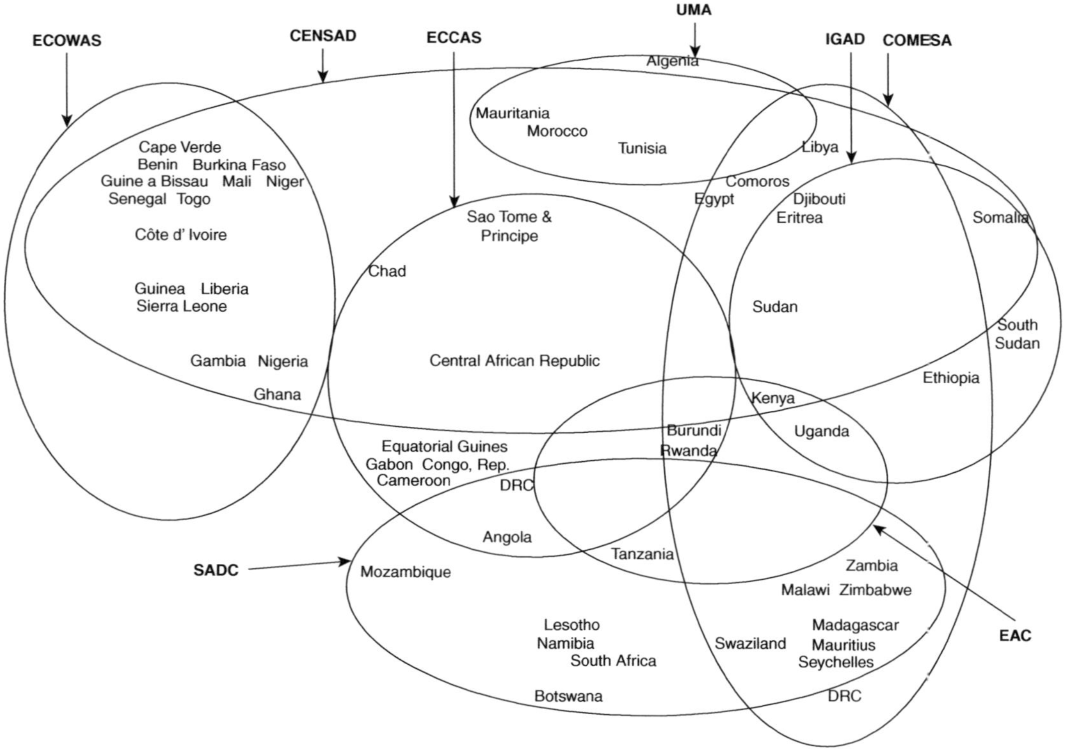

Figure 9.1 Eight Major Regional Economic Blocs in Africa
Note: South Sudan is also a member of the EAC. DRC (Democratic Republic of Congo) is listed at two different places in this figure.

groupings and also reveals the challenges and opportunities for regional economic integration in Africa. Given (a) how ambitious the EAC has been in its quest to deepen the level of integration of its members, (b) the dialogue between COMESA, the EAC, and SADC, ongoing since 2001, and (c) the overlap in membership in the three regional blocs, it was apparent that any union of the current regional groupings would start with them.

COMESA-EAC-SADC TRIPARTITE FREE TRADE AREA (CES-TFTA)

If one were simply to add the number of countries on the membership lists of COMESA, the EAC, and SADC, there would be a total of 40 countries.[1] However, due to overlapping membership, the actual number of individual countries is 27. A decision to develop a roadmap for a tripartite free trade area comprised of COMESA, the EAC, and SADC was reached in 2008 by the leaders of the member countries (COMESA, EAC, SADC, 2008). The CES-TFTA was launched in Egypt in June 2015 (ICTSD, 2015a, 2015b). The CES-TFTA will come into force after ratification by two-thirds of the CES-TFTA members.

The CES-TFTA could almost be described as a merger of not three but five large regional blocs. All members of the Southern African Customs Union (SACU) are members of SADC. Similarly, all members of IGAD are also members of COMESA, with the exception of Somalia and South Sudan (but South Sudan is a member of the EAC).[2]

Table 9.1 shows selected features of the CES-TFTA. Information for the CEN-SAD has been included to provide some casual comparison. As a reminder, because of the overlap in membership, the aggregate numbers for the CES-TFTA are not a horizontal summation of the numbers of the individual economic blocs. It should also be noted that there is an overlap between the CEN-SAD and the members of the CES-TFTA, as Figure 9.1 shows.

The CES-TFTA is the second largest economic bloc in Africa, in terms of the number of countries and economic size, as shown in Table 9.1. The largest bloc is the CEN-SAD. However, the CEN-SAD does not function as a true free trade area. The CEN-SAD members have done little to reduce barriers. Moreover, it has been relatively inactive since it lost its founder and primary supporter, President Gaddafi of Libya, in 2011.

Table 9.1 *Selected Features of the CES-TFTA and the CEN-SAD, 2013*

	CES-TFTA				CEN-SAD	Africa
	COMESA	EAC	SADC	Total		
Number of countries	19	6	15	27	29	54
GDP (millions of dollars)	657,220	131,998	658,381	1,222,916	1,318,178	2,356,378
Population (millions)	470	164	294	653	582	1,109
Area (square kilometers in thousands)	10,655	2,326	9,645	18,047	14,487	29,484

Source: World Bank (2014).

COMESA, the EAC, and SADC launched the CES-TFTA with the clear intention to liberalize trade. Actually, the delay in launching it was due in part to the fact that these three economic blocs were engaged in serious discussions to form a real free trade area. Their main objectives, as a Tripartite FTA, are:

- Harmonization and improvement of functionality of regional trading arrangements and programs, including establishing a Tripartite Free trade Area encompassing its 26 member countries – a major step towards establishment of the African Economic Community[3];
- Enhancement of trade facilitation to improve the flow of goods along regional transport corridors by lowering transit times and the cost of trading;
- Joint planning and implementation of infrastructure programs, which mainly involve surface (road, rail, border posts, seaports) and air transport, ICT, and energy; and
- Free movement of business persons within the Tripartite region (SADC, 2011).

Several factors support the efforts of the CES-TFTA to be a true free trade area. At the same time, some real challenges must be overcome before the CES-TFTA becomes a full-fledged free trade area. While the discussion in the following two sections is presented in the context of the CES-TFTA, it is applicable to the African continent as a whole.

FACTORS THAT SUPPORT THE EFFORTS OF THE CES-TFTA TO BE A FULL-FLEDGED FREE TRADE AREA

(a) The establishment of an African Economic Community is a stated goal of the African Union. The CES-TFTA was not only an aspiration of the three blocs but also of the whole African continent. As such, it is an endeavor that had, and will continue to have, the political and institutional support of the AU.

(b) The three economic blocs overlap each other. The fact that the leaders of these countries interact frequently with each other suggests they know each other well, an important element for deeper trade relations. When fully functional, the CES-TFTA will also provide welcome relief as a way to reduce some of the costly duplication of overlapping memberships. For example, some secretariat committees of the three regional blocs could be consolidated and thus reduce labor and operation costs.

(c) The Doha Round of the World Trade Organization (WTO), launched in 2001, is at an impasse and not many would be surprised if the Doha Round were officially declared dead. The lack of progress in multilateral negotiations under the auspices of the WTO has allowed countries ample diplomatic space to focus on economic integration (Hartman, 2013).

(d) The anti-trade sentiment that gained prevalence in the late 1990s as the WTO was trying to launch a round of negotiations has weakened. African countries, in general, have moved from their inward looking, centrally planned economies of the first three decades after independence to more liberalized economies, allowing freer trade and growth in the private sector.

(e) There seems to be an ongoing movement, involving even the strongest economies, to establish large free trade areas. The United States and 11 other countries have been negotiating the establishment of a free trade area to be called the Trans-Pacific Partnership (TPP), though the United States pulled out of the TPP deal in 2017, immediately after President Trump came to power. Likewise, China and 21 other countries are working to establish the Free Trade Area of the Asia-Pacific (FTAAP). One could say that enlargement of free trade areas is the current trend, notwithstanding the "British Exit" (Brexit) – the United Kingdom's decision in 2016 to leave the EU. Africa does not intend to be left behind. Needless to say, the EU has already shown what a large economic union can represent – economic and political strength. Both economies of scale and conventional gains from trade favor free trade interactions. Nonetheless, the CES-TFTA faces real challenges in becoming a full-fledged free trade area.

CHALLENGES FACED BY THE CES-TFTA IN BECOMING A FULL-FLEDGED FREE TRADE AREA

(a) The overlap between these three economic blocs has helped speed up the process to establish the CES-TFTA. However, it has also been a challenge. Countries need to determine what positions to take in which group. For example, Kenya's position may not be completely the same when it is negotiating as a member of the EAC as when it is negotiating as a member of COMESA. In some ways, it might have been easier if the membership of the three groups did not intersect. That way, each group would have its own clear position on various issues. They would bring a joint position to the table without the complexity of some members having to determine what position to take within each group.

It is important to acknowledge that even if these three economic blocs did not intersect, reaching a unified position on any particular issue in any given group is never an easy task. Member countries often have conflicting interests. The situation is complicated further by the fact that at the time the CES-TFTA was launched, some countries had not even ratified the free trade provision in their own groups. For example, while the Democratic Republic of Congo, Eritrea, Ethiopia, and Seychelles are signatory members of the COMESA Treaty (the first three being among the founding members of COMESA), as of June 2015, they were not yet members of the COMESA free trade area.[4] Uganda, also a founding member of COMESA, joined the COMESA free trade area only in March 2015 (Agritrade, 2014; Makonnen and Lulie, 2014; Zamfir, 2015). Three of fifteen SADC members – Angola, Democratic Republic of Congo, and Seychelles – are not yet in the SADC free trade area. Countries that were hesitant to join the free trade area in their own economic bloc are going to be even more apprehensive about ratifying the CES-TFTA.

(b) Related to the challenge noted in part (a) above, some members of the CES-TFTA belong to additional groups. Some of these groups, such as IGAD and SACU, are effectively within the CES-TFTA, while others, such as the CEN-SAD, ECCAS, and UMA, are not. Officially, SACU is not one of the eight building blocks, but its level of integration is deeper than that of SADC. This raises some questions. In the CES-TFTA, do SACU members, for example, negotiate as a group or as individual countries in SADC? Does it depend on the specifics of what is being negotiated? Apparently, countries can come to the negotiations under different coalitions or as individual countries, as they see fit, after weighing their interests, something that can delay reaching agreements in the CES-TFTA.

Part of what has complicated and prolonged the negotiations by COMESA, the EAC and SADC is that not only were the minimum requirements for a free trade area different, but member countries from the same regional blocs also made different tariff reduction offers. In fact, even at the launching of the CES-TFTA, some countries had not yet made any tariff reduction offers, as revealed by a media release by SADC just days before the launch of the CES-TFTA (SADC, 2015).

> Ministers reiterated the importance of making tariff offers and concluding related negotiations expeditiously. In this regard they decided that Member States that had not exchanged tariff offers do so within 6–12 months and those that have exchanged and are negotiating tariff offers should endeavor to conclude within 12 months.

Yet another complication has to do with IGAD. IGAD has eight members, seven of which are members of COMESA or the EAC and thus are members of the CES-TFTA. However, Somalia, an IGAD member that does not belong to either COMESA or the EAC, is left out. This weakens Somalia's membership in IGAD (which was weak to begin with, given its fragile government) as the other members of IGAD focus their attention on trade opportunities in the expanded market.

(c) Each economic bloc is dealing with its own challenges, especially regarding non-tariff barriers. None of the three regional blocs has a functioning dispute settlement mechanism. Outstanding disputes, whether they are due to arbitrary restrictions on trade, disagreement on the country of origin certification, the lack of uniform sanitary and phytosanitary certification procedures, or something else, will not disappear just because the CES-TFTA has been launched. In fact, unless those disputes are addressed effectively, they could be exacerbated in the CES-TFTA. The sheer number of countries in itself will create more disputes and might also intensify existing disputes, as countries jockey for position in the expanded free trade area.

(d) The diversity of the countries that formed the CES-TFTA may present another challenge. Seventeen of the 27 countries are categorized as least developed, not including Zimbabwe. Based on the criteria used by the United Nations, Zimbabwe would be a least developed country, as well (since the collapse of its economy in 2006–08), but it has declined to be labeled as such (United Nations, 2008). In multilateral negotiations, least developed countries usually form a coalition to lobby for preferential treatment and support. Examples include the LDC group in the WTO and the LDC Group at the climate change negotiations.

While the LDCs in the CES-TFTA may try to form a coalition (and they are a majority), the LDC identity may not necessarily gain them sympathy or special attention. Such attention is doubtful when it is African countries dealing with other African countries. These countries know each other well enough to understand that some of these LDCs have that status because of their own poor domestic policies and economic structures that excessively favor the rich.

Consider Angola and Kenya, for illustration. According to World Bank data, in 2015, their GDP per capita (PPP) was $7,371 and $3,083, respectively. If the GDP per capita was the only criterion for economic classification, Angola would be classified as an upper middle-income country and Kenya as a lower middle-income country. Yet when you consider the Human Development Index (HDI), a better measure of the standard of living than the GDP per capita by itself, Kenya is ranked higher than Angola.[5] The UN classifies Angola as a least developed country, but not Kenya.[6] In fact, Kenya is a lower middle-income country. Thus, although Angola can wave its LDC identity card in the WTO for special attention, it is highly unlikely any country in the CES-TFTA would see Angola as being worthy of any special treatment. One can also expect many divisions even among the LDCs themselves, given their economic disparity. In 2015, the gross national income per capita (PPP) ranged from $7,371 (Angola) to $736 (Burundi).

(e) Domestic challenges in some of the member countries are also a challenge to the CES-TFTA. Libya, for example, is embroiled in a civil war with no clear resolution in sight. Eritrea poses another challenge. Even though African leaders seem to have a high tolerance for dictators, the repressive regime of President Isaias Afewerki of Eritrea may find itself rejected at CES-TFTA and other regional meetings.

THE WAY FORWARD FOR THE CES-TFTA

The challenges described above are not insurmountable, although domestic challenges can be too complex to be handled at the regional level. They require solutions that are agreeable to all members. Regarding the overlap between the three economic blocs, countries that have membership in more than one group should be asked to choose one economic bloc from which they will be negotiating in the CES-TFTA. In other words, countries should not be given the opportunity to take two different positions as they try to protect their conflicting interests in different groups. The process should be similar to how African countries have negotiated (and are negotiating) Economic Partnership Agreements (EPAs) with the European Union (EU). As discussed in Chapter 1, African countries choose to negotiate with the EU from one of the regional economic blocs to which they belong. At the same time, in the CES-TFTA, countries should only negotiate from a given bloc (COMESA, the EAC, or SADC), but not as individual countries. Short of that, the CES-TFTA would not really be a union of three economic blocs, but rather 27 countries forming a free trade area.

Each group should be asked to resolve any internal disputes that might creep into the CES-TFTA. In addition, the CES-TFTA should endeavor to establish a dispute settlement authority that is autonomous and whose decisions are binding. When a trade dispute is not resolved through consultations, it is important that it to be resolved through a legal process rather than a political one, which is typically unpredictable. The EAC has an elaborate dispute settlement mechanism on paper, but it has not yet been put into operation.

APPLICATIONS FROM COUNTRIES WANTING TO JOIN THE EAC

While negotiations were underway to establish the CES-TFTA, three countries applied to join the EAC. These were Somalia, South Sudan, and Sudan. In addition, the Democratic Republic of Congo applied for observer status in the EAC, intending to apply for full membership in the future. While South Sudan's application did not look promising given its political instability, it was accepted into the EAC in 2016. None of the other countries have been accepted into or received official observer status in the EAC.

Sudan's application was quickly rejected on the grounds that it did not meet the "geographical proximity" criterion (East African Community, 2002, Article 3). This criterion requires that a country applying for membership share a border with a member of the EAC. Before South Sudan became an independent state, Sudan shared its southern border with Kenya and Uganda. When South Sudan split from Sudan, the latter no longer shared its border with any member of the EAC. In fact, Sudan sent its application to join the EAC just a few days before South Sudan became an independent state. The application was never taken seriously. Now that South Sudan is a member of the EAC, Sudan can no longer be rejected on the grounds that it does not meet the "geographical proximity" criterion. Nonetheless, the historic animosity between South Sudan and Sudan eliminates the possibility of Sudan being accepted into the EAC in the foreseeable future.

It is interesting that South Sudan applied to join the EAC just a few months after its independence in 2011, before it conducted any preliminary studies to determine what the implications of joining the EAC would be. Such is the approach to regional economic integration by some countries. While some members of the EAC were eager to offer South Sudan full membership, others were hesitant. Initially, it was decided to wait until South Sudan met the prerequisites for membership. High up among the prerequisites is "adherence to universally acceptable principles of good governance, democracy, the rule of law, observance of human rights and social justice" (East African Community, 2002, Article 3). The civil war that broke out in South Sudan in 2013 severely weakened the government to the point that, as of 2015, talking about good governance with respect to South Sudan would have been disingenuous. There was hardly any real, functioning government. Although South Sudan received juridical statehood when it gained independence on July 9, 2011, it has been struggling to achieve empirical statehood.[7]

Nonetheless, considering the strong alliance between President Museveni of Uganda and the government of South Sudan, it appeared from the very beginning that South Sudan was not going to be kept waiting too long before it was welcomed into the EAC as a member. Moreover, "good governance" is an elastic term that can be stretched, twisted, and bent to fit one's interpretation.

The UN describes good governance as one that is "participatory, consensus oriented, accountable, transparent, responsive, effective and efficient, equitable and inclusive, and follows the rule of law. It assures that corruption is minimized, the views of minorities are taken into account and that the voices of the most vulnerable in society are heard in decision-making. It is also responsive to the present and future needs of society" (United Nations Economic and Social Commission for Asia and the Pacific, n. d.).

If this description of good governance is to be applied with sincerity, not only will all the current applicants be waiting for a long time, but the EAC itself would have to question the qualifications of some of its current members, Burundi in particular. Burundi was accepted into the EAC in 2007 when that country was relatively stable and its future looked promising. Given the current situation, that outlook has proven to be too optimistic. It is unlikely that the Burundi of 2016 would have been admitted into the EAC if the "good governance" criterion were enforced. This is one dilemma of the EAC. How can Burundi, for example, say that South Sudan or the Democratic Republic of Congo, for instance, does not qualify for membership in the EAC because of a lack of good governance? That would be hypocritical.

The EAC has so far been careful not to rush into accepting new members and can now only hope that accepting South Sudan was not a big mistake. It should continue to take a cautious approach, especially since it does not have a road map regarding how to help these applicants end their internal conflicts and establish good governance. Moreover, if the CES-TFTA functions as a genuine free trade area, there was no immediate reason for South Sudan to join the EAC. South Sudan should have applied to join COMESA, where it only needed to meet the requirements for a free trade area. Likewise, there is no immediate reason for the three other countries – Democratic Republic of Congo, Somalia, and Sudan – to join the EAC. Somalia should apply to COMESA and thus become a member of the CES-TFTA. Democratic Republic of Congo and Sudan are already members of the CES-TFTA through their membership in SADC and/or COMESA. As members of the CES-TFTA, these aspirants can enjoy the privileges of a free trade area with the EAC members, without directly being EAC members.

THE ROLE OF THE AFRICAN UNION IN CREATING A CONTINENT-WIDE FREE TRADE AREA

The launching of the CES-TFTA in June 2015 was a significant boost to the AU's aspiration to form a continental free trade area. As discussed in Chapter 1, the AU envisions the regional economic communities as building blocks for the African Economic Community, to create a Continental Free Trade Area (CFTA) by 2017 and a continental economic and monetary union by 2028. Needless to say, these target dates will be missed and new ones will be set. Most of these target dates are set at euphoric moments when leaders tend to put their own misgivings aside and appear oblivious to the challenges ahead.

Nonetheless, in the context of multilateral negotiations, missing a target date may not be that critical. In fact, as unrealistic as a target date might be, it can still serve an important function. It can provide a precise "review moment" when those who set it are obliged to come together to assess the progress they have made and, if needed, as is often the case, set a new target date. A target date can also provide some basis on which to hold accountable the institutions and government agencies that have been given the responsibility for implementation. In addition, a target date can provide a forecast that can help investors plan better for the future.

A major challenge for the AU is that while it sets target dates based on the aspirations of its members, it does not have the resources or the power needed to direct the course of action of any individual economic bloc. The AU is more like a cheerleader than someone who orchestrates change. If African countries want the AU to play an important role in directing individual blocs to broader and deeper integration, the AU must be empowered with financial resources and a mandate to set guidelines and frameworks for regional economic integration.

The AU has never been short of ideas or ambition. However, it has always been short of financial resources. For example, the AU budget for 2015 was only $522 million, a meager 0.02 percent of Africa's GDP or $0.47 per capita.[8] Worse still, the AU cannot even raise that amount on its own. African leaders have always talked about the need for financial independence (i.e., self-reliance), but even the AU itself, the greatest symbol of Africa's unity, is highly dependent on international donors (often referred to as partners). The AU depends on foreign funding for 60–70 percent of its budget (Southern Africa Foreign Policy Initiative, 2015), even when African leaders themselves find it embarrassing to do so. The AU has proposed taxes on plane tickets, hotel accommodations, and text messaging as sources of revenues, so it can be financially independent (Lebhour, 2015; Mwiti, 2015). Whether such proposals should be approved or not is beside the point. It is astounding that a group of 54 leaders of independent countries who are good at "bashing" Western donors are not able to finance a budget of $522 million. Is it really a question of ability or willingness? For the AU to exercise a meaningful, independent role in steering countries and regional economic blocs into a continent-wide free trade area, it needs financial resources from within Africa. For an endeavor principally grounded in self-determination, African countries should have ownership – responsibility for both the costs and direction of economic integration in Africa. This is compromised by dependence on foreign donors.

The AU also needs a mandate to establish certain guidelines with respect to economic integration. For example, considering that the ultimate objective is to have a continental economic and monetary union, the AU should set a maximum number of individual blocs that a country may join. As it is now, for a group like the CEN-SAD, all a country needs to do to join is to send an application. It will automatically be welcomed, regardless of its economic or political conditions.

The AU should also establish the minimum requirements of openness and operations for an economic bloc to be officially considered a free trade area, a customs union, a common market, or a monetary union. If the labels for these phases of integration were used with a common meaning, it would be easier, for example, for two free trade areas that want to merge to do so. They would all have a clear understanding of what the minimum threshold is. Part of what has complicated and prolonged the negotiations by COMESA, the EAC, and SADC to form the CES-TFTA is that their baselines for a free trade area have been different.

Even with the launching of the CES-TFTA, it is still hard to predict the path through which African countries may achieve a continent-wide free trade area. However, given the configuration of the current economic blocs, if, and this is a big if, the CEN-SAD were to become a genuine free trade area, it would be a major step towards continental free trade. The CEN-SAD and the CES-TFTA include all African countries except five – Algeria, Cameroon, Equatorial Guinea, Gabon, and the Republic of Congo. These five countries could apply to join the CEN-SAD. With institutional support from the AU, ECOWAS could play a leadership role in helping the CEN-SAD become a free trade area. Then when the CEN-SAD and the CES-TFTA unite, the whole African continent would be a free trade area. The AU can help facilitate discussions between the CEN-SAD and the CES-TFTA.

Another area in which the AU could play a direct role is with respect to dispute settlement. What is missing in regional economic blocs in Africa is an effective mechanism to resolve disputes and enforce the implementation of agreements. It is partly due to the lack of such a mechanism that countries often make big "commitments" when they have no intention to fulfill them. A reliable mechanism to resolve disputes and enforce commitments would eliminate that cavalier attitude. One can see how countries have become much more careful and deliberate in their negotiations in the WTO, compared to when they were negotiating in GATT. Compared to GATT, the WTO has a strong adjudicatory process to handle trade disputes.[9]

The AU should provide leadership in guiding the establishment of dispute settlement processes in regional economic blocs. It should establish a process to be used as a template for all regional groups; a standardized system would allow a seamless transition in resolving trade disputes when two or more regional blocs decide to unite. This does not mean the AU would need to reinvent the wheel. The Dispute Settlement Understanding (DSU) in the WTO provides a blueprint that could be modified to fit regional economic blocs in Africa. That is what the EAC did in crafting its dispute settlement process, although it has not yet been put into operation.

The AU should also support studies on economic integration by institutions such as the African Economic Research Consortium (AERC), the Economic Commission for Africa (ECA), and African regional blocs. It is imperative that steps towards deeper and broader integration are guided by careful multidisciplinary studies that consider both the short-term and long-term implications of each step.

One can understand that using regional economic groups as building blocks for a continent-wide free trade area is the most logical and practical way to proceed. However, the AU should explore specific areas of free trade that can be promoted on a continental level, even before a continent-wide free trade area is established. For example, the AU should carefully evaluate some countries' practice of banning exports of agricultural food products even to their neighbors. If the findings warrant it, the AU could require unhindered exports of agricultural products within Africa.

Thus, the AU should facilitate discussions that can produce broad-based decisions that would apply to all regional blocs. This does not suggest that the AU should override the decisions made by individual economic blocs. The AU's role is complementary. The AU and regional economic blocs should "feed off" each other. The strength of the AU depends on the strength of regional economic blocs and vice versa.

THE LEADERSHIP CHALLENGE

As of 2016, 15 of the 54 African leaders had been in power since before the turn of the 21st century.[10] Regional and continent-wide development strategies and initiatives developed by African leaders are often taken lightly or with disdain because the leaders who are developing them (who are also the messengers) lack credibility. Autocrats espousing African unity are quickly dismissed because they come across as power mongers or leaders seeking a diversion away from discontent at home.

It is important to point out that some African countries have leaders who are highly regarded – leaders who respect democracy and the people they serve. However, when African leaders are together in one conference hall, there are enough "bad apples" to make one question the sincerity of what comes out of their "collective" mouths. In fact, one must feel sorry for those African leaders who respect democracy; they sit at the same table with autocratic leaders and discuss, for example, a path towards a "United States of Africa," a vision that, to be authentic, must be grounded in true democracy. No wonder some presidents say very little about the AU meetings when they return to their countries. They seem to want to forget the experience as soon as possible.

If African countries think they can unite simply because they are African, a "United States of Africa" will remain wishful thinking. Likewise, if they think they can unite simply by talking about the ills of colonialism and neocolonialism, they are deceiving themselves. Yet that is the standard rhetoric from the AU, as exemplified by the words of President Nguema of Equatorial Guinea when opening the 23rd AU Summit in 2014, hosted by his country.

> Africa now has 50 years of independence, so we do not need to suffer neo-colonialism and perpetuate it. We have adopted measures that have led to the stagnation of parity of our currencies . . . Africa cannot be content to continue with the current dependence on the economies of the developed world. Africa is sailing upstream against a dependency that prevents them from moving toward sustainable development. Africa should rethink its relationship with the developed world to reduce as far as possible the gap that prevents access to development." (Azikiwe, 2014)

Note that Equatorial Guinea is among the most corrupt countries in the world. Nguema is a dictator who has been in power since 1979. However, it seems that as long as someone is willing to foot the bill, an AU summit can be hosted by anyone and can be assured of praise and applause from guests.[11]

The ills of colonialism are well known and the threat of neocolonialism, while often exaggerated, is real. However, "bashing" the West, even when it is justified, is not going to be sufficient to unify Africa. Autocratic African leaders only appear hypocritical when criticizing colonial rule. In fact, having autocrats and dictators as the spokespeople for African unity, drains the energy from those who are legitimately sincere about a united Africa. One hopes that the day will come when African countries that respect democracy will have the courage to form their own coalition within the AU. The unification of Africa, if it is to happen, will require that some countries be left behind and helped to catch up, if they so wish. There is no way of avoiding such a path, unless it is silently accepted that no one is really serious about creating a unified Africa.

A DISCONNECT IN THE DEBATE OVER REGIONAL ECONOMIC INTEGRATION IN AFRICA

To conclude this chapter, it is important to note a disconnect in the debate over regional economic integration in Africa. Even though regional economic integration is a regular topic at AU and regional conferences, the topic does not receive much attention in local or national politics. Parliamentary and even presidential candidates often face off without any mention of aspirations for economic integration. Politicians act as if the benefits of economic integration are either so obvious or the impact so far removed from their constituencies that it does not require much discussion. Whatever the case, they see no real need to discuss economic integration at political rallies.

In 1996, the parliament of Tanzania unanimously accepted the re-establishment of economic cooperation between Kenya, Tanzania, and Uganda. When the author spoke later with some members of parliament about specific potential effects of such cooperation on their constituencies, it was apparent that they had not given it much thought.

One must wonder how many members of parliament in COMESA, the EAC, and SADC countries have actually thought, for example, about the potential impact of the CES-TFTA on agricultural production or other economic activities in their constituencies. The debates over economic integration seem to be confined to secretariat headquarters. Since the specifics of the agreements are usually not readily available, lawmakers are not even fully aware of what is being negotiated, except in some very general terms, when they care to find out. Therefore, countries do not prepare contingency plans for massive displacements that might occur in certain sectors or in certain geographical areas. Likewise, they fail to prepare in time to take advantage of new trade opportunities.

Developed countries have various programs to assist workers who are displaced by major trade agreements. For example, even the few workers in the United States who were displaced by the production shifts due to the African Growth and Opportunity Act (AGOA) were eligible for trade-adjustment assistance. Trade-adjustment assistance includes unemployment compensation, retraining, job-search support, relocation allowance, and small business startup assistance. Most African countries are not in any position to provide these services. However, by just being aware of the displacement of workers that would occur in certain sectors, countries can negotiate for adequate transitional periods. Likewise, to take full advantage of the new markets, vocational training programs may need to be more tailored to meet the needs of the new markets. Yet, there seems to be a very casual, "wait and see" approach towards integration that has allowed leaders to make unrealistic proposals.

For example, a far-reaching suggestion (some would consider it radical) such as forming a United States of Africa is tossed around by AU leaders at their summit as if they have already discussed it with their own people. One must wonder if these leaders have even been given a mandate by their people to discuss such an idea. Even more perplexing, African leaders have not explained to their people what that suggestion actually means.

In other countries, before trade agreements are voted on, it is common to have heated debates about them, let alone about higher levels of integration. Lawmakers, associations of producers and consumers, labor unions, environmental groups, and other organizations engage fully in discussions to push the outcome one way or the other. For example, the proposal to establish the North American Free Trade Area (NAFTA) was hotly debated for many months by various stakeholders in Canada, Mexico, and the United States, before it was established in 1994. The strong sentiments and divisions that were expressed and experienced regarding NAFTA resurfaced in the United States in 2015 and 2016 as politicians were debating the proposed Trans Pacific Partnership (TPP), leaving its future uncertain. The objective here is not to discuss the US debate about trade, but rather to point out that, in other countries, lawmakers and various stakeholders become fully engaged in debating proposals for trade agreements. Going back to the CES-TFTA, the hope is that lawmakers in each country will try to be well informed before voting to ratify or reject it.

The decision to join an economic bloc or unite economic blocs must be well informed and made through a democratic process. Otherwise, the implementation phase will, inevitably, be problematic. As suggested by the discussion in Chapters 5 and 6, there is a wide gap between what countries agree to do and what they actually end up doing. That happens partly because in the negotiations phase, countries do not go into the "nitty-gritty" aspects of the agreements. Countries "commit" to a schedule to remove trade barriers either without any real intention of doing so or before evaluating the impact of such reductions.

The intra-group imports for some countries are less than 10 percent of their total imports, yet they claim that reducing tariffs on intra-regional trade would have a severe impact on their government revenue. That was one of the excuses given by COMESA and ECOWAS countries for failing to bring tariffs down to the scheduled levels for years. Even if this excuse were valid, it would still leave one wondering why the revenue problem was not anticipated before the agreement was reached.

In 2012, two years after the establishment of the EAC Common Market, Tanzania increased work permit fees by 33 percent for workers from the other EAC states (Omondi, 2012). Responding to complaints and pressure from other member countries, Tanzania explained that "it will not rush to waive work permit fees for East Africans seeking jobs in Tanzania because such a move not only needs legal review but also a thorough assessment of its advantages and disadvantages" (Kisanga, 2013). It is quite reasonable that such a policy change calls for careful analysis of its potential impact on domestic employment. However, Tanzania should have conducted a preliminary assessment of the "advantages and disadvantages" of work permit fees before it committed itself to a common market agreement. Agreements that are reached prematurely lead to poor and haphazard implementation with costly implications. African countries are not under any particular external pressure to rush into any agreements – they should carefully consider the implications of agreements before committing to them.

Notes

1. Madagascar was suspended from COMESA in 2009, but was welcomed back in 2014.
2. Although Sudan is a founding member of COMESA, South Sudan (which separated from Sudan in 2011) is not yet an official member of COMESA (The Upper Nile Times, 2015).
3. South Sudan joined the EAC in 2016, thus bringing the number of countries in the CES-TFTA to 27.
4. The Democratic Republic of Congo and Ethiopia are expected to join the COMESA free trade area in the near future.
5. HDI is calculated based on life expectancy, the average number of years of formal schooling, and the GDP per capita. In 2013, Kenya and Angola were ranked 147th and 149th, respectively, in the HDI rankings (UNDP, 2014).
6. The UN uses three criteria to determine whether a country is an LDC or not: income per capita, the human assets index (nutrition, mortality rate for children, access to secondary education, and adult literacy), and the economic vulnerability index.
7. Juridical statehood implies being recognized by the international community as a state. Being a member of the UN is the most obvious way of demonstrating juridical statehood. Empirical statehood implies having a stable and effective

government that can promote development and exercise authority over its territory (Jackson and Rosberg, 1985). For example, Iraq, Somalia, South Sudan, and Syria (to mention just a few countries) currently have juridical statehood but not empirical statehood.

8. From that budget, $143 million was for operational costs and $379 million was for various programs.
9. GATT was established in 1947 and became operational in 1948. It was replaced by the WTO in 1995. The Dispute Settlement Understanding (DSU) of the WTO Agreement represents a major difference between the WTO and GATT. Under GATT, dispute settlements were processed primarily through diplomatic channels, instead of using GATT's adjudicatory process. The dispute mechanism under GATT was limited because each and every stage of the dispute settlement process required a positive consensus. It meant that the process could be delayed or blocked by a respondent or a losing party.
10. The numbers in parentheses are the number of years these leaders have been in power consecutively as of 2016:

    Algeria, Abdelaziz Bouteflika (17); Angola, José Eduardo dos Santos (37); Cameroon, Paul Biya (34); Chad, Idriss Déby (26); Congo (Republic), Denis Sassou Nguesso (19); Djibouti, Ismaïl Omar Guelleh (17); Equatorial Guinea, Teodoro Obiang Nguema Mbasogo (37); Eritrea, Isaias Afewerki (23); Gambia, Yahya Jammeh (22); Lesotho, Letsie III (20); Morocco, Mohammed VI (17); Sudan, Omar al-Bashir (27); Swaziland, King Mswati III (30); Uganda, Yoweri Museveni (30); and Zimbabwe, Robert Mugabe (36).
11. Incidentally, the CES-TFTA was launched in Egypt, a country that in 2013 was suspended from the AU for a year. Egypt was accused of ousting its first democratically elected president, Mohamed Morsi. Egypt was allowed back into the AU in 2014, even though Morsi remained in jail and, just three weeks before the launching of the CES-TFTA, was given a death sentence. At the launching of the CES-TFTA, the d-word (democracy) was very carefully avoided. Note the point here is not to make any judgment about what should have happened to Morsi, but rather to highlight how democracy is often taken lightly or not respected at all.

10

Conclusion

This book has examined efforts by African countries to integrate their economies. The focus has been on the East African Community (EAC), which is currently the most ambitious regional bloc in Africa. Since many benefits are associated with regional economic blocs and these blocs do not violate World Trade Organization (WTO) principles, African countries can and should continue their efforts to integrate.

To elaborate on the WTO principles, one of the core concepts is what is called the *most favored nation* (MFN) principle. This principle prevents WTO members from implementing trade policies that favor some members and discriminate against others. There are two exceptions to this principle. One is an Enabling Clause that allows "developed countries to 'accord differential and more favourable treatment to developing countries, without according such treatment to other contracting parties'" (OECD, 1983: 15). A program called the Generalized System of Preferences (GSP) is based on this exception. While there is the possibility of developed countries using the GSP program discriminatorily, this exception has not caused much debate. The other exception to the MFN principle is made by GATT Article XXIV for free trade areas and other levels of economic integration; the formation of regional economic blocs is permitted under this exception.

Allowing the establishment of economic blocs raises the perennial question as to whether the proliferation of regionalism complements or hurts the multilateralism to which the WTO aspires. On the one hand, allowing the establishment of economic blocs can lead to multilateral reductions of trade barriers (applying to all WTO members) as each bloc becomes more open. On the other hand, when most of a country's major trading partners are within various economic blocs to which it belongs, it may have a casual attitude towards negotiations in the WTO. In other words, economic blocs may render the WTO less important. The failure of the WTO to conclude the Doha Round of negotiations launched in 2001 has added to the proliferation of economic blocs, although the cause and effect is not that straightforward. The stalemate in the WTO and the proliferation of economic blocs feed into each other such that they are both the cause and effect of each other, notwithstanding other factors.[1] That said, the WTO and economic blocs will continue to coexist in the foreseeable future.

The quest for regional economic integration in Africa is not a fad that will somehow fade away with time. It is an effort that has been sustained since African countries were fighting for independence. African leaders have been consistent in their calls to unify and strengthen African countries and devise collective actions to bring social and economic development to the African people. Although actions on the ground have not in fact matched the political rhetoric, steps are still being taken here and there to integrate the economies of African countries.

While the ills of colonialism could never be justified by the incidental benefits, the colonial administration did leave Kenya, Tanzania (then Tanganyika), and Uganda joint institutions with which to integrate their economies. The first EAC was built on the foundation of colonial era institutions. In the end, the first EAC collapsed for a number of reasons: real and perceived unequal distribution of the benefits of integration (with Kenya ostensibly getting the lion's share of it), external factors such as the skyrocketing oil prices of the early 1970s, the instability caused by Ugandan dictator Idi Amin, and ideological differences, particularly between Kenya and Tanzania.

Still, the EAC was resurrected and came back with tremendous energy. The EAC is the most ambitious of all regional economic blocs in Africa at this point in history. The protocols to establish an EAC customs union and an EAC common market came into force in 2005 and 2015, respectively. The EAC is planning to have a monetary union by 2023, with the ultimate goal of establishing a political federation. The EAC has clearly made tremendous progress in the last 15 years in reducing trade barriers on intra-regional trade. It has also expanded to include Burundi and Rwanda in 2007 and South Sudan in 2016. In addition, it has joined with COMESA and SADC to form the CES-TFTA.

Nonetheless, as the discussion in this book has shown, major gaps exist between what the EAC countries have agreed to do and what they have actually done. Considering the prevalence of non-tariff barriers, one can even say that the EAC has often taken a few steps backward after taking some steps forward.

The optimism that one might feel in forecasting the trajectory of the EAC's level of integration is tempered by the fact that there is a backlog of agreements that have not yet been fully implemented. The gaps between what was agreed upon and what has actually been done weaken the foundation on which a political federation may be built. It is important for the EAC and all other regional economic blocs to identify current gaps and form a reasonable plan to address them. The gaps are a result of overcommitment or hasty commitments by the member countries. Some of the gaps should be eliminated by revisiting and revising the agreements that created them. It seems, for example, that the EAC may need to go back to the drawing board regarding some elements of the common market, especially the process for acquiring work permits.

The EAC countries are approaching the establishment of a monetary union with the explicit understanding that it requires considerable preparation, including meeting the macroeconomic convergence criteria to which they agreed. Whether the criteria and the ten-year period for the convergence process are optimal depends on many factors, including the level of commitment of the member countries. However, some challenges experienced in implementing the agreements related to the customs union and common market could have been preempted, had the EAC countries agreed upon convergence criteria for those levels of integration as well. For example, one criterion for the establishment of a common market should have been that each country issue identification cards.

Economic integration is not a race to be won simply by crossing the finish line (that is, establishing a political federation). One can cross the finish line but collapse immediately thereafter due to poor health and exhaustion. The Arab Federation of Iraq and Jordan "breathed" for only six months; it lasted from February to July 1958. The United Arab Republic that united Egypt and Syria existed for three years, from 1958 to 1961. The West Indies Federation survived for four years, from 1958 to 1962.

Of course, the idea for an East African federation has been considered on and off for almost a century, so it may not be fair to accuse the EAC of rushing. Nonetheless, readiness is not determined by how long an idea has been floating around. An important criterion for a viable federation is maturity in democracy – demonstrated respect for human rights, free and fair elections, respect for free speech, respect for a country's constitution, and separation of power between the branches of government. Such maturity provides a vitally important environment for an honest and open debate and a meaningful referendum on federalism. The EAC has not reached such maturity yet. As such, it must exercise the utmost caution in its ambition to become a political federation.

The speed of integration, both on paper and in practice, has relied too much on the personalities of the leaders. For whatever reasons, in 2013–2015, Kenya, Rwanda, and Uganda seemed to have wanted a faster pace towards integration and appeared impatient with Burundi and Tanzania. The leaders of Kenya, Rwanda, and Uganda came to be known, euphemistically, as the "coalition of the willing" (*The Citizen*, 2014). Still, it was an ad hoc coalition, without strong roots to hold it steady. The dynamics of that leadership changed when President Magufuli of Tanzania came to power in 2015. His leadership style matches that of Presidents Kagame and Museveni of Rwanda and Uganda, respectively, and he quickly established a close working relationship with them. In fact, some commentators have wondered whether Magufuli would be the region's next Kagame (DeFreese, 2016). As of August 2016, Magufuli had made only one trip outside of the country, and it was to Rwanda. That visit in April of 2016 and Kagame's visit to Tanzania three months later thawed the cold relationship that existed between Rwanda and Tanzania prior to Magufuli coming to power (Odhiambo, 2016).

In many ways, the decision by Uganda to change its initial deal with Kenya and reroute a proposed oil pipeline to go through Tanzania (instead of Kenya) was based on a cost-benefit analysis. However, the decision and apparent quickness with which it was made, also signal a good rapport between Magufuli and Museveni.

As the number of countries in the EAC has doubled from only three in 2007 to six in 2016, it has become important that the EAC uses, explicitly, the principle of "variable geometry" stated in Article 7(1)(e) of the EAC Treaty. This principle "allows for the progression in co-operation among groups within the Community for wider integration schemes in various fields and different speeds" (East African Community, 2002, 15). The EAC includes countries that are politically stable and ones that are (at least currently) marred by civil wars and political instability. On closer look, one will also see that the EAC countries vary widely in their institutional capacities and economic levels and stability. Needless to say, as demonstrated by the informal "coalition of the willing," at times some countries may want to move faster than others on a given area of integration.

If used constructively, the principle of variable geometry can preempt tension that might otherwise occur between those countries that feel held back and those that feel rushed. The principle of variable geometry should be used to encourage those countries that are ahead to help pull up those lagging behind. In other words, the principle of variable geometry must not become an opportunity to form a "clique" of nations within the EAC. Open dialogue among all members must be maintained.

Rather than granting South Sudan full membership into the EAC, the principle of variable geometry should have been applied to give South Sudan observer status. As one of this book reviewer remarked, that should be the approach used by the EAC for all countries applying to join the EAC. That is, before acceptance with full membership, a country applying to join the EAC should first be granted observer status. That would allow the EAC to focus on the prospective member country as it relates to a smaller set of programs and projects while the EAC assesses closely the preparedness of that country to become a full member.

The EAC accepted South Sudan too soon, considering that South Sudan had not yet achieved juridical statehood. Moreover, the EAC had neither a clear plan nor the means to help ensure political stability in South Sudan. The three-year transition period granted to South Sudan before it meets the requirements for a customs union is of no significance for a country with very poor public sector institutions.

Notwithstanding the challenges the EAC faces and the misgivings about its willingness to implement all of its commitments on time, the EAC has taken a number of steps towards integration in a rather short period of time. The EAC countries must be given credit for their resilience – for their ability to regroup and deepen their relationships after the ugly and bitter breakup of the first EAC. The EAC countries are open to each other now with regard to the trade of goods and services and the movement of people, much more so than they were in the 1990s. In that respect, the leaders of these countries must be commended for their overall commitment to regional integration. Of course, for the long-term stability of any advancement, major decisions, such as admitting new members or deepening the level of integration, must be made using fully inclusive democratic processes.

The EAC is operating in an economic and political environment that is more stable than the one that existed in the 1970s when the first EAC collapsed. Economic policies of EAC countries are essentially aligned with each other, the benefits of trade are not nearly as skewed in favor of one country as they were then, and the political environment, while not fully democratic in all countries, is significantly more open. With the multiparty system, even in those countries where the opposition parties are not accorded full constitutional rights, leaders are more accountable today than they were during the era of the one-party system. The likelihood of another Idi Amin in the EAC has been greatly reduced, if not eliminated. Given its current drive, the EAC has the potential to play a leadership role in moving the African continent as a whole towards greater integration, beginning with an active role in the CES-TFTA.

The launching of the CES-TFTA ushers in the hope that a continent-wide free trade area is on the horizon. But even if and when an authentic continent-wide free trade area is achieved, the identity of individual regional blocs will remain important. No matter how inclusive a continent-wide free trade area becomes, it will not be as cohesive as the individual regional groups can be. Opportunities can always be taken advantage of, and challenges handled, more effectively at the regional level than at the continent-wide level. For example, infrastructure projects can be navigated more efficiently at the regional level by the countries that will benefit directly from such projects.

The establishment of a continent-wide free trade area or an even higher level of integration is not going to eliminate conflicts in Africa. In general, conflicts are handled better at the regional level, of course, with support from the AU. Countries neighboring those with conflicts have more at stake, such as an influx of refugees and, therefore, are more determined and better positioned to help find a solution. In addition, those neighboring countries have more leverage in warning a country in its own bloc that is not "behaving" properly.

Regarding forming an "AU government" and creating the United States of Africa, it should not be expected anytime soon or even anytime at all. There are many reasons for this pessimistic outlook, but the key one is how African leaders have approached integration all along. They have focused almost solely on its impact on trade. Indeed, it is in trade that one can expect to see the immediate results of integration, but the discussion regarding integration must go beyond trade and capital flows, if African countries want to help and push each other to build governments that respect democracy and give an AU government a chance to materialize.

The conditions for integration have been framed purely in economic terms, with "good governance" mentioned more or less as an afterthought or as a cliché. All regional economic groups have annexes with detailed tariff reduction commitments, but none provide a threshold for "good governance." No one should deny any country the prerogative to have the form of government it wishes. However, for the term "good governance" to have any relevance, members of a regional group, and the AU as a whole, should have some explicit description of the minimum requirements for good governance and adhere to them. With good governance, regional economic integration can grow and expand to continent-wide integration. Given its dynamism and ambition, the EAC can play an important role in that integration.

Note

1. For a good discussion on multilateralism (implying actions by all WTO members) and regionalism, see Baldwin and Low (2009).

Bibliography

Acheson-Brown, Daniel (2001), "The Tanzanian Invasion of Uganda: A Just War?," *International Third World Studies Journal and Review*, 12, 1–11.

Ackello-Ogutu, C. and P.N. Echessah (1998), *Unrecorded Cross-Border Trade Between Tanzania and Her Neighbors: Implications for Food Security*. Washington, DC: U.S. Agency for International Development. www.afr-sd.org/publications/89tanztrade.pdf.

Adam, Christopher (2014), "Exchange Rate Arrangements in the Transition to East African Monetary Union." In Drummond, Paulo, et al. (editors), *The Quest for Regional Integration in the East African Community*, 159–197. Washington, DC: IMF.

African Development Bank Group (2013), *South Sudan: A Study on Competitiveness and Cross Border Trade with Neighbouring Countries*. Abidjan: African Development Bank Group.

African Development Bank Group (2015), *African Economic Outlook*. Abidjan: African Development Bank Group.

African Network on Debt and Development, et al. (2007), *Towards a People-Driven African Union: Current Obstacles and New Opportunities*. Harare: African Network on Debt and Development, et al.

African Trade Policy Centre (2007), *EPA Negotiations: African Countries Continental Review*. Addis Ababa: African Trade Policy Centre.

African Union (1999), *Fourth Extraordinary Session of the Assembly of Heads of State and Government: Sirte Declaration*. EAHG/Draft/Decl. (IV) Rev.1, September 8–9. Addis Ababa: African Union.

African Union (2006), *An AU Government: Towards the United States of Africa*. Addis Ababa: African Union.

Afrobarometer (2008), *Summary of Results of Round 4 Afrobarometer Survey in Kenya, 2008*. www.afrobarometer.org/files/documents/summary_results/ken_r4_sor.pdf.

Afrobarometer (2008a), *Summary of Results of Round 4 Afrobarometer Survey in Tanzania [2008]*. www.afrobarometer.org/files/documents/summary_results/tan_r4_sor.pdf.

Afrobarometer (2008b), *Summary of Results of Round 4 Afrobarometer Survey in Uganda [2008]*. www.afrobarometer.org/files/documents/summary_results/uga_r4_sor.pdf.

Aglietti, Stephanie (2014), "Rwandan Leader's Allies Seek Vote to Allow Him Third Term," *The Citizen* (Tanzania), October 24.

Agritrade CTA (2014), "Ethiopia, Uganda and DRC Commit to COMESA FTA," August 4, Agritrade CTA.

Ahmed, M. (2012), "Analysis of Incentives and Disincentives for Rice in Uganda," Technical Notes Series, Monitoring African Food and Agricultural Policies. Rome: Food and Agricultural Organization.

Ahmed, M. (2012a), "Analysis of Incentives and Disincentives for Maize in Uganda," Technical Notes Series, Monitoring African Food and Agricultural Policies. Rome: Food and Agricultural Organization.

Ake, Claude (1991), *A Political Economy of Africa*. New York: Longman.

Analo, Trevor (2015), "EAC Observer Team Says Burundi Presidential Poll Not Free or Fair," *The East African* (Nairobi), July 24.

Arezki, Rabah and Markus Brückner (2011), "Oil Rents, Corruption, and State Stability: Evidence from Panel Data Regressions," *European Economic Review*, 55 (7), 955–963.

Asante, S.K.B. (1997), *Regionalism and Africa's Development – Expectations, Reality and Challenges*. New York: St Martin's Press.

Asongu, Simplice (2014), "Are Proposed African Monetary Unions Optimal Currency Areas? Real Monetary and Fiscal Policy Convergence Analysis," *African Journal of Economic and Management Studies*, 5 (1), 9–29.

Auriol, Emmanuelle and Michael Warlters (2012), "The Marginal Cost of Public Funds and Tax Reform in Africa." *Journal of Development Economics*, 97 (1), 58–72.

Azikiwe, Abayomi (2014), "*Neo-Colonialism and 'Africa's Relations with the World,'*" *Global Research*, July 2.

Baldwin, Richard and Patrick Low (editors) (2009), *Multilateralizing Regionalism: Challenges for the Global Trading System*. Cambridge: Cambridge University Press.

Bariyo, Nicholas (2013), "Pipeline Riots Leave 7 Dead in Tanzania," *The Wall Street Journal*, January 28.

Barkan, Joel (1994), "Divergence and Convergence in Kenya and Tanzania: Pressures for Reform." In Joel Barkan (editor), *Beyond Capitalism vs. Socialism in Kenya & Tanzania*. Boulder: Lynne Rienner Publishers.

Barreiro-Hurle, J. (2012), "Analysis of Incentives and Disincentives for Maize in the United Republic of Tanzania," Technical Notes Series, Monitoring African Food and Agricultural Policies. Rome: Food and Agricultural Organization.

BBC News (2002), "Huge challenge for African Union," *BBC News*, July 8. http://news.bbc.co.uk/2/hi/africa/2115410.stm.

BBC News (2008), "Tanzanian PM to Resign Over Graft," *BBC News*, February 7. http://news.bbc.co.uk/2/hi/africa/7232141.stm.

BBC News (2010), "Kenya Corruption Costs Government Dearly," *BBC News*, December 3. www.bbc.com/news/world-africa-11913876.

BBC News (2013), "Why Has Tanzania Deported Thousands to Rwanda?," *BBC News*, September 2. www.bbc.com/news/world-africa-23930776.

BBC News (2014), "China to Build New East Africa Railway Line," *BBC News*, May 12. www.bbc.com/news/world-africa-27368877.

BBC News (2015), "Bagamoyo Port: Tanzania Begins Construction on Mega Project," *BBC News*, October 16. www.bbc.com/news/world-africa-34554524.

Beetsma, Roel and Massimo Giuliodori (2010), "The Macroeconomic Costs and Benefits of the EMU and Other Monetary Unions: An Overview of Recent Research," *Journal of Economic Literature*, 48, 603–641.

Ben Ltaifa, Nabil, et al. (2014), "Economic Convergence to Support the East African Monetary Union." In Drummond, Paulo, et al. (editors), *The Quest for Regional Integration in the East African Community*, 39–60. Washington, DC: IMF.

Bertelsmann Stiftung, BTI 2012. Burundi Country Report. Gütersloh: Bertelsmann Stiftung, 2012.

Bora, Bijit, et al. (2002), *Quantification of Non-Tariff Barriers*, Policy Issues in International Trade and Commodity Study Series No. 18. Geneva: United Nations Conference on Trade and Development.

Brenton, Paul and Isik Gözde (2012), *De-fragmenting Africa: Deepening Regional Trade Integration in Goods and Services*. Washington, DC: World Bank.

Buchanan, Rose Troup (2015), "Burundi Elections: President Pierre Nkurunziza Wins Third Term in Poll Denounced by Opposition and International Observers," *Independent* (UK), July 25.

Buiter, Willem (2010), "Economic, Political, and Institutional Prerequisites for Monetary Union Among the Members of the Gulf Cooperation Council." In MacDonald, Ronald and Abdulrazak Al Faris (editors), *Currency Union and Exchange Rate Issues: Lessons from the Gulf States*, 29–69. Dubai: Dubai Economic Council.

Byrnes, Rita, et al. (1992), *Uganda: A Country Study*. Washington, DC: Library of Congress.

Central Bank of Kenya (2015), *Monthly Economic Review – January 2015*. Nairobi: Central Bank of Kenya.

Central Bank of Lesotho (2006), *The Loti-Rand Peg: Benefits and Costs*, Central Bank of Lesotho Economic Review, No. 69. Maseru: Central Bank of Lesotho.

Chaurasia, Radhey (2005), *History of Middle East*. New Delhi: Atlantic Publishers and Distributors.

Clark, Phi and Zachary Kaufman (2013), "Rwanda: Recent History." In Iain Frame (editor), *Africa South of the Sahara 2014*. Oxford: Routledge.

COMESA (2002), *Procedures Manual on the Implementation of the Protocol on Rules of Origin for Products to Be Traded Between the Member States of the Common Market for Eastern and Southern Africa*. Lusaka: COMESA.

COMESA, EAC, SADC (2008), *Final Communique of the COMESA-EAC-SADC Tripartite Summit of Heads of State and Government*. www.tralac.org/wp-content/blogs.dir/12/files/2011/uploads/FinalCommuniqueKampala_20081022.pdf

Crabtree-Condor, Isabel and Leora Casey (2012), *Lay of the Land: Improving Land Governance to Stop Land Grabs*. Johannesburg: Action Aid International.

Deardorff, Allan and Robert Stern (1997), *Measurement of Non-Tariff Barriers*, OECD Economics Department Working Papers, No. 179. Paris: Organization for Economic Cooperation and Development.

DeFreese, Michelle (2016), "Is Magufuli the Region's Next Kagame?" *The World Post*, May 15.

Delf, George (1963), *Asians in East Africa*. London: Oxford University Press.

Delupis, Ingrid (1969), *The East African Community and Common Market*. London: Longman Group Limited.

Drummond, Paulo and Estelle Xue Liu (2013), *Africa's Rising Exposure to China: How Large Are Spillovers Through Trade*, IMF Working Paper 13/250. Washington, DC: International Monetary Fund.

Drummond, Paulo, et al. (2009), *Foreign Exchange Reserve Adequacy in East African Community Countries*. Washington, DC: IMF.

Drummond, Paulo, et al. (2014), *The Quest for Regional Integration in the East African Community*, 159–197. Washington, DC: IMF.

EAC Secretariat (2007), *Report of the Committee on East African Federation*. Arusha, Tanzania: East African Community.

EAC Secretariat (2007a), *Review of Reports from the National Consultative Committees (Kenya, Uganda, and Tanzania) on Fast-Tracking the East African Political Federation*. Arusha, Tanzania: East African Community.

EAC Secretariat (2009), *Application No. 1 of 2008: In the Matter of a Request by the Council of Ministers of the East African Community for an Advisory Opinion*. Arusha, Tanzania: East African Community.

EAC Secretariat (2011), *Report of the Team of Experts on Addressing the Fears, Concerns and Challenges of the East African Federation*. Arusha, Tanzania: East African Community.

EAC Secretariat (2014), *Schedule for the Realisation of the Monetary Union*. Arusha, Tanzania: East African Community.

East African Community (2002), *The Treaty for the Establishment of the East African Community*. Moshi, Tanzania: Printcare (T) Ltd.

East African Community (2004), *Programme and Modalities for the Elimination of Internal Tariffs* (Annex II to Protocol on the Establishment of the East African Customs Union). Arusha, Tanzania: East African Community.

East African Community (2004a), *EAC Common External Tariff* (Annex I to Protocol on the Establishment of the East African Customs Union). Arusha, Tanzania: East African Community.

East African Community (2004b), *Protocol on the Establishment of the East African Customs Union*. Arusha, Tanzania: East African Community.

East African Community (2004c), *The East African Community Customs Management Act, 2004*. Arusha, Tanzania: East African Community.

East African Community (2004d), *The East African Community Customs Union (Rules of Origin) Rules*. Arusha, Tanzania: East African Community.

East African Community (2008), *The East African Community Customs Management (Duty Remission) Regulations, 2008*. Arusha, Tanzania: East African Community.

East African Community (2009), *Protocol on the Establishment of the East African Community Common Market*. Arusha, Tanzania: East African Community.

East African Community (2009a), *The East African Community Common Market (Free Movement of Workers) Regulations – Annex II*. Arusha, Tanzania: East African Community.

East African Community (2012), *East African Community Gazette*, June 30, 2012. Arusha, Tanzania: East African Community.

East African Community (2012a), *Status of Elimination of Non-Tariff Barriers on the East African Community – Volume 5*. Arusha, Tanzania: East African Community.

East African Community (2012b), *Annex V: The East African Community Common Market Schedule of Commitments on the Progressive Liberalisation of Services.* Arusha, Tanzania: East African Community.

East African Community (2013), *Status of Elimination on Non-Tariff Barriers as per March, 2013.* Arusha, Tanzania: East African Community.

East African Community (2013a), *Reference No. 1 of 2011: The East African Law Society vs The Secretary General of the East African Community.* Arusha, Tanzania: East African Community.

East African Community (2013b), *Protocol on the Establishment of the East African Community Monetary Union.* Arusha, Tanzania: East African Community.

East African Community (2014), *East African Community Facts and Figures - 2014.* Arusha, Tanzania: East African Community.

East African Community (2015), *East African Community Facts and Figures - 2015.* Arusha, Tanzania: East African Community.

East African Community (2015a), *East African Community Gazette, June 19, 2015.* Arusha, Tanzania: East African Community.

East African Community and East African Business Council (2008), *Monitoring Mechanism for Elimination of Non-Tariff Barriers in EAC.* Arusha, Tanzania: East African Community.

East African Community and East African Business Council (2012), *The 2011 East African Community Business Climate Index Survey.* Arusha, Tanzania: East African Community.

Easterly, William and Yaw Nyarko (2008), *Is Brain Drain Good for Africa*, Brookings Global Economy and Development, Working Paper 19.

Elowson, Camilla and Cecilia Wiklund (2011), *ECCAS Capabilities in Peace and Security: A Scoping Study on Progress and Challenges.* Stockhlom: FOI – Swedish Defense Research Agency.

Eyakuze, Aidan and Ahmed Salim (2012), *The State of East Africa 2012: Deepening Integration, Intensifying Challenges.* Nairobi: Society for International Development.

Faye, Michael, et al. (2004), "The Challenges Facing Landlocked Developing Countries," *Journal of Human Development,"* 5 (1), 31–68.

FEWSNET, FAO, and WFP (2012), "East Africa Cross-Border Trade Bulletin: October-December 2011," Issue 4, February.

Friedman, Andrew (2012), "Kagame's Rwanda: Can an Authoritarian Development Model Be Squared with Democracy and Human Rights?" *Oregon Review of International Law*, 14 (1), 253–277.

Fugazza, Marco (2013), *The Economics Behind Non-Tariff Measures: Theoretical Insights and Empirical Evidence*, Policy Issues in International Trade and Commodities Study Series No. 57. Geneva: United Nations Conference on Trade and Development.

Gaffey, Conor (2016), "Tanzanian Faces Three Years in Jail or Fine for Insulting President on Facebook," *Newsweek*, June 9.

Gallagher, Kevin, et al. (2012), *The New Banks in Town: Chinese Finance in Latin America.* Washington, DC: Inter-American Dialogue.

Gatsiounis, Ionnis (2012), "Uganda Term-Limits Bill Grandfathers Museveni," *The Washington Times*, April 12. www.washingtontimes.com/news/2012/apr/23/uganda-term-limits-bill-grandfathers-museveni/

Gayathri, Amrutha (2013), "Uhuru Kenyatta, Indicted for Crimes Against Humanity, To Be Sworn In as Kenyan President; Will The ICC Drop Charges Against Kenyatta?" *International Business Times*, April 2013.

Gebe, Boni (2008), "Ghana's Foreign Policy at Independence and Implications for the 1966 Coup D'état," *The Journal of Pan African Studies*, 2 (3).

Genge, Manelisi, Francis Kornegay, and Stephen Rule (2000), "Formation of the African Union, African Economic Community and Pan-African Parliament," African Institute of South Africa Working Paper, 2000.

Gettleman, Jeffrey (2016), "U.N. Report Accuses Rwanda of Training Rebels to Oust Burundian Leader," *The New York Times*, February 4.

Global Financial Integrity (2010), *Illicit Financial Flows from Africa: Hidden Resource for Development*. Washington, DC: Global Financial Integrity.

Global Financial Integrity (2014), *Hiding in Plain Sight: Trade Misinvoicing and the Impact of Revenue Loss in Ghana, Kenya, Mozambique, Tanzania, and Uganda: 2002–2011*. Washington, DC: Global Financial Integrity.

Global Times (2013), "China-Africa Economic and Trade Cooperation." Beijing: Global Times. www.safpi.org/sites/default/files/publications/China-AfricaEconomic andTradeCooperation.pdf

Grewe, Wilhelm (author) and Michael Byers (translator) (2000), *The Epochs of International Law*, Part Four, Chapter Two, Section IV. Berlin: Walter de Gruyter.

Gundan, Farai (2014), "Kenya Joins Africa's Top 10 Economies After Rebasing of Its Gross Domestic Product (GDP)," *Forbes*, October 1.

Gupta, Abhijit (2008), "Cost of Holding Excess Reserves: The Indian Experience." Indian Council for Research on International Economic Relations, Working Paper 206. New Delhi: Indian Council for Research on International Economic Relations.

Gupta, Sanjeev and Jimmy McHugh (2012), "East African Monetary Union and Fiscal Policy: Current and Future Challenges." In Hamid Davoodi (editor), *The East African Community After Ten Years: Deepening Integration*, 59–75. Washington, DC: IMF.

Gupta, Sanjeev and Jimmy McHugh (2014), "The Fiscal Policy Challenges of Monetary Union in East Africa." In Drummond, Paulo, et al. (editors), *The Quest for Regional Integration in the East African Community*, 61–83. Washington, DC: IMF.

Hartman, Stephen (2013), "The WTO, the Doha Round Impasse, PTAs, and FTAs/RTAs," *International Trade Journal*, 27, 411–430.

Hazlewood, Arthur (1967), "The Treaty for East African Co-operation," *Standard Bank Review*. London: The Standard Bank Limited.

Hazlewood, Arthur (1975), *Economic Integration: The East African Experience*. New York: St. Martins Press.

Hilbers, Paul (2005), "Interaction on Monetary and Fiscal Policies: Why Central Bankers Worry About Government Budgets." In IMF, *Current Developments in Monetary and Financial Laws, Volume 4*, 159–166. Washington, DC: IMF.

Hope, Christopher (2017), "Scottish independence referendum: What Nicola Sturgeon said and what she really meant," *The Telegraph* (UK), March 13.

Hughes, A. J. (1963), East Africa: The Search for Unity. Baltimore: Penguin Books Ltd.

Human Rights Watch (2014), "Repression Across Borders: Attacks and Threats Against Rwandan Opponents and Critics Abroad." Nairobi: Human Rights Watch.

Humphreys, Charles and John Underwood (1989), "The External Debt Difficulties of Low-Income Africa." In Ishrat Hussain and Ishac Diwan (editors), *Dealing with the Debt Crisis*, 45–65. Washington, DC: World Bank.

Hyden, Goran (1980), *Beyond Ujamaa in Tanzania: Underdevelopment and Uncaptured Peasantry*. Berkeley: University of California Press.

ICTSD (2012), "African Union Aims for Continental Free Trade Area by 2017." *Bridges Weekly Trade Digest*, 16 (4), February 1. Geneva: International Centre for Trade and Sustainable Development.

ICTSD (2014), "Africa's Largest Free Trade Area Set to Launch in December." *Bridges Weekly Trade Digest*, 18 (36), October 30. Geneva: International Centre for Trade and Sustainable Development.

ICTSD (2014a), "EU and EAC Seal EPA Deal," *Bridges Africa*, October 20. Geneva: International Centre for Trade and Sustainable Development.

ICTSD (2015), "US, East African Community Ink Deal to Deepen Trade Ties." *Bridges Weekly Trade Digest*, 19 (8), March 5. Geneva: International Centre for Trade and Sustainable Development.

ICTSD (2015a), "Launch of African Tripartite FTA Set for June," *Bridges*, 19 (10), March 19. Geneva: International Centre for Trade and Sustainable Development.

Ihucha, Adam (2013), "Outcry as Tanzania Imposes New Levy on Kenyan Trucks," *The East African* (Kenya), August 24.

IMF (2000), *Poverty Reduction Strategy Papers – Progress in Implementation*. Washington, DC: IMF.

IMF (2012), *West African Economic and Monetary Union*, IMF Country Report No. 12/59. Washington, DC: IMF.

IMF (2012a), *Rwanda: Fourth Review Under the Policy Support Instrument and Request for Modification of Assessment Criteria*, May 22. Washington, DC: IMF.

IMF (2013), *Central African Economic and Monetary Union*, IMF Country Report No. 13/322. Washington, DC: IMF.

IMF (2013a), *Burundi: Second Review Under the Extended Credit Facility – Debt Sustainability Analysis*, January 30. Washington, DC: IMF.

IMF (2013b), *Kenya: Fifth Review Under the Three-Year Arrangement Under the Extended Credit Facility Request for a Waiver and Modification of Performance Criteria – Debt Sustainability Analysis*, April 1. Washington, DC: IMF.

IMF (2013c), *Uganda: Staff Report for the 2013 Article Consultation, Sixth Review Under the Policy Support Instrument, Request for a Three-Year Policy Support Instrument and Cancellation of Currency Policy Support Instrument*, June 17. Washington, DC: IMF.

IMF (2013d), *Regional Economic Outlook: Sub-Saharan Africa Building Momentum in a Multi-Speed World*. Washington, DC: IMF.

IMF (2016), *Economic Outlook Update World*. Washington, DC: IMF, July 19.

IMF/World Bank (2001), *Debt Relief for Poverty Reduction: The Role of the Enhanced HIPC Initiative*. Washington, DC: IMF/World Bank.

IMF/World Bank (2012), *Joint IMF/World Bank Debt Sustainability Analysis 2012 Update: Uganda*, May 18. Washington, DC: IMF/World Bank.

Information Service of the United Republic of Tanganyika and Zanzibar (1964), *Kampala Agreement*. Dar-es-Salaam: Mwananchi Publishing Co. Ltd.

Institute of Economic Affairs (2012), *Informal Sector and Taxation in Kenya*. Nairobi: Institute of Economic Affairs.

International Tax Compact (2010), *Addressing Tax Evasion and Tax Avoidance in Developing Countries*. Bonn: International Tax Compact.

Issa, Mohamed (2009), "EPA Scandal Dominated 2008, Shook Kikwete," *The East African* (Kenya), January 3.

Jackson, Robert and Carl Rosberg (1985), "The Marginality of African States." In Carter, Gwendolen and Patrick O'Meara (editors), *African Independence: The First Twenty-Five Years*. Bloomington: Indiana Press.

Jonung, Lars (2004), "The Political Economy of Monetary Unification: The Swedish Euro Referendum of 2003," *Cato Journal*, (24)(1/2).

Juma, Mussa (2014), "Rashid: Muungano ulikuwa siri ya Nyerere na Karume" [Rashid: The Union was a secret between Nyerere and Karume], *Mwananchi* (Tanzania), April 13.

Kabeera, Eric (2011), "Land – The Obstacle to EAC Integration," *The New Times* (Rwanda), December 12.

Kabendera, Erick (2014), "Tanzania House Committee Wants Heads to Roll over IPTL Saga," *The East African* (Kenya), November 22.

Kabendera, Erick (2016), "Magufuli Criticised as Tanzania Bans Rallies," *The East African* (Kenya), June 11.

Kabwe, Zitto (2013), "Transfer Pricing in Tanzania: My Experience in Tackling Tax Avoidance/Evasion Through Parliament." www.amiando.com/eventResources/H/z/P4jBx8U5eYQQ9B/Zitto_Kabwe.pdf

Kabwe, Zitto (2016), "Will the Real Opposition Emerge Under Magufuli's Presidency?," *The Citizen* (Tanzania), August 7.

Kamau, Charles, et al. (2012), "Tax Avoidance and Evasion as a Factor Influencing 'Creative Accounting Practice' Among Companies in Kenya," *Journal of Business Studies Quarterly*, 4 (2), 77–84.

Karugia, Joseph, et al. (2009), *The Impact of Non-Tariff Barriers on Maize and Beef Trade in East Africa*, ReSAKSS Working Paper No. 29. Nairobi: Regional Strategic Analysis and Knowledge Support System.

Kenya National Council for Law Reporting (2012), *East African Community Mediation Agreement Act*. Nairobi: Kenya National Council for Law Reporting.

Kenya Sugar Board (2010), *Kenya Sugar Industry Strategic Plan, 2010–2014*. Nairobi: Kenya Sugar Board.

Kiishweko, Orton (2012), "Curbing Tanzania's 'Land Grabbing Race,'" *Inter Press News Agency*, December 12. www.ipsnews.net/2012/12/curbing-tanzanias-land-grabbing-race/

Kisanga, David (2013), "Tanzania Is Not Ready to Abolish EAC Work Permit Fees-Ministry," *Ipp Media* (Tanzania), October 30.

Kituo cha Katiba (2010), *The Tanzania Union and the East African Integration Process: Lessons and Challenges*. Kampala, Uganda: Kituo cha katiba.

Kron, Josh (2011), "Uganda's Oil Could Be Gift That Becomes a Curse," *The New York Times*, November 25. www.nytimes.com/2011/11/26/world/africa/uganda-welcomes-oil-but-fears-graft-it-attracts.html

Lebhour, Karim (2015), "No Strings Attached: African Union Seeks Financial Independence," Foreign Bureaux Agence France-Presse (AFP) (February 1), Addis Ababa.

Leifer, Michael (1989), *ASEAN and the Security of South-East Asia*. London: Routledge.

Lesser, Caroline and Evdokia Moisé-Leeman (2009), *Informal Cross-Border Trade and Trade Facilitation Reform in Sub-Saharan Africa*, OECD Trade Policy Working Paper No. 86. Paris: Organization for Economic Cooperation and Development.

Lewin, Michael (2011), "Botswana's Success: Good Governance, Good Policies, and Good Luck." In Chuhan-Pole, Punam and Manka Angwafo (editors), *Yes Africa Can: Success Stories from a Dynamic Continent*, 81–90. Washington, DC: World Bank.

Ligami, Christabel (2013), "Kenya Loses Bid to Suspend Duty Remission Rule," *The East African* (Kenya), August 3.

Lofchie, Michael (1988), "Tanzania's Economic Recovery," *Current History* (May), pp. 209–212 and 227–229.

Lofchie, Michael (1989), *The Policy Factor: Agricultural Performance in Kenya and Tanzania*. Boulder, CO: Lynne Rienner Publishers.

Lury, D.A. (1965), *The Trade Statistics of the Countries of East Africa, 1945–1964, and African Population Estimates: Back Projections of Recent Census Results*. Nairobi: Institute for Development Studies, University College.

Magolanga, Elisha (2013), "Tens of Billions Swindled in New EPA-Style Scandal," *The Citizen* (Tanzania), August 19.

Mail and Guardian Africa (2016), "Uganda Finally Chooses Tanzania for Oil Pipeline Route, Leaves Kenya at the Altar," *Mail and Guardian Africa* (South Africa), April 23.

Makonnen, Tewodros and Hallelujah Lulie (2014), "Ethiopia, Regional Integration and the COMESA Free Trade Area," South African Institute of International Affairs.

Makoye, Kizito (2013), "Tanzania Committee Says Billions Lost to Corporate Tax Evasion." Thomson Reuters Foundation, October 14. www.trust.org/item/20131014094858-3frio.

Marari, Daniel (2015), "Of Tanzania's Cybercrimes Law and the Threat to Freedom of Expression and Information," *AfricLaw*, May 25.

Marere, Michael (2015), "The Cybercrimes Act, 2015: A Weed in the Garden of Freedom of Expression in Tanzania." Tumaini Univerity Makumira, Tanzania.

Marketing Development Bureau, Ministry of Agriculture, Tanzania (1986), *Import Intensity of Major Crops in Mainland Tanzania*, 1985/86. Dar-es-Salaam: Ministry of Agriculture, Tanzania.

Marsh, Zoe and G.W. Kingsnorth (1972), *A History of East Africa*. Cambridge: Cambridge University Press.

Masson, Paul (2012), "Effect of Oil and Gas Discoveries on the Proposed EAC Monetary Union," University of Toronto. www.trademarkea.com/download/Study-on-oil-and-gas-and-EAMU.pdf

Mayoyo, Patrick and Gitonga Marete (2011), "Sh 1.6bn Sugar Scam Unearthed," *Daily Nation*, (Kenya), April 28.

Mbashiru, Katare (2014), "Now's the Time for African Countries to Unite: Kikwete," *The Citizen* (Tanzania), April 27.

Mbogo, Steve (2012), "IGAD Prepares to Turn into a Free Trade Area," *The East African* (Kenya), December 15.

McAdams, Michael (2010), "Tanzania: Country Bans Middlemen from Its Onion Farms," *The East African* [Kenya], July 26.

McCarthy, Colin (2003), "*The South African Customs Union – A Case Study.* " Rome: Food and Agricultural Organization of the United Nations.
McVeigh, Tracy (2015), "Rwanda Votes to Give President Kagame Right to Rule Until 2034," *The Guardian* (UK), December 19.
Metzger, Martina (2008), *Regional Cooperation and Integration in Sub-Saharan Africa*, UNCTAD Discussion Paper, No. 189. Geneva: UNCTAD.
Mhagama, Hilda (2016), "Police Force Bans All Political Rallies – Until Further Notice," *Daily News* (Tanzania), June 8.
Ministry of Education and Vocational Training, Tanzania (2014), *Sera ya Elimu na Mafunzo – 2014* [Education and Training Policy – 2014]. Dar-es-Salaam: Ministry of Education and Vocational Training, Tanzania.
Ministry of Finance and Planning, Kenya (1987), *Statistical Abstract, 1987*. Nairobi: Ministry of Finance and Planning, Kenya.
Ministry of Finance, Tanzania (2013), *Tanzania National Debt Sustainability Analysis*. Dar-es-Salaam: The Ministry of Finance.
Mkali, Harid (2012), *East African Federation: Blessing or Blight?*" London: Ivydale Press.
Mold, Andrew and Rodgers Mukwaya (2014), "The Implications of the GDP Rebasing Exercise for Uganda and the EAC." Addis Ababa, Ethiopia: United Nations Economic Commission for Africa.
Mortimer, Caroline (2017), "Shetland Islands Could Go Independent if Scotland Leaves UK, Former Chancellor Claims," *Independent* (UK), April 9.
Msekwa, Pius (2013), "New Constitution an Interim Step Ahead of EAC Federation," *The Citizen* (Tanzania), June 12.
Mshomba, Richard (1993), "The Magnitude of Coffee Arabica Smuggled from Northern Tanzania into Kenya," *Eastern Africa Economic Review* 9 (1), 165–175.
Mshomba, Richard (2009), *Africa and the World Trade Organization*. New York: Cambridge University Press.
Mshomba, Richard (2010), "Trade Is Not the Enemy – Nor Is It a 'Magic Bullet,'" *Journal of African Development*, 12 (2), 27–31.
Mshomba, Richard (2015), "Tanzania's New Education Policy: We Need Details," *The Citizen* (Tanzania), March 22.
Mtulya, Athuman (2014), "Kenya Locks Out [Tanzania] TZ Tour Operators' Cars," *The Citizen* (Tanzania), June 7.
Mtulya, Athuman (2016), "Ignore CCM Manifesto at Your Peril, Govt Workers Warned," *The Citizen* (Tanzania), July 24.
Mtulya, Athuman, et al. (2015), "Zanzibar in Crisis: The Way Forward, *The Citizen* (Tanzania), October 31.
Mugarula, Florence (2015),"Tanzania Hits Kenya Where It Hurts," *The Citizen* (Tanzania), March 19.
Mugisa, Evarist, et al. (2009), *An Evaluation of the Implementation and Impact of the East African Community Customs Union*. Arusha, Tanzania: The East African Community.
Muhammad, Andrew, et al. (2011), *International Evidence on Food Consumption Patterns: An Update Using 2005 International Comparison Program Data*. Washington, DC: United States Department of Agriculture.
Mumo, Muthoki (2014), "East Africa Leaders Agree on Key Infrastructure Projects," *The East African* (Kenya), May 3.

Mundell, Robert (1961), "A Theory of Optimum Currency Areas," *American Economic Review*, 51 (4), 657–665.

Musila, Jacob (2005), "The Intensity of Trade Creation and Trade Diversion in COMESA, ECCAS, and ECOWAS: A Comparative Analysis," *Journal of African Economies*, 14 (1), 117–141.

Mwakikagile, Godfrey (2002), *Nyerere and Africa: End of an Era*. Atlanta: Protea Publishers.

Mwakikagile, Godfrey (2008), *The Union of Tanganyika and Zanzibar: Product of The Cold War?* Dar-es-Salaam, Tanzania: New Africa Press.

Mwalimu, Saumu and Katare Mbashiru (2013), "10,000 Foreign Teachers Face Deportation," *The Citizen* (Tanzania), September 13.

Mwananchi (2008), "Watakaouza Chakula Moro Kushtakiwa" [those in Morogoro who will sell food crops to be prosecuted], *Mwananchi* [Tanzania], June 2008.

Mwananchi (2013), "Mgogoro wa Gesi Mtwara: Pinda Azima Uasi" [Natural gas conflict in Mtwara: Pinda calms unrest], *Mwananchi* (Tanzania), Januari 30.

Mwananchi (2016), "Jukwaa la Wahariri lapinga *Mseto* kufungiwa" [Tanzania Editors Forum objects to the ban on *Mseto*], *Mwananchi* (Tanzania), August 13.

Mwapachu, Juma (2012), *Challenging the Frontiers of African Integration: The Dynamics of Policies, Politics and Transformation in the East African Community*. Dar-es-Salaam: E&D Vision Publishing.

Mwiti, Lee (2015), "12 Facts Proud Africans Don't Want to Know About the Au's Cash Situation - But We'll Tell You Anyway," *Mail & Guardian, Africa*, February 4.

Nabudere, Dan (1980), *Imperialism and Revolution in Uganda*. Dar-es-Salaam: Tanzania Publishing House.

National Treasury, Kenya (2013), *Quarterly Economic and Budgetary Review*, Second Quarter 2013/2014. Nairobi: The National Treasury.

Ndegwa, Philip (1963), *Some Aspects of Inter-territorial Trade in East Africa in Recent Years*, EDRP, 16. Kampala: Makerere Institute of Social Research. http://opendocs.ids.ac.uk/opendocs/bitstream/handle/123456789/1575/EDRP16-327389.pdf?sequence=1.

Ndegwa, Philip (1965), *The Common Market and Development in East Africa*. Nairobi: East African Publishing House.

Ndikumana, Léonce and James K. Boyce (2008), "New Estimates of Capital Flight from Sub-Saharan African Countries: Linkages with External Borrowing and Policy Options." Political Economy Research Institute, Working Paper No. 166. Amherst: University of Massachusetts.

Ndumbaro, Damas (2015), The Cyber Law and Freedom of Expression: The Tanzanian Perspective.

Neely, Christopher (2000), "Are Changes in Foreign Exchange Reserves Well Correlated with Official Intervention?" St. Louis: Economic Review of the Federal Reserve Bank of St. Louis.

New Vision (2012), "The Cost of Corruption Is Huge. We Look Back at Nine Graft Scandals That Have Tossed Uganda Here and There in the Recent Past," November 11. http://allafrica.com/stories/201211120092.html.

Ngo-Eyok, Suzanne (2013), "Advocacy for Free Trade." *Rural 21 -The International Journal of Rural Development*, February 16–17.

Nkrumah, Kwame (1963), *Africa Must Unite*. New York: F.A. Praeger.

Nuzulack, Dausen (2014), "Msekwa Atoboa Siri ya Muungano" [Msekwa reveals the secret behind the Union], *Mwananchi* (Tanzania), April 11.

Nyerere, Julius (1960), *East African Federation: Freedom and Unity*. Dar-es-Salaam: Tanganyika Standard Limited.

Nyerere, Julius (1961), *The Second Scramble*. Dar-es-Salaam: Tanganyika Standard Limited.

Ochieng, David and David Majanja (2010), "Sub-Saharan Africa and the WTO Dispute Settlement: The Case of Kenya." In Shaffer, Gregory and Ricardo Meléndez-Ortiz (editors), *Dispute Settlement at the WTO: The Developing Country Experience*, 301–341. New York: Cambridge University Press.

O'Connell, Stephen (1997), "Macroeconomic Harmonization, Trade Reform, and Regional Trade in Sub-Saharan Africa." In Ademola Oyejide, et al. (editors), *Regional Integration and Trade Liberalization in Sub-Saharan Africa*, 89–158. New York: St. Martin's Press.

Odeke, Julius (2012), "Review Law on Mad Cow Disease to Lift Ban, Uganda Tells Kenya," *The Independent*, Kampala, December 2012. www.independent.co.ug/news/news/7112-review-law-on-mad-cow-disease-to-lift-ban-uganda-tells-kenya.

Odhiambo, Allan (2016), "Magufuli's Rwanda Trip Sets Stage for New Order in East Africa," *Business Daily* (Kenya), April 6.

OECD (1983), *The Generalized System of Preferences: Review of the First Decade*. Paris: OECD.

Official Journal of the European Union (2015), *Commission Implementing Regulation (EU) 2015/776 of 18 May 2015*. Brussels: The European Union.

Ogalo, Victor (2012), "Achievements and Challenges of Implementation of the EAC Common Market Protocol in Kenya," *Conference on the East African Community Common Market Protocol for Movement of Labour*, Nairobi, Kenya.

Okafor, Harrison (2013), "Estimating the Costs and Benefits of a Common Currency for the Second West African Monetary Zone (WAMZ)," *Journal of Economics and Behavioral Studies*, Vol. 5, No. 2, pp. 57–68.

Olingo, Allan (2016), "No Deal with EU as Tanzania, Uganda Refuse to Sign Up," *The East African* (Kenya), July 16.

Omondi, George (2010), "Uganda, Kenyan Traders Differ over EAC Tax Rules," *Business Daily* (Kenya), November 1.

Omondi, George (2012), "Dar Work Permit Fee Raise Rocks Bloc," *Business Daily* (Kenya), August 6.

Omondi, George (2013), "Uganda's New Levy on Industrial Imports to Benefit Kenyan Firms" *Business Daily* [Kenya], June 13.

Omondi, George (2014), "IMF Boss Cautions East Africa on Monetary Union," *The East African* (Kenya), January 7.

Organization of African Unity (1963), *OAU Charter*. Addis Ababa: Organization of African Unity.

Organization of African Unity (1980), *Lagos Plan of Action for the Economic Development of Africa*. Addis-Ababa: Organization of African Unity

Organization of African Unity (1991), *Treaty Establishing the African Economic Community*. Addis-Ababa: Organization of African Unity.

Organization of African Unity (1999), *Sirte Declaration*. www.africa-union.org/Docs_AUGovernment/decisions/Sirte_Declaration_1999.pdf

Otage, Steve (2013), "Uganda's Sugar Imports Stuck at Busia Border," *Sunday Monitor* [Uganda], May 11.

Otieno, Elisha (2009), "Tanzania Farmers Defy Ban to Smuggle Maize into Kenya," *Business Daily* [Kenya], June 11.

Oucho, John (2010), "Undercurrents of Post-Election Violence in Kenya: Issues in the Long-Term Agenda." In Kanyinga, Karuti and Duncan Okello (editors), *Tensions and Reversals in Democratic Transitions: The Kenya 2007 General Elections*, 491–532. Nairobi: Society for International Development and Institute for Development Studies, University of Nairobi.

Pakenham, Thomas (1991), *The Scramble for Africa: White Man's Conquest of the Dark Continent from 1976–1912*. New York: Avon Books.

Republic of Rwanda (2003), *The Constitution of the Republic of Rwanda Adopted on 26 May 2003*. Kigali: Republic of Rwanda.

Republic of Rwanda (2015), *The Constitution of the Republic of Rwanda of 2003 Revised in 2015*. Kigali: Republic of Rwanda.

Review of African Political Economy (1994), "The Formation of IGADD," *Review of African Political Economy*, 21 (59), 93–96.

Rice, Robert (1979), "The Tanzanian Price Control System: Theory, Practice and Some Possible Improvements." In Kwan Kim, et al. (editors), *Papers on the Political Economy of Tanzania*, 95–110. Nairobi: Heinemann Educational Books Ltd.

Rodney, Walter (1989), *How Europe Underdeveloped Africa*. Nairobi: East African Educational Publishers.

Rogers, David (2015), "Chinese Firms Win $9bn Tanzanian Rail Scheme Amid East African Transport Boom," *Global Construction Review*, June 4.

Royce, Ed (2014), "Chairman Royce Decries Targeted Killings of Rwandan Regime Critics Abroad," March 12. http://foreignaffairs.house.gov/press-release/chairman-royce-decries-targeted-killings-rwandan-regime-critics-abroad

Rugemalira, Josephat (2005), "Theoretical and Practical Challenges in a Tanzanian English Medium Primary School," Göteborg Working Papers on Asian and African Languages and Literatures, 66–84.

Ruhangisa, John (2011), "The East African Court of Justice: Ten Years of Operation (Achievements and Challenges)." Paper presented at a Workshop on the Role of the EACJ in EAC Integration, Kampala, Uganda, November 1–2, 2011.

Rusuhuzwa, Thomas and Robert Masson (2012), "Design and Implementation of a Common Currency Area in the East African Community," Working Paper No. 451, Department of Economics, University of Toronto.

Rwebangira, Redempta (2016), "Tanzania Bans Mseto Newspaper for Three Years," *The East African* (Nairobi), August 11.

SADC (2011), *Towards a Common Future*. www.sadc.int/about-sadc/continental-inter regional-integration/tripartite-cooperation/.

SADC (2015), "Joint Meeting of the COMESA-EAC-SADC Tripartite Sectoral Ministerial Committee," May 31, SADC. www.sadc.int/files/3814/3317/4024/Joint_Meeting_of_the_COMESA-EAC-SADC_Tripartite_Sectoral_Ministerial_Committee.pdf.

Save Virunga (2013), "What Happened When Chad Found Oil?" http://save virunga.com/2013/12/15/what-happened-when-chad-found-oil-quel-souvenir-a-documentary/.

Schenkel, Mark (2012), "Exodus of Ugandan Teachers to Rwanda," *Radio Netherlands*, March 16. www.rnw.nl/africa/article/exodus-ugandan-teachers-rwanda.

Schneider, James (2015), Why the Fuss over Mugabe?, *Aljazeera*, February 3. www.aljazeera.com/indepth/opinion/2015/02/mugabe-au-zimbabwe-africa-150203042211499.html.

Secretary of State for the Colonies (1925), *East Africa: Report on East Africa Commission*. London: His Majesty's Stationery Office. www.scribd.com/doc/55821771/CAB-24–173-Report-of-the-East-Africa-Commission-1925.

Secretary of State for the Colonies (1956), *East African Commission Headquarters*. HC Deb 22 February 1956, vol. 549 cc369–70. http://hansard.millbanksystems.com/commons/1956/feb/22/east-africa-high-commission-headquarters.

Secretary of State for the Colonies (1961), *East Africa Report of the Economic and Fiscal Commission*. London: His Majesty's Stationery Office.

Shinyekwa, Isaac and Lawrence Othieno (2013), *Trade Creation & Diversion Effects of the East African Community Regional Trade Agreement: A Gravity Model Analysis*, Economic Policy Research Centre, Research Series No. 112. Kampala, Uganda: Economic Policy Research Centre.

Shivji, Issa (1999), "The Land Acts 1999: A Cause for Celebration or a Celebration of a Cause?," Keynote address to the Workshop on Land held [in] Morogoro, Tanzania, February 19–20. www.mokoro.co.uk/files/13/file/lria/land_acts_1999_cause_for_celebration.pdf

Short C., et al. (2012), "Analysis of Incentives and Disincentives for Rice in Kenya," Technical Notes Series, Monitoring African Food and Agricultural Policies. Rome: Food and Agricultural Organization.

Short C., et al. (2012a), "Analysis of Incentives and Disincentives for Maize in Kenya," Technical Notes Series, Monitoring African Food and Agricultural Policies. Rome: Food and Agricultural Organization.

Simon, Sheldon (1982), *The ASEAN States and Regional Security*. Stanford: Hoover Institution Press, Stanford University.

Sircar, Parbati Kumar (1990), *Development Through Integration: Lessons from East Africa*. Delhi: Kalinga Publications.

Skarstein, Rune and Samuel Wangwe (1986), *Industrial Development in Tanzania: Some Crisis Issues*. Uppsala and Dar-es-Salaam: Scandinavian Institute of African Studies and Tanzania Publishing House.

Smith, David (2013), "Mugabe Revives Gaddafi's United States of Africa Dream," *The Guardian* (UK), January 21.

Smith, David (2014), "Paul Kagame Hints at Seeking Third Term as Rwandan President," *The Guardian*, April 23.

Southern Africa Foreign Policy Initiative (2015), "Budget of the African Union for the 2014 Financial Year," Southern Africa Foreign Policy Initiative, June 3.

Stahl, Heinz-Michael (2005), *East African Customs Union Tariff Liberalisation Impacts in Perspective*. Arusha, Tanzania: East African Community.

Sturman, Kathryn (2007), "New Growth on Deep Roots: Prospects for an African Union Government," ISS Paper 146. Pretoria and Nairobi: Institute for Security Studies.

Tambwe, Masembe (2012), "East Africa: Sitta – Land Is Out of EAC 'Empire,'" *Tanzania Daily News*, May 25.

Tandon, Yash (2010), "'Quiet Corruption'?: The World Bank on Africa." *Pambazuka News*, Issue 477, April 15. Nairobi: Fahamu Kenya. http://pambazuka.org/en/category/features/63693.

TANU (1967), *The Arusha Declaration and TANU's Policy on Socialism and Self-Reliance*. Dar-es-Salaam: Publicity Section of TANU.

Tanzania Gender Networking Program (2015), *The Kilimanjaro Initiative*, Tanzania Gender Networking Program. www.landcoalition.org/sites/default/files/documents/news/arusha_planning_meeting_report.pdf

Tavlas, George (2007), *The Benefits and Costs of Monetary Union in Southern Africa: A Critical Survey of Literature*, South African Reserve Working Paper, WP/07/04. Pretoria: South African Reserve Bank.

Tax Justice Network-Africa (2012), *Taxation and the Informal Sector*, Volume 3. Nairobi: Tax Justice Network-Africa. www.taxjusticeafrica.net/sites/default/files/Taxation%20and%20the%20Informal%20Sector.pdf.

Tax Justice Network-Africa (2012a), *Tax Competition in East Africa: Race to the Bottom?* Nairobi: Tax Justice Network-Africa. www.actionaid.org/sites/files/actionaid/eac_report.pdf.

Taylor, Ian (2003), "Globalization and Regionalization in Africa: Reactions to Attempts at Neo-Liberal Regionalism," *Review of International Political Economy*, 10 (2), 310–330.

The Citizen (2014), "The Coalition of the Willing Emerges Again," *The Citizen* (Tanzania), January 13.

The Citizen (2015), "Dar Still Adamant on Key EAC Protocol," *The Citizen* (Tanzania), March 17.

The Citizen (2015a), "JK, Uhuru End Row on Tourist Vans, KQ flights," *The Citizen* (Tanzania), March 23.

The Citizen (2016), "Dar, Kigali Vow to Tackle Trade Hurdles," *The Citizen* (Tanzania), May 21.

The Citizen Reporter (2013), "TZ Renounces Trilateral Talks," *The Citizen* (Tanzania), October 22.

The East African Development Bank (1977), *Ten-Year Report, 1967–1977*. Kampala: Sapoba Bookshop Press.

The Guardian (2014), "Tanzanian PM Under Pressure to Resign over Alleged Fraudulent Payments," *The Guardian* (London), November 28.

The Herald (2011), "Museveni Tipped to Win," *The Herald* (Zimbabwe), February 16. www.herald.co.zw/museveni-tipped-to-win/.

The International Economy (2007), "Is the IMF Obsolete?" Washington, DC: The International Economy.

The London Evening Post (2014), "U.S. Urges Burundi Not to Change Country's Constitution," *The London Evening Post*, April 11.

The New York Times (2016), "UN: Promise of Peace and Justice 'Squandered' in South Sudan," *The New York Times*, July 28.

The Observer (2011), "Will Museveni Follow Beigye to Retirement?" *The Observer* (Uganda), August 1.

The Observer (2012), "How Term Limits Were Kicked Out in 2005," *The Observer* (Uganda), May 13.

The United Republic of Tanzania (1999), *Land Act, 1999*. Dar-es-Salaam: The United Republic of Tanzania.

The United Republic of Tanzania (1999a), *Village Land Act, 1999*. Dar-es-Salaam: The United Republic of Tanzania.

The Upper Nile Times (2015), "Embarrassed. Finance Minister Deng Athorbei Stormed COMESA Meeting Uninvited: South Sudan Is Not a Member," *The Upper Nile Times* (South Sudan) April 8.

Thompson, Virginia and Richard Adloff (1960), *The Emerging States of French Equatorial Africa*. London: Oxford University Press.

Tinbergen, Jan (1962), *Shaping the World Economy*. New York: The Twentieth Century Fund.

Transparency International (2006), *The 2006 Transparency International Corruption Perceptions Index*. www.infoplease.com/ipa/A0781359.html.

Transparency International (2015), *Corruption Perceptions Index 2014*. www.transparency.org/cpi2014/results.

Transparency International, Kenya (2012), *Bribery as a Non-Tariff Barrier to Trade: A Case Study of East African Trade Corridors*. Nairobi: Transparency International, Kenya.

Transparency International, UK (2011), "House of Commons International Development Committee Inquiry into Financial Crime and Development: Bribery Cases - BAE Tanzania." www.transparency.org.uk/component/cckjseblod/?task=download&file=publication_file&id=170.

Tulya-Muhika, Sam (1995), *Lessons from the Rise and Fall of the East African Community*. Germany: Friedrich-Ebert-Stiftung.

Ubwani, Zephania (2011), "Tanzania acts to Curb Maize Smuggling," *Daily Nation* [Kenya], July 9.

Ubwani, Zephania (2014), "Tanzania Loses Serengeti Road Case," *The Citizen* (Tanzania), June 21.

Ubwani, Zephania (2015), "JK, Kagame Break the Ice at EAC Summit," *The Citizen* (Tanzania), February 21.

Uganda Bureau of Statistics (2006), *External Trade Statistics Bulletin, Volume 4–2006*. Kampala, Uganda: Uganda Bureau of Statistics.

Uma, Julius (2011), "Kenyan Envoy Backs South Sudan's EAC Bid," *Sudan Tribune*, December 14, 2011: www.sudantribune.com/spip.php?iframe&page=imprimable&id_ article=40988.

Umbricht, Victor (1989), *Multilateral Mediation Practical Experiences and Lessons*. Boston: Martinus Nijhoff Publishers.

UNCTAD (2009), *Economic Development in Africa Report 2009: Strengthening Regional Economic Integration for Africa's Development*. Geneva: UNCTAD.

UNCTAD (2012), *Trade Liberalization, Investment and Economic Integration in African Regional Economic Communities Towards the African Common Market*. Geneva: UNCTAD.

UNCTAD (2012a), *Mobile Money for Business Development in the East African Community*. Geneva: UNCTAD.

UNCTAD (2012b), *Trade Liberalization, Investment and Economic Integration in African Regional Economic Communities Towards the African Common Market*. Geneva: UNCTAD.

UNCTAD (2013), *Intra-African Trade: Unlocking Private Sector Dynamism*. Geneva: UNCTAD.

UNCTAD (2015), *The State of Commodity Dependence 2014*. Geneva: UNCTAD.

UNDP (2014), *Human Development Report 2014 – Sustaining Human Progress: Reducing Vulnerabilities and Building Resilience*. New York: UNDP.

United Nations (1945), *Charter of the United Nations and Stature of the International Court of Justice*. New York: United Nations.

United Nations (1946), *Trusteeship Agreement for the Territory of Tanganyika: As Approved by the General Assembly on 13 December 1946*. New York: United Nations.

United Nations (2008), *Handbook on the Least Developed Country Category: Inclusion, Graduation and Special Support Measures*. New York: United Nations.

United Nations (2013), "Graduation of Countries from the Least Developed Country Category." http://unohrlls.org/custom-content/uploads/2013/12/Resolution-on-graduation-of-Equatorial-Guinea-and-Vanuatu.pdf.

United Nations Economic and Social Commission for Asia and the Pacific (no date), "What Is Good Governance?" Bangkok: United Nations Economic and Social Commission for Asia and the Pacific. www.unescap.org/sites/default/files/good-governance.pdf

United Nations World Tourism Organization (2015), *UNWTO Tourism Highlights, 2015 Edition*. Madrid: United Nations World Tourism Organization.

Verick, Sher (2008), *The Impact of Globalization on the Informal Sector in Africa*. Addis Ababa: Economic and Social Policy Division, UNECA.

Viljoen, Willemien (2016), "Brexit: Scapegoat for EAC Countries to Back Out of the EPA," Tralac Trade Law Centre (South Africa), July 27.

Wahome, Mwaniki (2014), "Ugandan Sugar Barons Finally Find Way to Export Sweetener to Kenya," *Daily Nation* (Kenya).

Walusimbi-Mkanga, George and Geoffrey Bakunda (2012), *An Assessment of the Implementation of the EAC Common Market Protocol Commitments of the Free Movement of Workers*. Arusha, Tanzania: East African Business Council and East African Employers' Organizations.

Wang, Jian-Ye, et al. (2007), "The Common Monetary Area in Southern Africa: Shocks, Adjustment, and Policy," IMF Working Paper. Washington, DC, International Monetary Fund.

World Bank (1981), *World Development Report*. New York: Oxford University Press.

World Bank (1987), *The World Bank/IFC Oral History Program*. Marko Zlatich's Interview of Victor Umbricht, February 4, 1987. http://siteresources.worldbank.org/EXTARCHIVES/Resources/Victor_ Umbricht_Oral_History_Transcript _44_02.pdf.

World Bank (1994), *Adjustment in Africa: Reforms, Results, and the Road Ahead*. New York: Oxford University Press.

World Bank (2010), "Silent and Lethal: How Quiet Corruption Undermines Africa's Development Efforts," in *African Development Indicators 2010*, pp. XI–29. Washington, DC: World Bank.

World Bank (2010a), *Global Development Finance: External Debt of Developing Countries*. Washington, DC: World Bank.

World Bank (2013), *Kenya Economic Outlook: Time to Shift Gears – Accelerating Growth and Poverty Reduction in The New Kenya*. Nairobi: The World Bank.

World Bank (2013a), *World Development Indicators*. Washington, DC: World Bank.

World Bank (2014), *World Development Indicators 2014*. Washington, DC: World Bank.

World Bank (2015), *World Development Indicators 2015*. Washington, DC: World Bank.

World Bank and East African Community (2014), *East African Common Market Scorecard 2014: Tracking EAC Compliance in the Movement of Capital, Services and Goods*. Washington, DC, and Arusha, Tanzania: World Bank and East African Community.

World Bank/IMF (2012), *Joint World Bank/IMF Debt Sustainability Analysis: United Republic of Tanzania*, June 22. Washington, DC: World Bank/IMF.

WTO (2013), "The Least Developed Get Eight Years More Leeway on Protecting Intellectual Property," *WTO: June 11 and 12, 2013 News Items*. Geneva: WTO www.wto.org/english/news_e/news13_e/trip_11jun13_e.htm.

Yabi, Gilles (2010), *The Role of ECOWAS in Managing Political Crisis and Conflict: The Case of Guinea and Guinea-Bissau*. Abuja, Nigeria: Friedrich-Ebert-Stiftung.

Zamfir, Ionel (2015), "The Tripartite Free Trade Area Project Integration in Southern and Eastern Africa," European Parliamentary Research Service.

Index